WITHDRAWN

FILM MUSIC 1

GARLAND REFERENCE LIBRARY
OF THE HUMANITIES
(VOL. 966)

RUDY BEHLMER
RICHARD H. BUSH
GAYLORD CARTER
BERNARD HERRMANN
DENNIS JAMES
KATHRYN KALINAK
EDDY LAWRENCE MANSON
DAVID RAKSIN
WILLIAM H. ROSAR
GREGORY ROSE
FRED STEINER
STEVEN D. WESCOTT
H. STEPHEN WRIGHT
LESLIE T. ZADOR

FILM MUSIC 1

edited, with an introduction, by
Clifford McCarty

GARLAND PUBLISHING, INC. • NEW YORK & LONDON
1989

© 1989 The Society for the Preservation of Film Music
"Holding a Nineteenth Century Pedal at Twentieth Century-Fox,"
  © 1989 David Raksin
All rights reserved

Library of Congress Cataloging-in-Publication Data
Film music 1.
  (Garland reference library of the humanities ; vol. 966)
  Includes bibliographies and index.
  Contents: The materials of film music / H. Stephen Wright—Tumult, battle, and blaze / Rudy Behlmer—Performing with silent films / Dennis James—[etc.]
  1. Motion picture music—History and criticism.
I. McCarty, Clifford, 1929– . II. Title: Film music one. III. Series.
ML2075.F448   1989   782.8′5   88-31035
ISBN 0–8240–1939–3 (alk. paper)

Printed on acid-free, 250-year-life paper
Manufactured in the United States of America

To the Memory of
Lawrence Morton
(1904–1987)

CONTENTS

Introduction: The Literature of Film Music
    Clifford McCarty   ix

The Materials of Film Music: Their Nature and Accessibility
    H. Stephen Wright   3

"Tumult, Battle and Blaze" : Looking Back on the 1920s—and Since—with Gaylord Carter, the Dean of Theater Organists
    Rudy Behlmer   19

Performing with Silent Films
    Dennis James   61

What Were Musicians Saying About Movie Music During the First Decade of Sound? A Symposium of Selected Writings
    Fred Steiner   81

Stravinsky and MGM
    William H. Rosar   109

Max Steiner and the Classical Hollywood Film Score: An Analysis of The Informer
    Kathryn Kalinak   123

The Music of Flash Gordon *and* Buck Rogers
        Richard H. Bush   143

Holding a Nineteenth Century Pedal at Twentieth Century-Fox
        David Raksin   167

Miklós Rózsa's Ben-Hur: *The Musical-Dramatic Function of the Hollywood* Leitmotiv
        Steven D. Wescott   183

A Conversation with Bernard Herrmann
        Leslie T. Zador and Gregory Rose   209

The Film Composer in Concert and the Concert Composer in Film
        Eddy Lawrence Manson   255

Contributors   271

Index   275

Introduction:
The Literature of Film Music

Clifford McCarty

Is there a literature of film music?

"The tendency has been to suppose not," wrote Martin Marks,[1] and as late as 1977 Roy Prendergast declared that with the exception of a few articles by Lawrence Morton, no body of intelligent and perceptive writing on film music existed.[2] Even in 1953, however, Morton himself recognized the existence of a "sizable" literature,[3] and with the publication of Steven Wescott's bibliography,[4] Marks' conclusion that "there is in fact an extensive literature on the subject" was documented beyond any question.

Of what has this literature consisted?[5]

The earliest examples, appearing in this country in 1909, took three forms: trade paper editorials, letters and articles calling for "better" music; cue sheets (lists of "musical suggestions" cued to each sequence in a picture); and anthologies of music for motion picture accompaniment. These materials were read and used by musicians from lowly nickelodeon pianists to conductors of large theater orchestras.

A regular column on music was inaugurated by *Moving Picture World* in 1910, the beginning of a decade that saw motion pictures enjoy a phenomenal growth in popularity. The number of movie theaters increased proportionately, as did the musical materials to assist in the accompaniment of an unprecedented number of films. These published materials—columns, articles, cue sheets, music anthologies, performance handbooks—though mostly of a practical nature, also took notice of aesthetic matters, and various theories of film music were advanced and illustrated. Throughout the silent period the materials became more detailed, sophisticated, and encyclopedic.

With the coming of sound there was a noticeable change: musicians had been the principal contributors to the literature, but now they were joined by filmmakers and theorists, especially those in Europe (the first three books on music in the sound film, although published in English translations, were by Europeans).[6]

In America—and the following sketch deals solely with periodical literature in this country—the magazine that most interestedly followed the film music scene was *Modern Music*, which espoused the ideas of the *avant-garde* and published articles by both theorists and composers. In 1936 *Modern Music* even engaged a (then) member of the *avant-garde*, George Antheil, to write a regular column on film music, a job he performed for four years. Under other hands, the column continued until the magazine's demise in 1946.

During the thirties other periodicals showed film music little consideration. *Etude*, America's most popular music magazine, often carried news of film music, but its primary concern was the use of music from the standard repertory *in* films rather than music composed specifically *for* films. The august *Musical Quarterly* ignored film music entirely during the decade (although one article had been published in 1929 and another would appear in 1941). *Pacific Coast Musician* featured occasional articles on film music, but they were mostly topical and the magazine had little circulation outside California.

Even film composers themselves did not seem much inclined to write about their profession. In the 1930s, in addition to Antheil, only Werner Janssen, Oscar Levant, Virgil Thomson, Ernst Toch, Herbert Stothart and Max Steiner published anything on film music, and only the last two were really *film* composers; the others had made (and were making) their mark elsewhere. Film composers probably were simply too busy to write about film music: they were trying to establish themselves in an industry that was producing a feature film every eighteen hours; improvements in sound recording were made almost monthly; scores were getting longer and orchestras bigger; composers from the concert hall were being wooed to Hollywood. It was a time of great excitement and constant change, and few of the participants had time to write anything down.

The 1940s, however, brought forth a relative deluge. In 1940 the quarterly *Films*, in its fourth and final issue, carried a symposium on

"Music in Films" by eleven participants. The same year also saw the first appearance of writings on film music by Aaron Copland, Louis Gruenberg, Erich Wolfgang Korngold, and even several "Hollywood" composers. Nineteen forty-one marked the debut of *Film Music Notes*, the first—and longest-lived—periodical devoted solely to film music. Its contents included articles, biographies, news items, and reviews of current scores—frequently with musical examples and often by the composers themselves.

A periodical that was especially hospitable to film music was *Hollywood Quarterly*.[7] From 1945 to 1951 its most prominent contributor on film music was Lawrence Morton, whose nineteen articles and columns included the first extended analysis of a film score published in America.[8] During this same six-year period Morton also contributed eighteen articles to *Film Music Notes*, including a special issue on Copland's *The Red Pony*.

Looking back from 1953, Morton (perhaps silently excluding his own writings) rendered a fairly dour characterization of the existing literature:

> ... it is far from comprehensive, it is scattered throughout a great number of periodicals, it is therefore not as accessible as it ought to be and, if the truth be told, it is not very distinguished. Some of it is pertinent but uninteresting, or interesting but fanciful; much of it is mere reportage, spot news; little of it has any permanent value.[9]

Morton stopped writing about film music in 1955, and two years later *Film Music Notes* (by then ominously called *Film and TV Music*) ceased publication. The only periodical that now gave film music a regular hearing was *Films in Review*, whose column "The Sound Track" commenced in 1952 and continues to this day. During its first decade this column was conducted by three writers, but since 1963 it has been in the hands of "Page Cook" (a pseudonym), a man of such passion, and with a style so unconstrained, that he has been known to invent words when the language's vocabulary failed him.

The 1960s, and indeed all the years since, provided both more and less: more in the number of words published about film music, less in the average value of those words. The only two periodicals committed to (mostly) serious articles about film music were Elmer Bernstein's short-lived *Film Music Notebook*, which printed valuable interviews with composers and close analyses of film scores,[10] and *Pro Musica*

Sana (1972–), published by the Miklós Rózsa Society with a natural emphasis on that composer's music.

A notable—if lamentable—addition to the literature of the sixties was the appearance, and flourishing, of amateur reviewing of film scores and amateur criticism of film music. In the vanguard of this trend were the newsletters and annuals (1965–76) issued by the Max Steiner Music Society, a group of *aficionados* whose qualifications in most instances consisted of an enthusiasm for the composer's music. Similar newsletters have since been devoted to Bernard Herrmann, Jerry Goldsmith, and others. Akin to the composer newsletters is a magazine that celebrates music for the fantastic film, *CinemaScore* (1979–), which indiscriminately juxtaposes unprofessional writing about film music with useful interviews and filmographies.

The writing and "criticism" prevalent in these "fanzines" is characterized by the contributors' ardor for a composer or a film genre and their insufficient understanding of either music or film. People who in their ignorance would rightly shrink from writing about poetry or sculpture display no apparent diffidence in writing about music—an art of which they often have little knowledge. These fans, on the other hand, sometimes perform useful functions by interviewing composers or conducting original research into film music history.

Another trend, observable since the 1970s, is toward academic criticism. Employing the language of semiology and structuralism (borrowed largely from French literature, philosophy, and anthropology), academicians have written primarily on theory and analysis, sometimes re-stating in their esoteric idiom observations made earlier in the literature by composers, filmmakers, and other critics. It is not clear how this language helps the reader to a better understanding of the subject. Academics, of all people, might be thought dedicated to clarification rather than obscuration, yet their style and vocabulary limit their audience for the most part to other academics.

Between the untutored effusions of the fans and the cloistered argot of the academicians lies a rather large area of communication in which writers can transmit a variety of theories, findings, insights, and experiences to the intelligent general reader without inviting the ridicule of the professional film musician. This language flourished briefly in *The Quarterly Journal of the Library of Congress*, which from 1978 to 1983 published six distinguished articles on film music, five of which were reprinted in book form.[11] The *Journal*'s writers followed Archibald

Introduction: The Literature of Film Music xiii

MacLeish's wise instruction that they "write *as* scholars but not necessarily *for* scholars."

The present volume is meant to continue this tradition of film music literature, as an ongoing (if irregular) forum for articles of permanent interest. After all the decades that have passed since film music began, it seems odd that no such forum has appeared before, yet this is the first anthology of new writings on film music to be published in English. The literature is already enormous, and it is not our purpose to add to it casually. Several forms are represented here—articles, essays, score analyses, interviews, and memoirs—all providing perceptive insights into a variety of film music topics. No such collection, of course, can hope to be comprehensive on such a complex subject, but each piece adds another tile to a gigantic mosaic of which more pieces are missing than present.[12]

Experiences in performing the musical accompaniment to silent pictures come from distinguished representatives of two generations of theater organists, Gaylord Carter and Dennis James. Fred Steiner surveys the responses of musicians to the challenges and opportunities posed by the coming of sound. Kathryn Kalinak and Steven D. Wescott provide two examples of a rare commodity, the extended score analysis; each will be revealing, even to those who know the scores well. Eddy Lawrence Manson tackles a long-standing issue—the movement of composers between the differing worlds of concert and film music. One of those who never effected the transition from concert hall to film was Igor Stravinsky, and William H. Rosar chronicles the great composer's first (though not last) encounter with Hollywood. The Flash Gordon films are representative of the method by which hundreds of films were fitted with musical scores from studio libraries, and Richard H. Bush has done exhaustive research into that method and its results. David Raksin's memoir of his days at Twentieth Century-Fox in the late thirties is recounted with the wit and style for which he is famous. Famous for another style was Bernard Herrmann, but his crusty manner should not come between the reader of his interview and the value of his experiences and opinions. H. Stephen Wright discusses a problem central to the study of film music: the accessibility of the music itself. It is appropriate that Mr. Wright's is the lead article in a book sponsored by the Society for the Preservation of Film Music.[13] The other pieces appear in chronological order by topic.

The contributions of Carter, James, Manson, Raksin, and Herrmann, though they do not constitute "scholarship" in the academic sense, nonetheless are important additions to the literature of film music: they are primary sources in the history of the subject, presented by those with first-hand experience in the composing and performing of music for motion pictures. It is, after all, from the labors of such practitioners that the studies by others can proceed.

Despite the thousands of writings on film music, there is much about the subject that is *terra incognita*. It is no exaggeration to say that hundreds of film composers are all but unknown—their careers unchronicled, their music seldom heard and wholly unexamined. Wescott's bibliography served two important functions: it revealed not only what had been accomplished but, *in absentia*, what remained to be done. The present volume and its projected successors now provide an outlet to encourage and stimulate writers to further our knowledge and understanding of film music through writings that serve both scholarship and the general reader. As film music approaches its centennial, historians, scholars, and musicologists have their work cut out for them.

NOTES

[1] Martin Marks, "Film Music: The Material, Literature, and Present State of Research," *Notes*, 36 (December 1979), 282–325; reprinted with additions and corrections in *The Journal of the University Film and Video Association*, 34, No. 1 (Winter 1982), 3–40.

[2] Roy M. Prendergast, *A Neglected Art: A Critical Study of Music in Films* (New York: New York University Press, 1977), p. vii.

[3] Lawrence Morton, "Foreword" to *Film Composers in America: A Checklist of Their Work*, by Clifford McCarty (Glendale, Calif.: John Valentine, 1953; reprinted, New York: Da Capo Press, 1972), p. xi.

[4] Steven D. Wescott, *A Comprehensive Bibliography of Music for Film and Television* (Detroit: Information Coordinators, 1985).

[5] The summary given here is necessarily brief. For a longer account (on which I have drawn) see Marks (n. 1), the best survey of film music literature and scholarship published to date.

[6] Leonid Sabaneev, *Music for the Films* (London: Pitman, 1935); Kurt London, *Film Music* (London: Faber & Faber, 1936); Hanns

Eisler, *Composing for the Films* (New York: Oxford University Press, 1947).

[7]Title changed to *The Quarterly of Film, Radio, and Television* (1951–1957) and then to *Film Quarterly* (1957–).

[8]Lawrence Morton, "The Music of 'Objective: Burma,'" *Hollywood Quarterly*, 1, No. 4 (July 1946), 378–395.

[9]Lawrence Morton, "Foreword," p. xi.

[10]*Film Music Notebook* (1974–1978) was actually the adjunct of a record club, the principal incentive to membership being the opportunity to purchase recordings produced exclusively for members. Fourteen such recordings were issued, along with thirteen numbers of the *Notebook*.

[11]Iris Newsom, ed., *Wonderful Inventions: Motion Pictures, Broadcasting, and Recorded Sound at the Library of Congress* (Washington: Library of Congress, 1985).

[12]It is my pleasure to acknowledge the valued counsel of the following in the assembling of this book's contents: Rudy Behlmer, William H. Rosar, Fred Steiner, Tony Thomas, and Leslie T. Zador. Their advice was sometimes heeded and sometimes not, and they are innocent of any faults the reader may find; those belong to the Editor.

[13]For information about the Society and membership, address the Society for the Preservation of Film Music, 10850 Wilshire Blvd., Suite 770, Los Angeles, California 90024. Editorial matters should be addressed to the Editor, P.O. Box 89, Topanga, California 90290.

Film Music 1

The Materials of Film Music: Their Nature and Accessibility

H. Stephen Wright

In 1976, John Steven Lasher, record producer and head of the Entr'acte Recording Society (a record club devoted to film music) decided to issue a new recording of Max Steiner's music score for the 1933 fantasy film, *King Kong*; he appointed composer-conductor Fred Steiner (no relation to *Kong*'s composer) as conductor of the project. In an effort to locate performance materials for the recording, Fred Steiner contacted Bourne, the publishing house holding the rights to the score. Unfortunately, he found that Bourne possessed only a piano-conductor score lacking explicit instrumental indications. Dissatisfied with this, Steiner then turned to Mrs. Lee Steiner, the composer's widow, who provided Max Steiner's original manuscript sketches, which were in a condensed three-to-four-stave format. Since a full score and parts seemed to be otherwise unavailable, Lasher and Steiner decided that these manuscript sketches would be the basis of their recording. Christopher Palmer, an English musician who had reconstructed orchestrations of film scores for RCA's "Classic Film Scores" record series, was engaged to reconstruct a full score, basing his work on the sketches and the somewhat primitively recorded soundtrack of the original film.

During his search for *King Kong* performance materials, Fred Steiner had attempted, without success, to determine if the full score might still be in the possession of RKO (the studio which produced the film). On Steiner's behalf, film music historian William H. Rosar succeeded in contacting RKO's archives in Los Angeles. In late September of 1976, with the recording less than a month away, Steiner and Rosar visited the RKO archives and examined, at last, the full orchestral score of *King Kong*. Of course, Steiner would have preferred to use this score in the upcoming recording, even though Christopher Palmer had nearly completed his reconstruction; however, RKO refused to allow the score to be used, for obscure reasons relating to a remake of *King Kong* then in production. The most Steiner could do was study RKO's score in order to resolve the problematic areas of Max Steiner's manuscript sketches. In late October of 1976 Christopher Palmer's reconstructed version of *King Kong* was recorded in London.[1]

This little anecdote reveals, all at once, the problems under discussion here. There exists in the world today a huge body of contemporary music for which there is virtually no bibliographic control, very limited or nonexistent access, and only the most minimal attempts at preservation. The full impact of this problem is realized when one considers that this music, much of which must be "reconstructed" before it can be studied or played, is not the product of some distant, forgotten era, not the work of minds long since turned to dust—it is music of our time, much of it composed within our lifetimes by composers who are still very much alive.

The matter being examined here has to do with the efforts of the film music scholar who wishes to analyze a particular film score or perhaps the collected output of a certain film composer, and thus wishes to examine the music in some detail and force it to yield up its compositional secrets. To be sure, this is not an activity that is sweeping through the world of music scholarship like some epidemic; in fact, the study of film music is still an orphan, lacking widespread acceptance despite the efforts of a few dedicated individuals. Suffice it to say that there is much film music written with the utmost care by composers of impeccable academic credentials who regard their work with considerable seriousness, and scholars who wish to explore this new and unique area of music find enormous barriers strewn in their path. An article in *Cinema Journal*, a scholarly publication devoted to the study of films, attempted to explore the unusual music composed for Alfred Hitchcock's films by Bernard Herrmann. The article, by Royal S. Brown, goes into considerable detail on the subject, using musical score excerpts to illustrate certain points. However, when we look to the list of references at the end of the article to discover the source of the first excerpt, we find this statement: "Since the score . . . was unavailable to me, I can only assume from listening to the recording and film soundtrack that the keys and the notation are as I

The Materials of Film Music

have mentioned."[2] Without disputing the accuracy of Mr. Brown's ears, we can safely say that this lack of access to a score is not a desirable condition under which to conduct serious research. This barrier appears almost immediately to anyone attempting such research, and in fact, it may well be the largest obstacle to the widespread advancement of film music scholarship.

Physically speaking, what is film music? How does it physically manifest itself to the scholar? The first and most obvious format is the film itself, with its accompanying soundtrack of dialogue, sound effects and music. Aside from this, the music may exist in recorded form on the original music tracks of film (as they existed prior to being mixed into an integral soundtrack) and in commercially issued recordings. In graphic form, the music may exist in a published format, either in a form identical to that used in the film (this is so rare as to be virtually nonexistent; one of the few extant examples is Prokofiev's *Ivan the Terrible*, published by H. Sikorski) or in adapted form, such as concert suites or arrangements for other media. Unpublished manifestations may include the composer's original manuscript sketch, a full score (sometimes in the composer's hand, but more frequently prepared by an orchestrator, whose role will be discussed later in this article), orchestral parts, and a condensed conductor's score (often a copyist's rendering of the composer's manuscript sketch).

Considering each of the non-manuscript manifestations individually, it quickly becomes apparent that though none of them is completely without value, they cannot ultimately substitute for the original materials. Of course, the original film can never be disposed of; film is a synthetic art, and the nature of this synthesis is (or should be) at the center of all serious study of film music. As Martin Marks remarked in a review of film music literature, "The primary material of film music, both for the audience and the researcher, is not a recording or a score, but the film itself." [3] Yet this primary material cannot stand alone; analysis of the synthesis of film and music inevitably involves some deconstruction into component parts, one of which is the music itself, and no serious scholar would attempt to analyze a musical work without the written record of the composer's original intentions—assuming that such a record is available.

Original recordings of film music, divorced from the film, are also valuable inasmuch as they provide a representation of the score in which every musical element can be clearly heard; as Aaron Copland

and numerous other film composers have often complained, many details of a film score can be lost when the music is mixed with the other audio tracks.[4] (However, recent advances in film sound technology, such as multichannel sound and noise reduction systems, have helped to minimize this problem.) The original music tracks of a film are often unavailable to the researcher. If they exist at all, they are likely to be in film studio libraries which present their own peculiar problems to the scholar (problems which will be discussed later in this article).

Commercially produced soundtrack recordings are often an adequate substitute for original studio music tracks. However, unless the film music scholar happens to be engaged in the rather expensive hobby of collecting film soundtrack recordings, he is likely to have a problem securing these recordings for study. Film soundtrack recordings are issued not in an effort to aid the researcher, but in an attempt to exploit the commercial success of the film. Music libraries, especially those of the academic type, do not normally buy these recordings, since they are usually perceived as "popular" fare. Even if a scholar requests that a library purchase the soundtrack recording for a specific film, he is likely to be disappointed, since the recordings often go out of print soon after the film disappears from theaters. Those wishing to obtain such recordings must turn to a frightfully expensive collector's market in which prices have been known to reach hundreds of dollars for a single disc.[5]

Even when they are readily available, these recordings have a few drawbacks that impede their use as research materials. Since film music is often fragmentary in nature and eschews traditional musical forms (qualities which will be further discussed later), composers and record producers usually rearrange the order of sequences in a film score, cutting and splicing lengths of tape and even omitting entire sections in order to produce a musically satisfying experience for the home listener. Well-intentioned as this process may be, it causes difficulties for the researcher who desires an accurate aural representation of the score. The liner notes are frequently no help, for most film score recordings are very poorly annotated (recordings produced especially for collectors, such as the aforementioned Entr'acte recording of *King Kong*, are an exception to this; such recordings often include extensive liner notes, sometimes even including musical examples). The recording may also contain material that does not even appear in the film—such as

The Materials of Film Music

ludicrous "pop" versions of themes, arbitrarily inserted by greedy producers. Or, in many cases, the recording may be a complete re-recording of the score masquerading as an "original soundtrack," such as MGM's recording of Miklós Rózsa's *Ben-Hur*.

Even assuming that an ideal recording of a film score can be obtained to supplement the original film, this will not be sufficient for the scholar. As unerring as one's ears may be, it is still desirable to have a printed or manuscript copy of the film score for study purposes. However, if the researcher proceeds to his nearby music library to examine a copy of the score, he will almost certainly come away empty-handed—and unlike the situation with soundtrack recordings, this dead end is not at all the fault of the library in question. Film scores rarely appear in published form, and the published versions that do exist are unlikely to suit the needs of the film music scholar. These published manifestations include suites or other concert adaptations (usually prepared by the composer), commercially produced arrangements (usually adapted by someone other than the composer), and the original score itself.

The concert suite adapted from the film score is what our researcher is most likely to find when he visits the music library (assuming, of course, that he finds anything at all). These suites (or other adaptations) come into existence when a composer wishes to give his film work some life apart from the original film and expand his catalog of performable concert music in the process. Though this does not occur as much as some film music aficionados would like (partly due to lack of interest on the part of composers and publishers and partly due to problems of copyright which will be discussed shortly), many fine examples of this transformation exist. Prokofiev's cantata *Alexander Nevsky*, based on his 1938 film score, is one of the best known and most ambitious examples. Ralph Vaughan Williams adapted his strange and ethereal music for *Scott of the Antarctic* into an entire symphony, calling it *Sinfonia Antartica*. Aaron Copland converted several of his film scores into viable, well-known concert works, such as *The Red Pony* and *Music for Movies* (a suite comprised of material from *The City*, *Our Town*, and *Of Mice and Men*). Bernard Herrmann combined music from two Orson Welles-directed films, *Citizen Kane* and *The Magnificent Ambersons*, into a Welles "portrait" wittily entitled *Welles Raises Kane*. Leonard Bernstein's single venture into film scoring became the suite from *On the Waterfront*. More recent examples include

John Williams' seven-movement suite from *Star Wars*, and John Corigliano's *Three Hallucinations for Orchestra*, derived from his music for *Altered States*.

However, the degree of congruity between these various suites and the original scores is not always close. Film music, as was mentioned earlier, does not follow traditional musical forms; since it is an element in a dramatic art, it necessarily derives its form from the sequence of events in the drama itself. As composer Leonard Rosenman has stated, "functional music is impelled by literary ideas." [6] Thus classical forms do not often appear in film music (though there are exceptions, such as Jerry Goldsmith's use of the passacaglia form in *The Blue Max*), and when a composer converts a film score into a concert work he may wish to rewrite the work in order to impose an abstract form upon it. Furthermore, since the individual sequences of a film score are often very short—usually under three or four minutes—the composer may expand certain sections or combine others to make longer units. Finally, some musical elements (such as "sting" chords) may be meaningless without their visual counterparts and will be omitted. The implications of all these factors are that, depending upon the individual composer and the nature of the particular score, a concert suite may vary drastically from the original work as heard in the film.

The researcher may wish to consult other published versions of a film score, such as piano arrangements, but the value of these is quite limited since they are often the work of commercial arrangers who are aiming the product at a specific market. Some arrangements may accurately reflect the character of the original, such as David Raksin's elaborate solo piano version of his *Laura* published by Robbins, but many others are grossly oversimplified in an effort to appeal to the amateur musician. Needless to say, such simplifications are inadequate for the purposes of the film music scholar.

The answer, then, is to turn to the original score. However, the researcher who attempts to do so is immediately thwarted by the fact that film scores in their original, unadapted state are not published and thus unavailable for purchase. Of course, many films carry a notice in their screen credits that ascribes a "publication" function to the musical arm of the studio producing the film—such a credit might read "Music published by Twentieth Century-Fox Music" or something similar. But the music has been "published" only in the most superficial sense of the word. The music is simply copyrighted in the name of the studio, and a copy of the score and its accompanying instrumental parts are filed away in the studio's music library. The music is not made available for purchase, and orchestras who wish to rent the material are forced to pay astronomical fees (which even involve royalty payments for all of the copyists involved in the production of parts). In view of this, it is no wonder that some film composers have despaired of having their works played in concert. Composer John Williams even went so far as to say, "The scores [are] impossible to get . . . they're very, very guarded."[7] This whole process makes a complete mockery of the notice of "publication."

Before examining what the researcher's next step should be, it would be appropriate to consider why film scores do not get published in their original forms—and why so few of them are published in any form, cheap piano arrangement or otherwise. Since the earliest days of Hollywood, a situation has obtained in which the composer is often no more than an employee. The standard film music composition contract divests the composer of all rights to his musical offspring; these rights go to the employer (*i.e.*, the studio), who in the eyes of copyright law is technically the "composer." The actual composer has no say in the matter of publication; the studio itself has control over this and will only venture into publication if it will help exploit the film. Only a few of the most successful film composers have the stature necessary to negotiate a contract in which they retain some rights; most others must continue to submit to this arrangement if they want to continue composing for films.[8]

During the 1970s, the composers struck back in a protracted legal battle that ultimately brightened the situation somewhat. In 1972 a large group of film composers led by Elmer Bernstein filed a 300-million-dollar class action suit against the major film and television studios, charging them with conspiracy to monopolize the publication of film music and withhold copyrights from composers.[9] The Columbia Broadcasting System, along with a few other producers, immediately broke ranks and settled with the composers, agreeing to give them copyright control.[10] However, most of the studios chose to fight, refusing to compromise. An attorney for the producers summed up their position thusly: "When we buy a score, it's as if we are buying a suit of clothes. If we want to hang it in the closet and just leave it there, that's our business."[11]

After a number of reversals, the lawsuit was finally settled out of court in 1979. Under the terms of the settlement, the producer of a film has fifteen months after the release of a film to publish the music; if this is not done, the composer then has thirty months in which to seek publication. If the music is still unpublished after this thirty-month period, the rights then revert to the producer.[12] Although it is too early to tell if this change will have any significant effect on film music publishing, most composers seem to feel that their position has been improved. Walter Scharf's reaction was typical: "We've given them notice that they can't bury [music] in the cellar." [13]

But what of the vast amount of music that still occupies the "cellar" Scharf speaks of? The bulk of it still resides in the music libraries of the major film studios, untouched and unseen. The physical and bibliographic inaccessibility of these libraries is still a considerable obstacle to research. Studio music libraries are not listed in any library directory. Though they usually have good internal bibliographic control in the form of elaborate card indexes, there is no external bibliographic control at all. A researcher who does not have access to these libraries can only guess at the contents by examining a list of films produced by a particular studio. The researcher must then either travel to the appropriate studio library or query the librarian to determine if a particular score is held. Even so, there is no guarantee of access or cooperation. Studio music libraries are designed to meet the internal needs of the studio, not the unprofitable demands of the scholar.

One should not infer from these dark comments that the door is always closed. For a scholarly analysis of Bernard Herrmann's music for *Psycho*, Fred Steiner based all of his work not on the manuscript materials (which were still in the composer's possession at the time), but on the score in the Paramount Pictures music library. In the bibliography appended to his published analysis, Steiner even gives the shelf location of the *Psycho* materials.[14] However, it should be noted that Steiner is himself a film composer and is thus on somewhat more intimate terms with Hollywood music libraries than the average music scholar.

Perhaps the ideal studio music library is that of Warner Bros. Conductor Charles Gerhardt, who helmed the extensive "Classic Film Scores" series of film music recordings for RCA in the 1970s, commented that serious problems with materials constantly emerged when repertory was being assembled for the series—except when the

The Materials of Film Music

music in question was from a Warner Bros. film. For the many scores created for that studio by Erich Wolfgang Korngold, Max Steiner, and others, Gerhardt reported that full scores and complete sets of parts were always available.[15] Furthermore, Warner Bros. has shown a concern for the research value of its collection that is unique in Hollywood. The Warner Bros. music scores are now held at the University of Southern California (Special Collections, Doheny Library) and can be viewed by special arrangement.

An interesting study in contrast is provided by the Metro-Goldwyn-Mayer music library. In 1957 the MGM music library actually claimed that it was "second in size only to the Music Division of the Library of Congress," containing approximately two million musical compositions and one million recordings; MGM valued this collection at five million dollars.[16] However, this awareness of the importance of the collection—an awareness implicit in these extravagant claims—was not sustained. In 1969 an event occurred that has since become known as "the score burning."[17] MGM felt that it needed more storage space and decided to create it by disposing of all full scores and sets of orchestral parts, keeping only the cryptically notated conductor's scores. Published materials went to the library of California State University at Long Beach, which extracted fewer than 200 items judged to be valuable and consigned the remainder to a landfill.[18] The full impact of this action manifested itself rather slowly; sometime later composer Maurice Jarre, engaged to conduct some of his film music for a guest appearance with a major orchestra, called MGM to inquire about borrowing some performance materials and was curtly informed that they no longer existed.[19] Jarre was not the only composer to receive such a shock; virtually every MGM music score composed up to that time was irretrievably destroyed.

It should be pointed out that in many cases composers retain their original manuscripts; however, most of these are not full scores. Due to the crushing demands of Hollywood production schedules, composers are forced to limit their utterances to a compressed "sketch" of about three to five staves, which contains all necessary information about instrumental coloration; this sketch is handed over to a colleague who expands it into a full score, thus allowing the composer to eliminate the time-consuming process of preparing a manuscript score. The full score, and the parts prepared from it, become the basis of studio library holdings; the manuscript sketch is often retained by the composer. It is these manuscript materials that frequently become the basis of non-studio film music archives.

As might be expected, some of the major film music collections are in California. One of these is at the University of California at Los Angeles, which holds major collections of manuscripts of Alex North (including the famous "discarded score" North wrote for *2001: A Space Odyssey*), Ernst Toch, Henry Mancini, Jeff Alexander, André Previn, William Lava, and many others. The music library also includes a large collection of film score recordings by Alfred Newman, as well as vast numbers of miscellaneous items of other Hollywood composers. According to music librarian Stephen M. Fry, all of the film music collections at UCLA have printed inventories (though these vary widely in format), and an online index of film composers is planned.[20]

The University of Southern California has the distinction of housing three major film music collections. The Alfred Newman collection encompasses twenty cartons of material, including manuscript scores and recordings. The Dimitri Tiomkin collection, which consumes 125 feet of shelf space, includes most of Tiomkin's film scores as well as personal papers and correspondence. USC's third major holding, the Warner Bros. collection, has already been mentioned. Other composers represented at USC include George Duning and Maurice Jarre.[21]

One of the largest manuscript collections of film music is, surprisingly, at the University of Wyoming. Their Archive Collection of Film Music contains manuscript music of Bronislau Kaper, William Axt, Gail Kubik, Carmen Dragon, Walter Scharf, and many, many others.[22]

Other major collections are scattered throughout the United States. At Syracuse University, manuscripts of Miklós Rózsa and Franz Waxman can be found.[23] Fifty-two of Bernard Herrmann's manuscripts are held at the Music Library of the University of California at Santa Barbara.[24] The Archives Division of the State Historical Society of Wisconsin possesses an Ernest Gold collection.[25] Other major collections can be found at California State University at Long Beach, the University of Oregon, and the University of Santa Clara.[26]

Of course, mention must be made of the Library of Congress Music Division, which has managed to secure manuscripts of some of the most significant film scores ever produced. Included in its collection are *Citizen Kane*, by Bernard Herrmann; *Laura*, by David Raksin; *On the Waterfront*, by Leonard Bernstein; and *The Heiress*, by Aaron Copland.[27] Numerous film scores acquired through copyright registration, mostly in conductor's score format, are also held. Four manuscript film scores by Erich Wolfgang Korngold are also held by the Music Division.[28] The Library of Congress also recently completed a project to establish bibliographic control over its film music holdings through the construction of a card "finding aid"; this project also involved the microfilming of the entire film score collection. The Copyright Office collections also hold a great many film scores not selected for cataloging by the Library of Congress; limited bibliographic access to these materials is provided by the Copyright Office's computer system.[29]

This is the situation as it stands today. Though it could certainly be much worse, it is hardly ideal. Much film music, perhaps too much, is still languishing in studio libraries, bibliographically inaccessible, awaiting perhaps another "score burning." Manuscript collections are widely dispersed and often uncataloged. Soundtrack recordings become increasingly evanescent. All of this presents a formidable barrier to the scholar. In an article on this problem, film music critic Robert Fiedel bemoans the geographic scattering of existing film music collections. He suggests a "national film music archive," which would be charged with preserving manuscript scores and original recordings, and further suggests that the Library of Congress, with its superior knowledge of preservation procedures, would be the ideal location.[30] Fiedel is quite correct as to the need for better bibliographic control of existing collections, but his proposal for a national archive is a bit over-idealistic. The geographic problem has been with scholars in many fields for some time, and undoubtedly will continue to be. Fiedel is not a librarian or an archivist, and thus may be forgiven these grandiose notions; but in the spirit of his proposal, some other suggestions are offered herewith:

1. Composers should be strongly encouraged to deposit their manuscript materials in the Library of Congress or an academic music library.

2. Existing collections of film music should be extensively and accurately cataloged, so that scholars can easily determine their contents without having to travel long distances and rummage at random through boxes of unsorted material.

3. Increased provisions for preservation of film score materials, such as microfilming, should be made by holders of major collections.

4. A *union catalog of film music* should be created, in which all major film music collections are described in sufficient detail to enable scholars to determine where a particular composer's materials are held. Currently, three sources exist that partially fill this function. The first is Linda Harris Mehr's *Motion Pictures, Television, and Radio: A Union Catalogue of Manuscript and Special Collections in the Western United States* (Boston: G.K. Hall, 1977); the second is *Resources of American Music History: A Directory of Source Materials from Colonial Times to the Present*, edited by D.W. Krummel and others (Urbana: University of Illinois Press, 1981); and the third is *Directory of Music Research Libraries: Volume I, Canada and the United States*, 2nd rev. ed. [RISM C/I] (Kassel: Bärenreiter, 1983). All of these works index major film music collections; however, because film music is not their focus, the depth of information provided in them is not sufficient to compensate for the lack of a film music union catalog.

5. Finally, studio music libraries should be apprised of the historical importance of their holdings and encouraged to make greater provisions for scholarly access to their materials. It is perhaps too much to expect studio libraries to produce published versions of their catalogs, but if they could be persuaded to provide some general information about themselves for the proposed union catalog, this would be a great step forward. The Music Library Association is currently negotiating with the Music Publishers Association in the hope of providing increased study access to rental music;[31] perhaps a similar understanding could be achieved with the film studios, who are now quite reluctant to allow materials to leave their libraries.

One last factor, a somewhat disheartening one, cannot be overlooked. None of the proposals outlined here can be achieved without funding; consequently, any progress will necessarily require the concentrated efforts of at least a few music librarians who are willing to plead the case of film music and divert some energy, as well as seed money, toward the ideal of total bibliographic control and access. Just as many old films produced on nitrate stock are in danger of dissolving, the huge body of film music this century has produced also threatens to vanish, both literally and bibliographically. In 1948 musicologist Manfred F. Bukofzer speculated that in the future, film music "may be regarded as the most characteristic music of the 20th century."[32] This prediction may indeed come to pass, but if the process of control and preservation does not accelerate now, future generations interested in the film music art will have no place to begin.

NOTES

[1] This account of the events preceding Entr'acte's recording of *King Kong* is based on John Steven Lasher, "The Mightiest Kong of All," *Main Title*, 2, No. 2 (1976), [6–7]; and a written account provided by William H. Rosar.

[2] Royal S. Brown, "Herrmann, Hitchcock, and the Music of the Irrational," *Cinema Journal*, 21, No. 2 (1982), 48.

[3] Martin Marks, "Film Music: The Material, Literature, and Present State of Research," *Notes*, 36 (1979), 283.

[4] Aaron Copland, *What to Listen For in Music*, Rev. ed. (New York: McGraw-Hill, 1957), p. 156.

[5] Ken Sutak, "The Investment Market in Movie Music Albums," *High Fidelity*, 22, No. 7 (1972), 62–66.

[6] Leonard Rosenman, "Leonard Rosenman on Film Music," in *Film Score: The View from the Podium*, ed. Tony Thomas (South Brunswick, N.J.: A.S. Barnes, 1979), p. 243.

[7] John Williams, as quoted in John Caps, "Keeping in Touch with John Williams," *Soundtrack*, 1, No. 1 (1982), 3.

[8] Leonard Zissu, "The Copyright Dilemma of the Screen Composer," *Hollywood Quarterly*, 1 (1946), 317–318.

[9] For a detailed statement of the composers' argument, see Elmer Bernstein, "The Film Composers vs. the Studios: A Three Hundred Million Dollar Complaint," *Film Music Notebook*, 2, No. 1 (1976), 31–39.

[10] Herm Schoenfeld, "Historic CBS Deal Gives Composers Full Copyright Control in TV & Films," *Variety*, 27 September 1972, pp. 45, 48.

[11] Unnamed attorney, as quoted in Gene Lees, "When the Music Stopped," *High Fidelity*, 22, No. 7 (1972), 20.

[12] "Writers Suit May Be Settled," *Billboard*, 31 March 1979, p. 160.

[13] Walter Scharf, as quoted in Cynthia Kirk, "Composers' Bargaining Tack Seen Altered by Bernstein C'right Case," *Variety*, 9 April 1980, p. 81.

[14] Fred Steiner, "Herrmann's 'Black-and-White' Music for Hitchcock's *Psycho*: Part II," *Film Music Notebook*, 1, No. 2 (1974–1975), 46.

[15] Charles Gerhardt and Christopher Palmer, jacket notes, *The Spectacular World of Classic Film Scores*, RCA, ARL 1–2792, 1978.

[16] Clifford McCarty, "Filmusic [sic] Librarian," *Films in Review*, 8 (1957), 292.

[17] Elmer Bernstein, "Collection News," *Film Music Notebook*, 3, No. 3 (1977), 2.

[18] Letter to the author from Don A. Hennessee, 22 June 1987. Mr. Hennessee was a reference librarian at California State University at Long Beach at the time. He attempted to halt the destruction of the MGM collection but was powerless to do so.

[19] Lees, p. 20.

[20] Letter to the author from Stephen M. Fry, 6 April 1983.

[21] Linda Harris Mehr, ed., *Motion Pictures, Television, and Radio: A Union Catalogue of Manuscript and Special Collections in the Western United States* (Boston: G.K. Hall, 1977), s.v. University of Southern California.

[22] D.W. Krummel et al., eds., *Resources of American Music History: A Directory of Source Materials from Colonial Times to the Present* (Urbana: University of Illinois Press, 1981), pp. 385–386.

[23] Krummel, pp. 271–272.

[24] "Notes for *Notes*," *Notes*, 39 (1983), 839.

[25] Krummel, p. 377.

[26] Mehr, s.v. California State University, Long Beach; University of Oregon; and University of Santa Clara.

[27] "*Citizen Kane* Score Acquired," *Library of Congress Information Bulletin*, 19 November 1976, p. 710.

[28] "Korngold Scores Given to Library," *Library of Congress Information Bulletin*, 20 February 1981, p. 62.

[29] Letter to the author from Gillian B. Anderson, 27 June 1983.

[30] Robert Fiedel, "Saving the Score," *American Film*, 3, No. 1 (1977), 32, 71.

[31] Music Library Association and Music Publishers Association, *White Paper Consideration by MLA/MPA on Distribution of Rental Music* (n.p., n.d.).

[32] Manfred F. Bukofzer, "Forms and Functions of the Music Library," *Notes: Supplement for Members*, No. 3 (1948), p. 4.

"Tumult, Battle and Blaze": Looking Back on the 1920s—and Since— with Gaylord Carter, the Dean of Theater Organists

Rudy Behlmer

Gaylord Carter, a master musician from the golden age of the silent film, is still considerably active in that field at the age of 82. And his genuine enthusiasm has not left him.

For three years, beginning in 1926, he was the featured organist in conjunction with a large orchestra at the prestigious Million Dollar Theatre in downtown Los Angeles, followed by engagements at other major picture palaces. After the advent of sound pictures he discovered a new career playing for "Amos 'n' Andy" and other popular radio shows during the 1930s and '40s. During World War II he served as an officer in the Navy, and after the war became the musical director and organist for several television shows.

In 1960 he began his special presentations of silent film classics accompanied by organ in theaters throughout the U.S. and in Canada, England, France, and Australia. Carter has also composed and recorded organ scores for the Mary Pickford Company, the Harold Lloyd Corporation, the Museum of Modern Art, the British Broadcasting Corporation, and Blackhawk Films. In addition, he has done several albums for various record companies.

In 1986 and 1987 he composed and played scores for seven classic Paramount films of the 1920s which have been released on videocassette in honor of that studio's 75th anniversary. *Wings* was the forerunner of the group, followed by *The Wedding March, The Ten Commandments, Old Ironsides, Running Wild, The Docks of New York, The Last Command,* and *The Covered Wagon.*

The following interview was done at Carter's home overlooking the Pacific Ocean in San Pedro on October 29, 1986, and on February 21, 1987. We concentrated primarily on his earlier career and the procedures and ambience of playing for silent films in the 1920s up to and including the transition to sound motion pictures. The conversations have been edited.

BEHLMER: Gaylord, I know that you came to Los Angeles in 1922 and started at a theater when you were only 17.

CARTER: The Sunshine Theatre at 54th and South Park Avenue. I don't think it's there anymore. It was a little neighborhood theater. We had just come from Wichita, Kansas, and I didn't have a dime to get in to see the shows. So I got a job playing piano in the theater—which was quite a ways from where we lived. It involved getting on a streetcar after school and going out to this place, and then coming home—and coming and going I'd study algebra and Latin on the streetcar.

BEHLMER: How did you happen to get the job?

CARTER: Well, my dad brought us out here. He was in a real estate office down on Hill Street. And the woman who owned the theater came in and wanted to sell the theater and listed it with my dad. And then she said, "By the way, do you know anybody who would play the piano for our movies?" And my dad said, "Well, my son would probably be interested in that." I mean, if that isn't a shot in the dark!

BEHLMER: Now up to this point, you had never . . .

CARTER: No. Back in Wichita we'd had kiddie matinees, when they had the Keystone Kops and things, and I'd go in and play the piano for a couple of bucks on Saturday afternoons. I was still in high school. So, when we came out here, this was kind of a natural way to go. But it never occurred to me. I didn't go and ask anybody for a job.

Gaylord Carter at the Wurlitzer Theatre Organ, San Gabriel Civic Auditorium, 1975

BEHLMER: Was that a regular piano at the Sunshine?

CARTER: It was more than a piano. It was a Wurlitzer unit orchestra, which consisted of a piano keyboard, two little sets of pipes—one a flute sound and one a kind of string sound—and then various handles that you'd pull down if you wanted a crash, or a whistle, or a toot, or a bang or something. And it also had rolls. There were two places to play player rolls. So you could score. You could set up maybe a "hurry" in one of these things and a love theme on the other, and you'd go back and forth on these things. I played the feature picture, and I'd play the rolls during the serial and sometimes during the comedies. You could put on the little mandolin effect that would give you the plinky piano sound, which I used to use a lot and still do. I like that music. Along about the middle of the second show at night, the manager, who was a very nice guy, came down and relieved me and said, "Well, there's hardly anybody left; I think I'll play rolls until the end of the picture and you can go home."

BEHLMER: After you had gotten your experience there, how did you manage to segue into the big houses?

CARTER: That was interesting. After I'd been there about a year, the manager got a chance to buy a little theater organ. It was a two-manual Robert Morton. It had drums and xylophones and bells and tambourines and castanets and the whole *schmeer*. Not very many pipes, but enough. And I learned to play theater organ with that little two-manual. I was getting $16 a week; then they raised my pay to $25 a week, with the organ. And then they sold the house. And I didn't like the new owners; they didn't appreciate what I was trying to do. So I quit and started going to UCLA. I had an organist friend—in fact, I took organ lessons from him—and he occasionally substituted at a little theater in Inglewood called the Seville. It was on West Boulevard. And he said, "Why don't you go down there and play one night a week, and keep your finger in by substituting for this gal?" So I remember I had a little Model-T Ford; and after I'd come home from UCLA I'd rattle out to this place on West Boulevard, and they had a very nice theater organ there—a little Estey. The organist wasn't much of a musician, and she didn't know quite what to do. When great events would take place on the screen like the crashing of the chandelier in *The Phantom of the*

Opera, she wouldn't do anything. So I went down and said, "Honey, you've got to make a crash there!" She said, "How do you do that?" [*Laughs.*] Well, it wasn't long until the management decided that she wasn't quite filling the bill and they gave the job to me, and I hated to take her place but I did.

BEHLMER: Where are we in time, now?

CARTER: We're in 1926, because one of the big drawing cards in those days for silent movies in little theaters like that was Harold Lloyd. He always had his pictures on a percentage, and he would send a representative out to see that they were getting the proper percentage. The representative would buy the first ticket when the box office opened, and then would either buy the last one or get the number of the last one. Then they could claim their proper percentage. Nobody trusted anybody. And this guy had nothing to do while he was there, so he'd come in and sit down and listen to the picture. Later he went to Harold and said, "There's a kid out here in Inglewood who's really kicking the heck out of the score to this picture, and he's helping the movie by what he's doing." So Lloyd apparently came out and listened. While I didn't meet him at the time, he recommended me to the management of the Publix Theatres in downtown Los Angeles. They had at that time the Million Dollar, the Metropolitan—later on called the Paramount—and the Rialto, all in downtown L.A. And they had brought me down to be at the Million Dollar Theatre, which was the main presentation house! When I went there about the end of August in '26, the feature picture was *The Temptress* with Greta Garbo. There was a small symphony orchestra playing the music for the feature, and I would spell the orchestra. We'd share most of the films, and then I'd play the last one at night.

BEHLMER: When you say you'd "share," you wouldn't play along *with* the orchestra?

CARTER: No, I wouldn't play with them.

BEHLMER: It would be either the orchestra or you.

CARTER: They would play about 30 minutes, and then we'd find a place where there was, let's say, an oboe solo, and I'd start playing the oboe solo on the organ and the oboe would drop out and then gradually everybody else would drop out and I would bring in the full organ, and we would do that in such a way that people wouldn't realize that the orchestra had stopped playing.

BEHLMER: Then the orchestra could take a break.

CARTER: They'd take a break for about 20 minutes. They'd quietly take off from the orchestra pit and fade.

BEHLMER: Was that more or less the pattern all over?

CARTER: Yes. What they wanted to do was find somebody who could play in an orchestral manner. And there were some who could and some who couldn't. The minute the organ started, you suddenly went from the opera house into the cathedral or [*laughs*] a very small church.

BEHLMER: What size orchestra?

CARTER: Thirty-six people, and the director was Leo Forbstein, who later on became Music Director for Warner Bros. In addition to the feature picture, which we shared, there was an orchestral overture always and I would usually come in on the finale for that. Then there would be a stage show. When I first went there, Paul Whiteman, with his great orchestra, was on the stage. He introduced the *Rhapsody in Blue*, and I want to tell you, that was an experience. It was.

BEHLMER: They were on the stage versus the pit.

CARTER: They were on the stage and there was the regular orchestra in the pit, so you can imagine how many musicians there were. Whiteman had an orchestra with close to 30 people on the stage, and there were 36 in the pit. They didn't play together, but there they were. The orchestra played the newsreel and I would play the cartoon. Then for the last show at night the orchestra would start and play for about ten minutes and then I would play the rest of the last show. And when we did *Ben-Hur* at the Million Dollar Theatre the manager gave me a little description of what he wanted that I've been using ever since. He said, "Now Gaylord, while the people are coming in we want you to keep some music going, but don't assault them with a lot of frantic organ. Just 'perfume the air with music'."

BEHLMER: [*Laughs.*] And you nodded knowingly.

CARTER: People were always late getting there, and I played for about an hour. *Ben-Hur* ran six months at the Million Dollar Theatre. I still have the score. I carried it home with me, and I still refer to it.

BEHLMER: When you were playing during this period, did the theater always use the score provided or did you use an alternate score?

CARTER: Well, Forbstein had a scorer—we also called him a synchronizer—and usually the score that we did there was his compilation. C.P. LanFranchi was his name. He was a very nice little Italian guy who liked to use a lot of Verdi and Puccini in his scores.

BEHLMER: How did he function, exactly?

CARTER: He had to get the music together and see that it fit, make proper cuts and arrange for the segues and do it so that when the orchestra got a hold of it, it all made sense.

BEHLMER: And, usually, the big theaters would all have their own synchronizer?

CARTER: Yeah, yeah. In *The Scarlet Letter* with Lillian Gish, which we premiered there, here is Lillian walking down the street with a crowd of villagers following her with nasty comments, throwing things, and she had on the scarlet letter, and for this LanFranchi introduced the "Via Appia" from *The Pines of Rome*. And I was so impressed with that piece that I've used it in my compilation score to *The King of Kings* ever since.

BEHLMER: This was not the *Scarlet Letter* score that was sent out?

CARTER: No. In this particular case, LanFranchi scored *The Scarlet Letter*.

BEHLMER: He would do it for just that theater?

CARTER: For just that theater, yes.

BEHLMER: Based on your knowledge of other places, did this go on a lot? In all the major theaters?

CARTER: In all the major theaters, I would say. Now the *Ben-Hur* score was by David Mendoza and William Axt. They were at the Capitol Theatre in New York and they did most of the scores for MGM's big pictures at that time.

BEHLMER: But the theaters did not necessarily use their scores?

CARTER: They were available if you wanted.

BEHLMER: What percentage, would you say, used the scores that were supplied?

CARTER: I wouldn't even be able to hazard a guess. I would think that in the major cities they would use them. Maybe in places like Woodstock, Kansas, where they didn't have orchestras in the theaters, the organist would be invited to use it if he wanted to. But you know, we all had cue sheets in those days. When I was playing at the Seville and at the Sunshine Theatre, when the manager would book the shows the film exchanges would give him a cue sheet and he would hand me eight or ten cue sheets at a time. In this way you'd know what you were up against—whether it was a drama or a comedy, whether it was an Indian picture or frozen north or tropical picture or what—and you'd also know if there was going to be a bugle call or a chime, or bells, or steamboat whistles; you'd know in advance, so you didn't get caught. When you're looking at a picture and you suddenly see a train whistle and you're not ready for it, it's gone.

I remember one time we did a picture with Gilda Gray called *The Devil Dancer*. It was a Goldwyn picture, and Goldwyn, instead of having Leo Forbstein and his scorer LanFranchi do a score for that, hired Carli Elinor, who was musical director at the Carthay Circle Theatre, to compile and arrange it. Well, Forbstein was so annoyed—they're all dead now, so I can tell you this—Forbstein said, "Now Gaylord, you play Elinor's score, but don't play it too good." [*Both laugh.*] Now another case, when we did *Beau Geste* with Ronald Colman, there was a score that was provided. I don't remember whether this was Hugo . . .

BEHLMER: . . . Riesenfeld. Yes, it was.

CARTER: We got the score from the Forum Theatre. It was just full of wonderful music, including the music that was written for the score—"Brother Theme" and the "Legion March." I remember that score. I went out and borrowed the music and still have it.

BEHLMER: Was it a compilation score?

CARTER: Right. Some original material . . . just very few things.

BEHLMER: What was the determining factor in this instance?

CARTER: It was Paramount. They insisted that we use the score that they had at the Forum.

BEHLMER: Would they "insist" a lot? Did different studios . . .

CARTER: Mostly it was recommended. I'll tell you another example of studio pressure. *The Student Prince* with Ramon Novarro premiered at the Million Dollar. Now, the studio wanted to avoid any royalties, so they told us they wouldn't let us use the Romberg score. They wanted us to use the score to Luders' *The Prince of Pilsen*, which didn't fit it *at all*. But there was so much fuss made. They previewed the picture out in Glendale. A friend of mine, Frank Lanterman, played the picture. They didn't want him to play the Romberg score and he said, "Well, I'm going to do it because everybody will expect it, and the other doesn't fit." Well, the studio was adamant in refusing to pay for the Romberg score. But by the time we got it, they had compromised. And we played the picture with the Romberg score. I couldn't conceive of doing it without it; it would have been pure corn. So we just took the

Romberg music and LanFranchi adapted it to the orchestra we had, made the orchestrations, and the studio went along with it.

BEHLMER: You did *The Last Command* in 1928, I recall you saying. Emil Jannings, William Powell, Evelyn Brent—who was very good, incidentally.

CARTER: Oh, she was. At the Million Dollar I had a great theme for her in the picture, written by Tchaikovsky, called "Intermezzo," transcribed from his Suite, Opus 43. I remember before we played *The Last Command*, during the preceding picture's run I had been working with this gal, Claire Forbes Crane. She played the Tchaikovsky Piano Concerto at the California Theatre with Carli Elinor. So the theme from the Tchaikovsky [*hums*] . . . I'm playing this for the trailer—previews of coming attractions. And Forbstein sends a representative down to me and says, "Leo wants to know what that is you're playing?" I said, "Tell him it's the main theme from the first movement of the Tchaikovsky Piano Concerto." So they used that as the main theme in the scoring for the picture. LanFranchi made an arrangement of this and they used it throughout.

BEHLMER: Since you were supplied with scores for so many of the films, compilations or otherwise, why would you not always use these scores?

CARTER: We'd often use the score if there was one available. I'd say only one picture in ten would have a score.

BEHLMER: If you used the score that went out with the picture, was it expensive?

CARTER: I don't believe so. You would have to rent the score. The theater would rent the parts, and on some occasions I expect they would buy the parts.

BEHLMER: I'm still not clear about the reason for doing another score when there was an "official" score available. Just somebody's whim? Or . . .

CARTER: I think that the local ego of the musical directors and/or conductors had something to do with it. They would probably go to management and say, anything we could do would be better.

BEHLMER: So it wouldn't necessarily have to be monetary or because of restrictions, or . . .

CARTER: I think it would have to do largely with whoever was concerned with it—the musical director and his budget.

BEHLMER: Did you use any of the very few completely original scores of the time?

CARTER: Mortimer Wilson did . . . *Thief of Bagdad*.

BEHLMER: There were two scores for *The Thief of Bagdad*, weren't there?

CARTER: At least. I had access to the Wilson score, and my feeling about it was that it wasn't very easily adapted to organ. My score consists of a theme for "The Thief" character that I composed, material from *Scheherazade* of course, and the main theme is "Ah, Moon of My Delight" from *In a Persian Garden* by Liza Lehmann—and it's a beautiful thing. Then I use the H. Bemberg "Hindu Song" for the holy man in the temple. I used a lot of stuff from the James Bradford cue sheet, but I never did use anything from the Mortimer Wilson score, which was completely original with nothing lifted from other sources. I don't think a lot of the orchestras could hack the Wilson score.

BEHLMER: In addition to Wilson, are you familiar with other composers who wrote purely original scores? I know that there were scores that had original themes and elements, some were entirely compiled, and some were partially original and partially compiled.

CARTER: There were very few completely original scores then. There were so many ideas as to what constituted good movie music. There was a firm called Belwin, one of the companies that specialized in movie music. And there were all kinds of writers. There was an English composer . . . the guy that did *In a Persian Market*.

BEHLMER: Ketelbey.

CARTER: Yeah, Ketelbey. He wrote a lot of incidental music for silent movies. Then there was the Italian composer Riccardo Drigo. A lot of theaters didn't have synchronizers like LanFranchi. And they would rely on just putting stuff together, if they had a library; or go to a library and get the stuff and just find something that would fit, and then pass the parts out. But on the score for *The Devil Dancer* that Samuel Goldwyn insisted we use, I remember that LanFranchi wrote a theme that was real nice. But Goldwyn wanted to feature a well known Italian . . . sort of a boat song, Drigo's "Serenade" from *Harlequin's Millions*, and I remember that Leo Forbstein and LanFranchi thought that was way beneath us. [*Hums.*] It's a nice piece. Drigo was adding to his popularity as a composer by writing a lot of stuff for films. And I had quite a few of them.

BEHLMER: Do you remember whether James C. Bradford was a composer or primarily a compiler?

CARTER: He was a compiler. And I got the impression, having dealt with so many cue sheets of his, that he had certain favorite publishing companies, because certain little numbers would show up on all of his cue sheets. He may have been in the publishing business himself, or he may have had connections with the publishing business. There'd be a lot of things, especially J.S. Zamecnik and Domenico Savino titles, that were on his cue sheets all the time. But if a Wagnerian piece was indicated, he would have it in there.

BEHLMER: You don't recall him doing any original things?

CARTER: I don't think so. There may have been one or two. I think that he did cue sheets for all the motion picture companies.

BEHLMER: Who actually was responsible, if you were breaking down the compositions and compilations—were there staffs of people? I'm speaking now of the big scores, let's say one of the Hugo Riesenfeld scores or the *Ben-Hur* score.

CARTER: Oh, yes.

BEHLMER: Generally, did the man who was credited with it . . .

CARTER: He was just a supervisor.

BEHLMER: He would perhaps come up with the general pattern and then the other people . . .

CARTER: True. The Capitol Theatre in New York had an enormous staff, doing just this. We didn't do it to the same extent. Our staff at the Million Dollar consisted of Leo Forbstein, C.P. LanFranchi, and two librarians.

BEHLMER: What would their duties be, specifically?

CARTER: Knowing where to find the music that LanFranchi wanted.

BEHLMER: By "knowing where to find it"—you mean outside. Not in the library.

CARTER: Yeah, where to order it and where to buy it. They would be "procurers" of music. I remember, for instance, if he would want the Finale to *La Bohème*, with which I remember we ended *The Scarlet Letter*, there were lots of companies in Los Angeles then that had scores and parts of movie music on hand, and you could go down there and you could probably get a score of *La Bohème* with all the parts and just take out the parts you wanted.

BEHLMER: It would be a question of buying or renting it.

CARTER: You could do it both ways. I would say in our case they'd buy it and add it to the library in the theater. It was a huge library.

BEHLMER: What were the names of some of the companies where you could get this material?

CARTER: The main one was G. Schirmer, of course. Then there was Morse Preeman and Carl Fischer. They all had music stores here and you could get most of what you wanted, including the orchestra parts, from all of those sources.

BEHLMER: Did you have your own music library?

CARTER: Well, coming from a musical family—my father was a church organist and my mother taught piano—we had an awful lot of music in the house that was available to me, and so I could use Mendelssohn, Mozart, Beethoven, and so on.

BEHLMER: Once you established yourself in the theaters did you personally start acquiring music?

CARTER: Yes I did. While I was playing in some of the little theaters, there were certain pieces in the cue sheets we'd get that looked interesting. I'd go buy them. Then, when we got to the Million Dollar and the scores were being produced there, I bought copies of everything that we did and I've still got them. I've got an elaborate library of old movie music. It's going to go to the University of Cincinnati in my will.

BEHLMER: On these compilation scores did you keep seeing the same material come up over and over again? Certain things that worked . . .

CARTER: Especially with James Bradford. He had a little piece called "Le Retour," which is a kind of perpetual motion thing. I bet he had that in a hundred cue sheets I saw. I never did buy it, but it's a little piece, a little rondo kind of thing. Incidentally, I have a few students that I coach in scoring. They say, "What do you use here?" Well, I say, "Something neutral." That means nothing to them. But to me it means something that isn't specific but is in the mood of the action. It wouldn't be a special piece. So I have to come up with something. And I remember I have said, if I had a copy of "Le Retour," that's what we would use here.

BEHLMER: Maurice Baron—are you familiar with him?

CARTER: Oh, yes, yes.

BEHLMER: He was a composer, an arranger, and an orchestrator, right? In fact, he orchestrated some of the big David Mendoza and William Axt scores.

CARTER: Yes.

BEHLMER: Did he actually compose original material for silent films?

CARTER: He would compose what you would call dramatic agitatos. There's one called "Tumult, Battle and Blaze," which could be used for catastrophic scenes. He operated in New York. We played a lot of his music.

BEHLMER: For a rental fee?

CARTER: No, whenever I played his music it would come up in the score that people like LanFranchi had put together. I'd go out and buy it because I liked it. So I bought practically everything that we used of his, and I've still got it.

BEHLMER: You say you did use the supplied score for *Ben-Hur*?

CARTER: This was not a road show situation. We did it as a grind, which was very unusual for that time. But I don't remember the Million Dollar ever having a road show. So we didn't do an intermission for the picture. There's an intermission that comes almost right after the chariot race. The score I've got indicates where the intermission comes. It was a hard ticket, reserved seat show around the country. And I think in New York it was. The orchestra would play for about 45 minutes, and then I would play another half hour or so and the orchestra would finish the picture. This would be the main show in the afternoon, and then we'd have what was called the supper show, and I had an assistant that played that. I'd come in with the orchestra about 7:00 in the evening and we'd do the overture. At the time we did *Ben-Hur*, we had a wild chariot race on stage, with horses! The end of the thing was very short. The horses would dash across the stage with the chariots, the curtains would close, and we would go into the picture.

BEHLMER: And this was just part of the stage presentation?

CARTER: Yeah. They had a stage presentation that was known as an atmospheric prologue of the *Ben-Hur* type of thing. The last show at

Gaylord Carter, at the age of 21, at the Wurlitzer Organ of Los Angeles' Million Dollar Theatre, 1926

night the orchestra would play maybe the first ten minutes, and then I'd play the rest of it. There was an assistant manager there who was an awfully nice guy. He just loved the chariot race. And he liked the music. Of course, the music was all in a 9/8, you know.

BEHLMER: Full gallop!

CARTER: Oh, full gallop. And this went on for about eleven minutes. It was a *wild* thing! I was playing the music from the score. This assistant manager came down and sat in about the third row every night while we did the chariot race. So I never could loaf on that last show. He was *always* there. I had to play this chariot race *furiously*!

BEHLMER: The big performance of the evening—the eight o'clock show or thereabouts—that was still back and forth between . . .

CARTER: Yes, back and forth.

BEHLMER: So, the supper show you would have your assistant do. And that would be strictly organ.

CARTER: Strictly organ.

BEHLMER: And then the matinee, assuming there was a matinee . . .

CARTER: There'd be orchestra and organ.

BEHLMER: Of course the orchestra members were the same, day and night.

CARTER: Well, they'd work from about one till five, with a couple of rests, and then from about seven till ten. The last show started at ten. In the case of *Ben-Hur*, it was past midnight every night.

BEHLMER: Would you say this would be fairly typical of the big houses in which you worked?

CARTER: Yeah.

BEHLMER: And that probably would be similar around the country. But when you get into the smaller theaters, that's a different act.

CARTER: In the smaller theaters it was mostly organ. In some cases piano. But mostly organ.

BEHLMER: In the evening, did you wear tuxes? I'm speaking of you and the rest of the musicians.

CARTER: Yeah, we all wore tuxes at the Million Dollar. Day and night.

BEHLMER: And was that standard operating procedure?

CARTER: At the big houses, yeah. They were just regular black tuxedos, and they got all worn out and frazzled and you looked like a bum.

BEHLMER: We think of Leo Forbstein mostly as the musical director at Warner Bros. later when sound came in. But at this time he was the musical director at the Million Dollar.

CARTER: He would supervise the scoring, but LanFranchi actually did it.

BEHLMER: Did Forbstein conduct at all of the performances?

CARTER: Very rarely, very rarely. Sometimes at the premiere.

BEHLMER: Didn't Forbstein want to conduct?

CARTER: No, he had an assistant to conduct. I think Forbstein would conduct the overture. And the newsreel, usually.

BEHLMER: This was at most performances?

CARTER: Yeah, at most performances. His associate conductor or assistant conductor would conduct the picture.

"Tumult, Battle and Blaze"

BEHLMER: According to what Ray Heindorf told me, Forbstein conducted only occasionally on the scoring stage at Warners in the 1930s and '40s. He didn't compose.

CARTER: No, he was not a composer. He was mostly an administrator. I remember one time I was playing at the edge of the stage; the curtain was right above the organ. One time Leo Forbstein came, looked down at me and said, "Gaylord, you're playing the wrong notes."

BEHLMER: Really?

CARTER: Yes. He and the stage manager used to play pinochle in a room right below the organ chambers.

BEHLMER: Well, do you think he was kidding you?

CARTER: No, I don't think so. I probably played something wrong. I think I remember the piece. I think it was the primary theme from *Swan Lake* [*sings*].

BEHLMER: That only happened one time?

CARTER: Only once, yes. After that, I was very careful.

BEHLMER: That's very funny. In between pinochle hands. Would Forbstein decide what scores would be modified, or which ones would be done by LanFranchi?

CARTER: He would decide.

BEHLMER: And he would be at most of the rehearsals, I would imagine.

CARTER: Oh yes.

BEHLMER: Speaking of rehearsals, let's talk about that for a minute. Since you were changing the bill frequently . . . At the Million Dollar, though, things would run longer . . .

CARTER: I think the shortest thing we ever had there was two weeks. *Tell It to the Marines* with Lon Chaney ran for a month, and *The Temptress* with Greta Garbo ran for, I think, about two months. I enjoyed that. And we had a great LanFranchi compilation score for it.

BEHLMER: What would be a pattern for rehearsing, since obviously the theater was going all the time? When the new picture was coming up, when *did* you rehearse?

CARTER: Well, Forbstein, when we'd start scoring a new picture, would tell me how much the orchestra was going to do and how much I was going to do, and then he would hand me his score, his guide. LanFranchi would hand me the main themes, and I would incorporate them into my organ music for that part of the picture that I would do. Now, in the case of *Ben-Hur*, of course, I played the score as written for my part. When we would have a picture like *Ben-Hur*, about three days in advance of the opening we would have rehearsals in the morning, and the orchestra would be all splendid musicians. They could read all this at sight.

BEHLMER: This would be rehearsal with the film?

CARTER: No, there would not be a rehearsal with the film. It would be just a rehearsal of the orchestra parts. Maybe there was a rehearsal with the film. I don't really remember. But I would have a rehearsal with the film, usually, because the operators would run the film the night before to be sure they had a good print, and I would just stay over, after my last thing, and I'd work on the score we had put together—with the film on that occasion.

BEHLMER: Would there be more than one or two rehearsals?

CARTER: On a major picture like *Ben-Hur*, we would rehearse for two mornings. On a smaller picture, like maybe *Chang* or whatever, one rehearsal.

BEHLMER: We're talking about three hours?

CARTER: About three hours for each rehearsal. Then the first performance in the afternoon of the opening day would be the rehearsal with the film. And that was kind of tricky. They would have a speedometer on the musical director's stand to be sure that the film was going at the speed that the scoring was done to.

BEHLMER: The speed of silent film varies.

CARTER: It really did. It started at about 18 frames a second and then I think it went to 19, and then to 20, and sound, of course, is 24 frames.

BEHLMER: Would there be an annotation on the score, saying it was to be projected at . . .

CARTER: *Ben-Hur* was designated, I think, at 20 frames. Now, of course, when we do it, we run it at 24 frames. I had an argument with a guy about that once. I was playing a concert version of the Galley Slave theme, and somebody said, "No galley slave could possibly keep up with that tempo." [*Laughs.*] And I said, "Well, we're running the film now at 24 frames, and it does go a little faster than the original. But if we ran *Ben-Hur* at 20 frames, we'd be there all night." I remember a few years ago we were running *The Thief of Bagdad* in San Francisco. It is a long, long movie—over two hours at 24 frames. And some projectionist up there said, "Well, this is a silent picture. Let's do it at silent speed (18 frames)." I was just dragging out this stuff unmercifully. And I didn't understand what was the matter. A buddy of mine with the theater realized it was going at the wrong speed and had the projectionist increase it.

BEHLMER: Unfortunately, that's a common mistake. People somehow feel that silent films should run at 16 or 18 frames, which, of course, is not, with rare exception, the case. If you don't have a rheostat, they're better off running at 24.

CARTER: A good example of the speed is in *The Winning of Barbara Worth*. Henry King *loved* closeups of Vilma Banky, and he just stayed on her face unmercifully. And if you take a picture like that and run it at silent speed, well . . . The only thing I've noticed that you have to be careful of is the Keystone Kops. That does get a little fast at 24.

BEHLMER: Something like the Keystone Kops—we're talking about 1914, 1915—then they *were* going around 16 or 18, and, of course, they were deliberately under-cranking to speed up the action anyway. But you get into *The Winning of Barbara Worth*—late '20s—that was about 24.

CARTER: Very close to it.

BEHLMER: Particularly that '26–'27 period. Well, getting back to the rehearsal routine: that procedure you described pretty much would be the way it was done during those days?

CARTER: I would say so, except if a theater was trying to fit it into the budget, and the rehearsal costs were high. The reason that studio musicians, certain ones, are in such demand today is because they *instantly* can make sense of what's there. You don't have to have long rehearsals. And with the orchestra of the Million Dollar Theatre, these were musicians comparable to the L.A. Philharmonic. I remember we had a bass player that filled in for our bass once, and they got the chief of the bass section of the Philharmonic Orchestra, Fred Huber. He played so loud on this bass that it drowned out the whole orchestra. You never heard such a thing. Oh, it was incredible.

BEHLMER: For a musician, the Million Dollar was considered to be a good job.

CARTER: Oh, it was a good job.

BEHLMER: I would imagine there wasn't much turnover.

CARTER: Very little turnover in the three years that I was there.

BEHLMER: They wouldn't be doing other things as well. They couldn't. There wasn't any time.

"Tumult, Battle and Blaze"

CARTER: No, they couldn't. It wasn't like today where the Philharmonic people are playing in the studios, and the studio people are playing television. When I first went down to the Million Dollar Theatre, I was just some interim guy they hired until they were supposed to find somebody good. And I understand that my job was saved by the guy who was taking care of the organ—we had maintenance every night. You'd get some valves that would stick and wind lines that would leak. And I was nearly always there practicing when he got there. I was the only organist in town who was practicing late at night. And he went to the head man and said, "Look, this kid is really knocking himself out there." So, I stayed at the Million Dollar until they closed.

BEHLMER: You were strongly motivated.

CARTER: I was enormously motivated by the scores that we were using. By what LanFranchi was doing. I was with the best. I was with the very best. And I had an opportunity to study how they were putting it together and what they did and the music that they used. So this was an absolutely marvelous experience for a kid.

BEHLMER: Obviously the movie theaters were open seven days a week. Did you and the orchestra ever have any days off?

CARTER: Yes, the union required that you have a day off.

BEHLMER: How would you work it with the orchestra?

CARTER: They would stagger it. There'd be a few guys off each day.

BEHLMER: Would they have replacements?

CARTER: They would have replacements, and the replacements were usually very good musicians. Very often they would be from the L.A. Philharmonic. I had a day off and my assistant just filled in on those days. Later on, when I got to be a featured performer in the theaters, the union made some allowances for the fact that I was advertised and should be there. So I think that I played seven days, but it wasn't difficult. I only played ten minutes at a time about four times a day as a featured performer.

BEHLMER: Did they put a spotlight on you when . . .

CARTER: Only if you were going to do a special solo. Now, at the Million Dollar, I didn't do a solo until just before I left.

BEHLMER: Now, when you say solo, you mean—

CARTER: Item five on the program.

BEHLMER: Gaylord Carter . . .

CARTER: . . . at the organ.

BEHLMER: In those days, in some of the theaters, did you have the elevator, with the organ coming up?

CARTER: Well, not at the Million Dollar. It just sat on the floor of the orchestra pit. But when I went to the United Artists, they had it there. They had it at the Paramount. You'd come up to what was called "picture level." That would mean the top of the organ console would be about even with the stage. And most of the control boards had the picture level on them—if you were coming from the depths down below. But at the Million Dollar, we just walked down the aisle and through a little sliding door onto the organ. The one in the Chicago Theatre—I was so surprised to discover that the organ elevator, the one that Jesse Crawford made famous, rose only four feet.

BEHLMER: Were there any other players at the time with whom you were particularly impressed—I mean organists who were doing motion picture music?

CARTER: Oh, sure. Most of the ones that were my predecessors at the Million Dollar—Jesse Crawford had played there, of course. We all listened to him because he was the kingpin. I used to think that his arrangements were over-simplified. "When the Organ Played at Twilight" was one of his big numbers. Milton Charles had played at the Million Dollar, and Henry B. Murtagh. But the best of all during that period were Albert Hay Malotte, who wrote "The Lord's Prayer" music, and Alexander Schreiner, the chief organist of the Tabernacle in Salt Lake City. He was organist at the Paramount Theatre at one time.

BEHLMER: In Los Angeles?

CARTER: Los Angeles, uh-huh. It was called the Metropolitan when he was there. I would go and hear him play these dazzling solos. He would do something like "The Ride of the Valkyries," which would make your hair stand right up. Then they wanted something on a more popular style and they hired a man by the name of Herb Kern. And he came in and played "Isle of Capri" and that kind of thing. It wasn't very stimulating. Both Schreiner and Malotte were magnificent organists. An awful lot of other organists who were in this particular field got by with a minimum of scholarship, so that when you found somebody who really knew something about the organ and was in addition a profound student of music, it was a great thing. Then the scores took life and soared and did great credit to what was going on on the screen.

BEHLMER: I imagine some of the others were rather mechanical.

CARTER: Yeah, well they relied on the cue sheet, and it said to play some piece for $3/4$ of a minute and that's what they'd do. They watched their clock instead of watching the screen. It was a period, like anything else, where you had every conceivable combination of talent and experience. I kind of had my own ideas about things through the organ being a part of my family setup, and so I used to think that most of the organists in the theaters didn't have any actual classical background in organ playing. They didn't make it sound like an organ. Did you know when sound arrived, the *Los Angeles Times* came out with a story, and the headline said, "Sound Films Drive Organists From Theatres. Managers Rejoice." [*Laughs.*]

BEHLMER: Before sound, did you, as so many people did, feel that this was all going to go on . . .

CARTER: Indefinitely. Forever. Of course. It wasn't a question of, well, one of these days they're going to do something else.

BEHLMER: So it must have been a major shock to virtually all of the musicians when sound really took over.

CARTER: It emptied the theaters of musicians. And of course they hated the organists who stayed on. I stayed for about three years, I think, after sound came in.

BEHLMER: Of the organists playing at the time, there are only a few of you still around.

CARTER: Yeah, there are not very many. One of the best is Lloyd Del Castillo, who played in Boston and had a theater organ school there, training theater organists. He's still alive and in his middle 90s. And of course Ann Leaf. She was at the Metropolitan.

BEHLMER: Were there many women organists?

CARTER: There were quite a few.

BEHLMER: Throughout the country?

CARTER: Yes. My two assistants at the Million Dollar were both gals.

BEHLMER: You were saying some of the other organists that were still around . . .

CARTER: There's one who was in the Chicago area; he's now in Atlanta. He's older than I am, if that's possible—John Muri. There are several kids that are doing this. One is a house organist at the Ohio Theatre in Columbus, Dennis James. He'll tell you that he heard there was a guy going to play a silent movie at the Tower Theater in Philadelphia, and he went. And it was me. He said, that night, "That's what I want to do." He'll tell you that. Before he went into competition.

BEHLMER: Is there much of a market for young people?

CARTER: No, not really. If you're going to make a profession of this, I don't think you can depend on making an adequate living playing organ concerts.

BEHLMER: I heard that the Eastman School of Music in Rochester was founded to coach musicians for silent movie theaters, including organists.

CARTER: Yes, yes. They had a department there . . .

BEHLMER: I understand that was the primary purpose in founding it.

CARTER: Well, I know that Eastman, in his big theater there, in connection with the school, had a huge organ. It was a big four-manual Austin organ and he had it installed backstage so the music would come through the screen. Well, in doing this, he just deadened the organ beyond belief, because it was playing in this area backstage and none of it was getting out. And this was before the days of amplification. It didn't work out.

BEHLMER: Let's talk about that transition period from silent to sound films for a minute, Gaylord, because I think most people think sound-on-film or disk started and live musical accompaniment ended. But obviously there was a transition.

CARTER: There was a transition. Nobody recognized this as a *monumental* change. We all thought it was just a fad. We didn't think it would last.

BEHLMER: During that period, did you still have the big orchestras?

CARTER: They kept the large orchestras for a while, and they did presentations. I remember they brought Rubinoff and his violin to the Paramount, and they had big things there with the orchestra. The orchestra stayed on for a while, then I stayed on for a while as a soloist. The organ would rise out of the pit, and I'd play presentations. Then they brought Milton Charles to the Paramount and moved me to the United Artists.

BEHLMER: Both of these theaters were downtown?

CARTER: Yeah. And this would be in about 1931, I think.

BEHLMER: Did the United Artists have a stage policy at that time?

CARTER: Just an organ policy. They had a wonderful organ there. And I stayed there and did the organ solos for quite a while. About a six-minute specialty. The organ would come up and I'd play.

BEHLMER: You eventually went to the Egyptian, didn't you?

CARTER: Yes, after the Warner Bros. Hollywood.

BEHLMER: How long did you stay at the Warner Bros. theater?

CARTER: I was there about two and a half years.

BEHLMER: At the Warner Bros. theater, as I recall, they did have an orchestra. There was a stage . . .

CARTER: There was a stage presentation, yeah.

BEHLMER: . . . in addition to the sound feature film, obviously.

CARTER: Yeah, it was a kind of vaudeville show.

BEHLMER: Then you went to the Egyptian because you got a better offer, or . . .?

CARTER: No, they changed policy and decided to drop the organ and not have any for a while. I went back to UCLA to do some postgraduate work, and one day I was walking by the Egyptian and dropped in. I had met the manager there, Harry Sugerman, and I said, "Hey, how about doing some organ shows for you?" He said, "Why not." And I went there for about half of what I'd been getting. But this was definitely the Depression era.

BEHLMER: You were doing an organ specialty?

CARTER: Yeah. I just played some popular tune, and I would occasionally have slides of current things on the screen and everybody would sing. And then I'd play a little organ solo. I remember one of the ones that they liked best was "Trees." And the best sing-a-long that we ever had was "Isle of Capri."

BEHLMER: Now we're talking '35 . . .

CARTER: We're talking '34, '35. And I stayed there until I got a call from KHJ radio, inviting me to come to work for them.

BEHLMER: We always tend to think of the "mighty Wurlitzer," but obviously there were others. What were some of the organs that were used then?

CARTER: Well, there's one called a Marr & Colton. The Wiltern, where I played for quite a while, had a Kimball—one of the great theater organs of all time. It's now in a big church in West Hollywood. And the organ at the Orpheum is still there. It was a Wurlitzer. The Million Dollar organ is gone. The big theater organs of those days were Wurlitzer, Marr & Colton, Kimball, and the Robert Morton.

BEHLMER: Were there major differences between them, or were they more or less the same?

CARTER: Wurlitzer was the Rolls-Royce of them. They were all good. Estey made some. I played an Estey at the Seville Theatre in Inglewood when I was there. But I play all kinds. There's another organ company that built organs in the Middle West called Barton, and they made very good organs. And Moller was another.

BEHLMER: What were the basic differences?

CARTER: The reason that Wurlitzer was so outstanding . . . they probably had the greatest mind in the history of theater organs, a guy by the name of Robert Hope-Jones. Hope-Jones was an Englishman who came to this country and opened an organ factory in Elmira, New York. He had the idea of increasing the pressure. Now, the toe of the pipe is in a chest, and when you put down a key it opens a valve, and the air under pressure in that chest goes into the pipe and makes the sound. Now, church organs have low pressure. But he thought that by increasing the pressure, you'd increase the brilliance of the reeds and the string tone, which is done with slender pipes. And mainly the tibia, which is a flute, and he designed it. It gives a nice kind of hooting sound. You play tibias and voxes together and that's how you play "Hearts and Flowers" and "I Love You Truly" and all those things on the tibia. Nobody has ever been able to duplicate that sound. The Robert Mortons, the Bartons, the Marr and Coltons, the Geneva, the Smith—they all had tibias. But none of them could touch the quality of the Wurlitzer tibia. And that made the Wurlitzer unique. Plus the fact that it looked like a Rolls-Royce.

BEHLMER: In terms of other capabilities, were they pretty much . . .

CARTER: Pretty much the same. They all had drums and bells and xylophones and tambourines, and steamboat whistles and . . .

BEHLMER: Were they all approximately the same size?

CARTER: Well, yes. The smallest one that I had at the Sunshine was four ranks of pipes, up to the biggest one, which is probably in Radio City Music Hall, which has maybe 42 sets of pipes. But that's nothing. You take a big organ like the Crystal Cathedral, it has 315 sets of pipes!

BEHLMER: What was this one machine that we were talking about earlier . . . the Fotoplayer?

CARTER: The Fotoplayer. That was a piano with two sets of pipes. A kind of a little flute sound, and a little . . .

BEHLMER: You mean it was a piano with partial organ . . .

CARTER: Yes, partially organ. You'd press a key and if you put down the stop that said flute, it would not only play the piano, it would play the flute too. They were kind of funny little things. They hooted, and . . .

"*Tumult, Battle and Blaze*"

BEHLMER: Were they popular?

CARTER: Oh, the smaller theaters that couldn't afford pipe organs had them. The first that I ever played was in the Kansas Theatre in Wichita.

BEHLMER: Would you say that most theaters had live accompaniment or automatic instruments—automatic pianos and automatic orchestras?

CARTER: I don't remember any automatic in Los Angeles. Now in Wichita, where I was, they had the Fotoplayers there. They would have two slots where you would put in piano rolls, and so you could put one in here and run it for a little while and then put one in here, and when you wanted to change the scene you'd bring in the second one. And they'd go back and forth, so you could score that way. I never heard of any theater in L.A. doing it.

BEHLMER: Forgetting L.A., would you say that in general throughout the country there would be considerable use of this or . . .

CARTER: I don't think so. I mean, they either had a piano player or an organist, or a small combo.

BEHLMER: How small a combo?

CARTER: I think maybe five or six people was the smallest. Because the music was arranged for at least one trumpet and one clarinet and maybe one trombone, and then strings. So, you take a place like the Mission Theatre in downtown Los Angeles, where they had the premiere of *The White Sister* with Ronald Colman and Lillian Gish . . .

BEHLMER: They didn't have a full orchestra?

CARTER: They had six pieces. A drum, a trumpet, trombone, clarinet, violin, and a cello, I think. Something like that. You wouldn't have a string quartet in a pit doing these things because they don't provide the kind of sound that's expected. The first thing you had to have, if you had any kind of a combo, was the drummer. So you could get the punches and rifle shots and cataclysmic things like an earthquake. You'd need a trumpet for bugle calls. And it would be nice to have a clarinet. You didn't have to have it. You had to have usually one violin and a second violin. You wouldn't have a viola, but you'd have a cello and maybe a bass. And you could make a lot of music with these. I'll never forget, while I was between the matinee and the evening shift, I dropped in to see *The White Sister*. And they did something that I had never heard before. There were some very dynamic scenes. And they always started with a tremendous tympani roll. It would just raise you out of your seat. We never did this at the Million Dollar. It was very startling. And another thing, it introduced me to "The Swan" from *Carnival of the Animals* by Saint-Saëns. That was the theme for *The White Sister*. [*Hums.*]

BEHLMER: For *Wings* in 1927, didn't they, at least at the road show performances, have some percussionists backstage or in the wings?

CARTER: Oh, I believe they did, yeah.

BEHLMER: So this would be in addition to the pit.

CARTER: For the battle scenes.

BEHLMER: The booms and the crashes and bombs and so forth were being done with the augmented tympani.

CARTER: The supplied Zamecnik score for *Wings* in the opening aerial battles indicated the Mendelssohn *Midsummer Night's Dream* scherzo, which I didn't think quite fit an aerial battle. And so I wrote another little thing for it. Of course, everybody said, "Gaylord, do you think you're better than Mendelssohn?" I would say to that, "Well, Mendelssohn was one of the world's greats, but he didn't write that for a movie."

BEHLMER: In the 1920s the assumption was that there were not many movie-going people who would be that familiar with the standard repertoire, so you could do a lot of things that you wouldn't dare do now—certain musical cliches as we now regard them.

"Tumult, Battle and Blaze"

CARTER: Oh, definitely! It was desirable to use the *William Tell* Overture for a chase, for example. Of course, that was before *The Lone Ranger*. It was acceptable.

BEHLMER: Would the Mission Theatre be considered a middle-of-the-range theater?

CARTER: Well, it was a first-run house.

BEHLMER: So a lot of first-run houses would have a six-piece ...

CARTER: Oh, yeah.

BEHLMER: In Los Angeles during the '20s—we're talking about what? Maybe three or four houses that would have a 38-piece orchestra?

CARTER: Yes, there was a house—the California Theatre—I believe it was on Main Street. That's where Carli Elinor had his orchestra. They had a big orchestra, maybe 24 to 26 to 30 pieces.

BEHLMER: Did you know Carli Elinor?

CARTER: Yes, I did. He was a little bit imperious.

BEHLMER: What about the Egyptian and the Chinese?

CARTER: They had about 24 to 30 pieces.

BEHLMER: What you'd call a large orchestra then would be 38?

CARTER: Oh, yes, that would be large. The Million Dollar had 38. Also the Paramount and maybe the Carthay Circle. That would be about it.

BEHLMER: That's interesting, because you think of the Chinese as being such a big house, and the Egyptian. You picture them having bigger orchestras.

CARTER: Well, the Chinese had one of the big orchestras. I think the Chinese opened with *The King of Kings*.

BEHLMER: You're right. In 1927.

CARTER: It was about a 30-piece orchestra. And Sid Grauman, he supervised everything. He told the musicians what to play. He told the director what to do. He was extremely knowledgeable. And the score for *The King of Kings* was . . .

BEHLMER: Hugo Riesenfeld is credited.

CARTER: Bradford also had a cue sheet. He used a lot of hymns in connection with the score, but for many years I've been using my own compilation. I never did feel that those hymns fit, *except* in the Resurrection Scene. There, a great light shines down on the tomb, where this big rock is. Well, that to me indicates a good spot to play Bach's "Break Forth O Beauteous Heavenly Light," one of the great hymns of all times. Bach harmonized it from somebody else's original, I think. The Bradford cue sheet didn't call for this. It called for "Nearer My God to Thee" and several other things. Anyway, I didn't feel we ought to load down that score with a lot of hymns, with the exception of "Break Forth . . .", but that was really a great thing for that particular scene.

BEHLMER: What else do you use for *The King of Kings*?

CARTER: Bach, Wagner, Saint-Saëns, Respighi, as well as some of my own material. And for my favorite part, when Jesus mends a little girl's doll, I play Leonard Bernstein's "Sanctus" from his *Mass*.

BEHLMER: In New York, although I know you didn't play there, would the big theaters, the Capitol for example . . .

CARTER: Oh, they had sixty musicians.

BEHLMER: Would they pretty much have the same situation with the organist in regard to spelling the players and so on?

CARTER: Oh, yes, yes.

BEHLMER: Gaylord, from your standpoint, what started the silent film revival with you going to various theaters that still had an organ throughout the country and accompanying a silent feature?

CARTER: Well, you remember Jim Day; he was my partner in these things. Jim was a film buff who always had been interested in reviving silent movies. He got a hold of two of Douglas Fairbanks' films: *The Mark of Zorro* and *The Thief of Bagdad* in 1959. We found this Rialto Theatre in South Pasadena, which was a nice place; it had a good organ and I remember we decided to do *The Mark of Zorro*, and we advertised it. You came and saw a packed house and everybody having a great time.

BEHLMER: As a matter of fact, I don't think I'd ever seen a film that was accompanied by a theater organ.

CARTER: Then you brought me to Channel 13 in Hollywood, where you were executive producer and directing, and you devised this weekly half-hour show we did "live" for quite some time. And it went from there.

BEHLMER: Which films, over the years, can you get the most mileage out of in your live revival presentations?

CARTER: Well, the best of course, the ones the people seem to get the most kick out of, are the comedies of Harold Lloyd. Any Harold Lloyd film does well. Although, more and more, people don't remember him. Another one is Buster Keaton. People remember him to a certain extent. And Charlie Chaplin. We always do well with *The Gold Rush*. And *The Circus* is one of my favorite pictures; Charlie Chaplin in *The Circus*. We've done well with that. Comedies I think do better, because people don't have the opportunity at home anymore to laugh in groups with TV. Three thousand people laughing in unison to these antics on the screen is quite an experience. I remember that Harold Lloyd told me once, "Gaylord, when they're laughing, play soft. It's when they're *not* laughing that I need you." Well, with Harold Lloyd they're laughing all the time. And Doug Fairbanks' *Mark of Zorro* and

Broken Blossoms with Lillian Gish go over very well—and, of course, Lon Chaney's *The Phantom of the Opera*.

You know, the combination of a great scene with music that fits is hard to beat. I had a little act that occasionally I did in schools and colleges. I would take the unmasking scene from *The Phantom of the Opera*, and we'd start with the scene where the gal is lying in this bed that he has put her in; she gets up and she's looking at the mirrors and things on her dressing table, and they all have her initials on them. I would play "Somebody Loves Me" (I Wonder Who). Then, we'd get to him playing the organ, and I would play "The Lost Chord." When she would rip the mask off, I would play "Hello, Dolly." Well, of course, this convulsed everybody. Then, while he's saying "What are you doing to me?" I play "You Made Me Love You" (I Didn't Wanna Do It). We'd stop it at the end of the sequence. And I'd say, "Now you've seen how it shouldn't be done; let me show you how it should be done." Then we would play the score. I'd play the "Dies Irae" from the *Fantastic Symphony* of Berlioz, which fits more or less what the Phantom is doing. And then when he stops and turns around, you can go to something else with dramatic content, maybe a little lower . . . probably put the vibratos back on. But anyway, everybody would laugh their head off when I was doing these other things, these tunes. Then, when we would do it straight, you could hear a pin drop. Because the music is just part of what you're seeing. And the students in high schools and colleges would be astounded by what this is all about. They've never heard of such a thing. They couldn't believe that there was ever anything like this going on. And they were wondering why it didn't keep going. Well, the reason of course is that it was no longer needed. But only in these special ways—"presentations."

BEHLMER: You knew Harold Lloyd pretty well.

CARTER: Yeah, we got to be good friends.

BEHLMER: He really kept his films in first-rate condition.

CARTER: Yes, he did. He had his own curator and his own vaults, and they're still more or less intact. They were sold to Time-Life. Time-Life exploited them to a certain extent, but I don't think they really knew quite what to do with them. They came to the conclusion that

Harold Lloyd and the organ were not particularly good for the small television screen, so they had a rock group put scores to his pictures. It didn't come off; it didn't work.

BEHLMER: Did he influence you in terms of what kind of music you would be using? Or, did he just leave it all up to you?

CARTER: In the very late thirties and the early forties, he came to me and said that he was thinking of reviving some of his pictures and he was going to run *The Freshman* in a theater down in East L.A. "We'll get a Hammond Organ and we'll try a score and see if the people laugh." He showed me the picture and he gave me some suggestions. For instance, he wanted to use "The Sweetheart of Sigma Chi" for the love theme and a little piece called "Oh, Harold," which he had copyrighted. And then "You Gotta Be a Football Hero" (To Get Along with the Beautiful Girls). He suggested all those. I probably would have come up with them. And, of course, the people laughed. He wanted me to use "I Love You" from *Little Jessie James*—that little piece. It was kinda his favorite love song.

BEHLMER: You know, the term "Mickey Mousing" has been used in conjunction with cartoon music and then carried over into live action films during the thirties which obviously evolved from catching things musically directly from the action on the screen. Did you do much of that consciously in the silent days, or were you just musically illustrating what was on the screen?

CARTER: Well, I think what I was doing could be called "Mickey Mousing." As far as I was concerned I was expressing in musical terms what I was seeing on the screen. I was rehearsing here just this morning—we're getting ready to do the score for Cecil B. DeMille's *The Ten Commandments* [1923] for Paramount Home Video, and I was visualizing some of the scenes without having the tape or the film here at the moment. It was so interesting to come up with what I wanted to do without being able to see the film. Because the film gives me the ideas, it gives me the feeling—the whole bit. There is a guy who does this kind of thing back East. He says that the music sets the mood for the picture. Not for me, it doesn't. The picture sets the mood and you comply with that. You'd be surprised how many tempos you get by people walking, running, gesticulating on screen. A perfect example are Laurel and Hardy. They're always going on a little walk, you know—you see them walking on the street and that would give you a tempo. I suppose that's "Mickey Mouse," I don't know. I discovered that guys like Laurel and Hardy sort of worked to a beat. I've got a picture called *That's My Wife*. They're having a fight in the living room and throwing things, and they're punching each other and kicking. If I can get a certain tempo, I can catch every one of those things right in the tempo that I'm in. It's like [*sings tempo*] kick, [*sings tempo*] pow! So they're doing this—whether they've got a metronome going or what they're doing, I don't know. Maybe it's subconscious with them that they're doing it to a beat. And that happens on many occasions with them: you'll discover that they're operating to a beat, to a certain rhythmic pattern.

BEHLMER: When you were exposed to these films for the first time—back in the twenties, not later on when you were doing them in repertory—did you draw on all kinds of things in your approach to creatively accompanying the film?

CARTER: A mixture. The thing that I think probably a lot of us are equipped with is creative self-expression. Now, that is a high-falutin' way of saying we were "faking." But "faking" comes at all levels. If you have no talent, you can't fake very good. But if you've got some talent, you fake pretty good.

BEHLMER: Did you compose music in the twenties?

CARTER: I'd jot down little things that came to my mind.

BEHLMER: Original things?

CARTER: Oh, sure.

BEHLMER: Did you have anything published?

CARTER: No. I carry it all in my head, most of it. I can write out a four-bar theme and do that with variations for an hour without referring to any notes.

BEHLMER: "Rhapsody on a Theme by Carter."

CARTER: Yes. Endless variations. Upside down, inside out, backwards, slow, fast . . . [*laughs*].

BEHLMER: In the late twenties, just before sound came in, there was a major emphasis on writing a theme for a big picture. I mean, "Diane," "Ramona," "Charmaine," etc. And some of those became standards. Do you happen to recall, was there some particular impetus for this?

CARTER: It was part of the promotion of the film.

BEHLMER: Did you use those themes when they were popular?

CARTER: If the film exchange provided a copy, which they occasionally did along with the cue sheet. There's another thing that we did in those days. The publishers would all have what they called professional copies printed of their published songs. And we'd go to their local offices like Robbins, or Berlin, or—there were all kinds of publishers; dozens. Every month you'd go and they'd give you all the sheet music to all their things. Now, occasionally among this stuff would be one of these songs written for a picture. And I remember I'd come home with a big stack of stuff and suddenly discover among them the theme of one of the pictures I was going to be doing. That's how I'd happen to get it. But what they were all trying to do was to get us to do song slides with their songs for sing-a-long.

BEHLMER: Sound effects: You were the master. Is there a certain way that you evolved your way of doing sound effects with the organ?

CARTER: Well, Harold Lloyd put it in a way that I thought was awfully good. He said, "Where it's possible, do the effects musically." In other words, when somebody gets hit, don't play a drum or cymbal. Play a chord. Which I was always in favor of anyway. Make it musical.

BEHLMER: Did you work out by experimenting and by trial and error a way that you could achieve a certain texture—a sound texture with the organ to get an effect?

CARTER: Oh, sure. For instance, there's a scene in *The Kid Brother* where Harold Lloyd has gone upstairs to get some bedding and he opens the door where his father is sleeping. And there's a very brief shot of his father. Well, I wanted to get a snore effect. Just that little tiny thing, not particularly to get a laugh, but I found on certain organs there's a thing called the post horn. It's kind of a nasty sizzly sound, very low. So I would use that for that little snore scene.

BEHLMER: Well, some of the effects you devised are unique.

CARTER: Again, it's your musical imagination. I've always thought that I could duplicate practically anything you could see with some kind of musical effect.

BEHLMER: Back then, in the reviews of the new films in the papers, did they talk much about the accompaniment?

CARTER: Very little. There was hardly ever a mention about me. I was doing a show at the Paramount, just before sound came in, and it said, "Gaylord Carter's score was adequate." Now that's being damned . . . with . . .

BEHLMER: How about, "Gaylord Carter's score was *barely* adequate."

CARTER: [*Laughs.*] I don't ever remember seeing a review where the orchestra was mentioned.

BEHLMER: Or the score?

CARTER: Or the score. No.

BEHLMER: Gaylord, how would you say your approach differs from that of other theater organists?

CARTER: Oh, I wouldn't know. [*Long pause.*] Well, I will say this: the fact that I was there and played the silent movies for eight years gave me an insight and an experience that you couldn't get any other way. In other words, I lived with these things for eight years, every day and night. Now the kids . . . I've got one coming in for a lesson this afternoon. He's working on a picture that we're doing, we've done half of it already—*The General* with Buster Keaton.

BEHLMER: I love *The General*.

CARTER: You've got to know when to play "Dixie" and when to play "Yankee Doodle"!

Performing with Silent Films

Dennis James

Reminiscences

My early memories of silent films are from television broadcasts in the late 1950s and early 60s of such retrospective documentary series as *Silents Please* and the travesty *Fractured Flickers*. Saturday mornings were reserved for silent short comedies often used for fillers between the regular cartoons. Experiencing only these broadcasts, usually accompanied by early piano or orchestra recordings of ragtime, jazz and "novelty" music, I had no notion then of the live musical and vast theatrical presentation forces utilized with the major silent films during their initial release.

I began accompanying silent films at Indiana University in 1969 as an undergraduate classical organ major studying for a solo concert career. Initially I was interested in only the films and attended my first campus screening after a friend mentioned there were weekly classroom showings for a Comparative Literature course. I vividly remember that first Wednesday night seeing these silent films. They were indeed completely silent. No sound accompanied them except for the occasional giggle of the student viewers. I was quite disappointed in the presentation and felt a tremendous void that made the films nearly unwatchable.

I noticed a piano at the front of the small auditorium and asked the professor, Indiana University's noted film author and teacher Harry Geduld, if I could play for the next show. He asked if I knew how to accompany films, and I thought there couldn't be much to it so I said "sure." The film was *The Great Train Robbery* (Edison, 1903, with

G.M. "Broncho Billy" Anderson; no original score extant). Being a ragtime piano fancier (pre-*The Sting*, mind you), I thought a quick rendition of Scott Joplin's "Maple Leaf Rag" would be just the thing. I began, and then noticed that once the opening titles and credits were finished, the music didn't fit the action at all. Grasping about, I mined my mental inventory of the early film music clichés I absorbed from those hours of television screenings. This worked, but the audience laughed uproariously—at me, I thought, not the film, since there weren't any visual comedy cues. I went into my own improvisation, stylistically matching the ragtime style and including a Stephen Foster tune when the dancers appeared on screen.

This piano debut became a weekly effort and various problems soon developed. For example, while playing for Laurel and Hardy's *Big Business* (Hal Roach, 1928) I saw Stanley reach for a doorbell. The film showed the bell, then a close-up of Stanley's finger heading directly toward the button. I played a bell effect just as Ollie brushed Stanley's hand away, not letting the doorbell ring at all.

After a few more such disastrously wrong assumptions about direct action cues, plot turns, and character thoughts, I began to think about screening the films in advance of performance. At first I made mental notes of the most obvious cues but soon devised a written shorthand for particular musical possibilities and thematic ideas during nonstop previews.

The Museum of Modern Art began sending out complete published piano scores to be played along with their films shown in the film class. I remember in particular *The Last Command* and *Greed* and how much easier it was for me to read through them than to make up my own music at each performance. These written scores intrigued me. Some were original scores distributed with the films during the initial releases in the 1920s. Others were newly prepared by the film performance staff at the Museum. Excerpts from standard classical piano and orchestra repertoire appeared throughout most of them. In performance these seemed to work fairly well, but some of the more recognizable melodies would often draw audible groans from the listeners. Of greatest value to me in the MOMA scores were the sight cues and performance instructions. For the first time I saw what was done by others to add music to a film and how they indicated methods of keeping the performance in synchronization.

Performing with Silent Films 63

During Summer break in 1969 I attended a screening of Douglas Fairbanks' *The Mark of Zorro* (United Artists, 1920) which was accompanied by the veteran theater organist, Gaylord Carter. I said to myself, "Hey, I can do that!" and returned to school quite enthused to try this sort of show.

I found an unused theater pipe organ in the school's radio/TV building and set about restoring it and preparing it for film shows. The organ was a 2-manual, 7-rank Estey, originally located in the Princess Theatre in downtown Bloomington, Indiana (where I.U. student Hoagy Carmichael performed with his college band during the twenties). Numerous electrical problems and the typical voicing deterioration plagued the organ. Once it was playable, however, the crew and I decided to add a few special effects. One effect proved to be more than special.

We rigged up a 38-caliber pistol to a pinball machine solenoid, and I was able to fire it from a remote control button on the organ console. The gun was so loud that we changed its label to "bomb," and decided its debut would be in the "exploding the cash box" scene in *The Great Train Robbery* (a performance scheduled in the tiny broadcast studio housing the organ). Right on cue I fired the "bomb," and some very surprised audience members reflexively jumped up out of their seats while others shouted in response. Smoke poured out of the organ chamber and created the surrealistic effect of a floating film image projected on the billowing clouds.

In 1970 the local student organ guild and I scheduled a screening of *The Phantom of the Opera* (Universal, 1925, with Lon Chaney) for the 3800-seat I.U. auditorium. I was unable to locate the original score, so I decided to compose a new one for the organ. Silent film organist Lee Erwin flew out from New York to give me an evening of invaluable instruction in the art of composing organ accompaniments to feature films.

I based my *Phantom* score on the Gounod version of *Faust* and assigned actual opera excerpts (the Waltz, and the Jewel and Spinning songs) to the appropriate filmed portrayals. I designated particular operatic motives for the various characters ("Mephistopheles" for the Phantom, "Faust" for Raoul, etc.). Instrumental interludes from the opera accompanied large segments of the film, and organ recital pieces from the French Romantic period served well for the scenes in which the Phantom played the pipe organ in his underground residence. I set

Dennis James at the organ of the Ohio Theatre in Columbus

the majority of the intertitles to recitative and decided to improvise the rest of the film score during performance.

I printed only four hundred tickets in the school's craft shop, hung my hand-printed posters on trees and dormitory walls, and painted "The Phantom Is Coming" on campus sidewalks. I was thoroughly surprised when a sell-out crowd of over four thousand turned up. The energy in the audience (possibly aided by the rampant marijuana consumption) was unequaled in all my performing experience. The program was a resounding success and turned into a silent film series at the I.U. auditorium that continues to this day.

Performance Practices

It is a fascinating experience to perform for a silent film. What in preliminary viewings seems to rush by, leaving little time to think, let alone perform, becomes quite slow in performance. One has "all the time in the world" to decide what to play and how to do it.

With repeated viewings, the various films' underlying rhythmic styles soon become quite familiar. I found that the film editing often directly suggested appropriate rhythms of music. Also, the varying levels of thematic development mirrored the overall film structure and the component scenes. There are predictable musical progressions indicated by the pacing in the films of a single comedian or the work of a leading actor or director for a single studio. One learns to start and end musical segments by matching the style of transition devices (iris close, superimposition, cut to title, etc.) used between scenes or by the particular vantage points of the camera within the body of the work.

Acute visual memory is an important aid to the accompaniment process, particularly for comedies. At the start of my silent film work I realized the importance of retaining the exact appearance and timing of direct sight cues (doors closing, knocks, people falling, etc.) and structure cues (scene fades, cuts, intertitles, etc.). Now, many years and hundreds of films later, I can mentally inventory them at sight. I prefer two screenings, however, the first to note my own emotional reactions as though I were a member of an audience seeing the film for the first time, the second to dissect the film into its component parts.

Sound effects, if tastefully inserted, can add entertaining realism to the films' presentation. I had read accounts of sound effects that were performed on stage behind the screen. To a screening of *Lilac Time* (First National, 1928) I decided to synchronize the sounds of World War I airplanes, such as revving motors, whistling dives, and the clatter of machine guns. Positioning speakers behind the screen, I set about finding source materials for an audio tape to be controlled from the organ console. I obtained a stereo recording of period airplanes but was not satisfied with the impressive yet, for me, unauthentic sounds. The campus radio station owned a large collection of 78-rpm recordings from the 1930s once used for the creation of sound effects for radio dramas. Played on my stereo turntable with a special 78-rpm cartridge, these were better but still not "right." Finally I played them on an old spring-wound Victrola and placed the recording microphone down the throat of its enormous metal horn. The resulting scratchy and compressed sound was ideally suited to the images on the screen.

Silence is a particularly useful tool in performing silent film scores. I discovered that stopping the music at moments of greatest intensity always works better than fortissimo music or grand harmonic suspensions. Evidence that silence can cause actual physical suspension in an audience occurred much later in my career during a performance in Meridian, Mississippi. While playing a theater pipe organ for *The Phantom of the Opera*, I reached the climactic moment. The Phantom, chased by an enraged mob (with torches, of course) along the streets of Paris, is cornered down by the river Seine beside Notre Dame. He turns to the mob and holds his hand up high, appearing to clench a lethal weapon. All screen action stops as the crowd draws back, and I stopped the music. The Phantom looks up, laughs, and opens his hand, revealing nothing inside. At that moment I would normally have begun the finale music leading to the closing theme. At that performance, however, the ground wire suddenly popped off the organ's electrical system, rendering the keys inoperable but still allowing air into the pipe chests. I discovered the nonfunctioning keys and, by instinct, turned the master switch off and back on. This sometimes clears an unknown problem. The audience was still in suspense and holding its collective breath. Then, a single Tuba pipe wept into speech as air leaked through its valve while the pressure sagged. The audience gasped an audible sigh; they needed that pathetic auditory cue to release them from the suspense.

Inadvertent silence has also caused memorable comments from patrons. While playing *Safety Last* (a 1923 Harold Lloyd comedy) in

San Diego, the organ broke down during the climbing-the-building sequence, action that takes up nearly half the film. For at least eight minutes the organ didn't play. Afterwards, a patron came up and told me how dramatic it was when the organ stopped and how well the silence added to the suspense.

The level of involvement by both performer and audience can become quite intense. I recall how totally involved I felt after one particular performance of *Lilac Time*. The music literally flowed out of me, and each cue was matched to perfection. Although I was more than familiar with the film, my performance caused me to react emotionally with tears and a quickened pulse at the climaxes. This intensity was felt by the audience, too. One woman said afterwards, "I thought you said this was a silent film!" Apparently the organ music, the dialogue intertitles, and Gary Cooper's image had combined to such an extent that her mind filled in the last element: she had actually imagined hearing him speak. At the same performance another patron said she hadn't known silent films had such lovely color. The film, of course, is in black and white!

Recreating Original Orchestral Scores

Broken Blossoms (United Artists, 1919, with Lillian Gish and Richard Barthelmess. Score by Louis F. Gottschalk.) Presented at the Indiana University auditorium on March 25, 1972.

By 1971 I had enough exposure on campus to attempt to stage a revival of an original film score complete with pit orchestra. I chose *Broken Blossoms*, the D.W. Griffith drama set in the Limehouse district of London, after seeing a reproduction of the first page of the original piano-conductor score (with the opening title, "It is a tale of Temple Bells") in an enchanting book by Ben M. Hall about the movie-palace era entitled *The Best Remaining Seats* (New York, 1961). Hall explained that in large metropolitan theaters orchestras usually accompanied the silent films, performing specially commissioned scores distributed with the film or locally compiled excerpts from the standard symphonic repertory.

I wrote to Ben Hall and received by return mail a photocopy of the entire piano-conductor score. But there were no instrumental parts. Since Hall had no idea where to get the parts and I had no contacts in the silent film world whatsoever, problems were beginning to emerge. Geoff Simon, an Australian conducting student and conductor of the Bloomington Symphony, offered to help with the project and to present the film at the Indiana University auditorium as a Bloomington Symphony project. I obtained a print of the film (complete, thank goodness), and we screened it at home while playing through the score on the piano.

It was obvious to us at the outset that the score had to be somewhat altered for our revival performance. Of prime importance was the fact that we were forced to run the film at a faster speed than originally intended. Although we could change the speed on our standard two-speed projector (the original projection speed of *Blossoms* was close to the modern 18 frames per second "silent speed"), the theater's equipment could run only at sound speed of 24 fps.

In addition, there was the necessity of altering the order of some of the musical segments because they simply did not match the action portrayed. We also found a wide variety of musical quality in the score's individual cues. Few matched stylistically and at times the musical choice was actually ludicrous. I later determined that the score was made up of a compilation of both preexisting published film music (including one of my favorites, "The Crafty Spy" by Gaston Borch) and classical symphonic and operatic excerpts. There was also some newly composed material by Gottschalk (*e.g.*, the two waltz themes assigned to the Lillian Gish character).

Working with only the piano reduction of the score, we had no clue as to the size of the orchestra. Finding a *Madame Butterfly* excerpt included in the score determined our "grand opera" instrumentation for 55 performers. This proved to be far greater than the original orchestration, which was turned up years later and called for a standard theater orchestra. Geoff Simon proceeded to organize a group of fellow music students, and throughout a school vacation we scheduled marathon copying sessions. First, the entire score was orchestrated (by Simon) cue by cue. Then volunteer copyists hand-copied individual parts from the master score.

While examining accounts of the early days of film accompaniment, I found that in the large metropolitan areas the orchestra generally played only the evening performances. Sometimes the orchestra performed only the weekend shows. The matinees and early evening performances were left to the theater organ soloist, who would perform either a transcription of the original score or one of his own selection (either improvised or compiled). There was also the common practice of having the orchestra begin the presentation and perform perhaps the first ten minutes of the film, at which point the organist would slip in and take over. The orchestra would leave the pit and return for the closing minutes and grand finale, often staying on to accompany the next vaudeville presentation or live prologue.

I have found intriguing stories at the Ohio Theatre of how off-duty time was spent by the musicians. Some of the more colorful tales involve an accommodating hotel located just around the corner. In Jack Courtnay's *Theatre Organ World* (London, 1946), organist W. Lloyd Webber recalled that "the trumpet player had come back from the local (pub) rather worse for drink, so they wanted the organ to provide his part, which it did with gusto!"

In order to insert an organ part into *Broken Blossoms*, I followed the performance practice of the organ as related to the orchestra in the smaller "general release" theaters during road tour presentations. With a reduced complement of orchestral players, the organ was used to expand the overall texture. The organist would also play whenever the music was too difficult for the local musicians or when the synchronization was lost by an inept or under-rehearsed conductor. Alternating musical cues between the organ and the orchestra made the synchronization much easier to control in performance.

I searched the *Blossoms* score for segments that suited the solo organ texture and reassigned these to the organ. I then found places where the drama could be heightened by the addition of organ pedal tones and large chords on top of the orchestra. Finally, the conductor suggested we treat the organ as another solo instrument in the orchestra and have it take occasional solo passages or play in tandem with other solo instruments.

My next performance of the film with full orchestra was in 1978 for the 50th Anniversary of the Ohio Theatre. This 1928 deluxe presentation house and flagship of the Loew's midwest chain had recently been converted into a home for the Columbus performing arts. The silent film show served as my tribute to the theater's origins. For this performance the Columbus Symphony was in the pit and was conducted by Evan Whallon. He and I had gone through the score to tighten many sections and add additional sight cues, making more exact synchronization possible.

Most silent film scores had only the minimal number of cues necessary for synchronization. Often the instructions included comments such as "Repeat until next cue." It would appear that provincial musicians were quite adept at knowing what to do with a minimum of instruction. Perhaps this ability grew from either the routine of accompanying new films every week or the experience of performing vaudeville with its widely varied scores and accompanimental demands. In any case, there are distressingly few direct sight cues in any of the silent film scores I have turned up to date. In fact, the norm was a simple starting cue for each scene's music and an exit cue coming, at times, several minutes later and offering no visual cues to provide a frame of reference during the interim. A major part of my preparation process has been the insertion of additional sight cues, frequently in each line of the conductor's score, and consisting of the majority of the film's intertitles which can be easily seen peripherally during performance.

Critical to the acceptance of this style of silent film production at the Ohio was the naming of *Blossoms* as the "Best Theatrical Event of 1978" by the local newspaper. This silent film performance edged out fine productions by various arts organizations and paved the way for future projects.

Robin Hood (United Artists, 1922, with Douglas Fairbanks. Score by Victor L. Schertzinger.) Presented at the Ohio Theatre on May 2, 1981.

Three years after the Ohio's orchestral presentation of *Broken Blossoms* I was asked to create another silent film evening with the Columbus Symphony Orchestra. Budgetary restrictions again allowed only a single musical rehearsal for the score and a single "dress" rehearsal with the film before the public performance. I had discovered the music for Douglas Fairbanks' *Robin Hood* in an archive and decided it looked simple enough to rework. The piano-conductor score and most of the orchestral parts had survived, with only the trumpet and first violin parts missing. The full orchestral score was not published, a common practice of the period, so I would have to compose replacement parts.

I obtained a print of the film and played the score on my studio practice organ. The necessity of running the film at 24 fps caused synchronization cues in the score to vary with the film. While

First page of the piano-conductor score for *Robin Hood* (1922)

matching overall segments to the various start and end cues indicated, I timed and played them through and established a metronome count for performance. Then I modified the music to fit by structuring the original imprecise repeats and deleting measures while retaining the original harmonic progression. (Repeats in silent film scores are often labelled "Repeat Until . . .," followed by a sight cue. Under this system, the end of a "repeat" rarely has harmonic resolution and is subject to a ragged break. By adding visual cues to the score, the repeats can be restructured to provide clean breaks and harmonic resolutions at the end or logical progressions between sections.) Finally, I recorded the results. When I was satisfied with the visual/audio match, I reviewed this synchronization and inserted the new detailed sight cues into the score.

The title page of the score acknowledges *Robin Hood* as "composed by Victor L. Schertzinger" with the additional notation, "compiled and arranged by Victor L. Schertzinger and A.H. Cokayne." The music appears to be all newly composed with the exception of the song "O Promise Me" from Reginald De Koven's 1890 light opera *Robin Hood*, which is used for the grand love theme when Robin Hood and Maid Marian are reunited in the convent garden. There was, however, quite a contrast in the quality of orchestral part writing in certain sections of the score. The musicians decided that the Cokayne credit referred not to an actual person but to an "influence" on the arranger of the more inept segments.

I would classify most of the score's music as atmospheric—providing a musical "frame" for the screen image and establishing a general tone without character or action detail. This was in keeping with all but the very late silent film scores (such as the 1926 *Don Juan*). Musical passages carefully tailored to character and plot developments were virtually nonexistent. In the *Robin Hood* score, however, there were a few instances of direct screen action cues besides those required for the musical cue divisions. These included "Three Horn Blasts" (trumpet calls signaling appropriate military maneuvers by the band of Merry Men) and certain percussion effects cues (drum rolls synchronized to onscreen drums and an extended tympani roll to match a falcon's flight). The major overall problem with the score was the over-repetition of the marches and tournament music. I assigned alternate repetitions of the marches to the orchestra and the organ (with the organ sometimes playing them in different but related keys). The organ also handled the slow themes quite well, so I reassigned a few of them to the organ either in their entirety or with the solo melody line over an orchestral accompaniment.

I found that the organ worked best as a relief instrument, providing the orchestra with a much needed rest after lengthy chase or dramatic sections. I inserted several organ improvisation sections where, in performance, I could create music based on the musical themes already established for individual characters. The organ also served to emphasize the drama by punctuating the *forte* orchestral "sting" chords during the chase scenes near the end of the film. I found that I was able to fill in between orchestral music cues when the synchronization slipped a bit and open holes appeared in the score. As my conductors have all said, it is much better to be "on top" of the score in performance and sometimes come out a few measures ahead in a given cue than to lag behind and cause the score to drag the film.

The missing trumpet and first violin parts became quite a puzzle to replace. I hired a small component of the orchestra to play through the score for an audio tape. I assigned the parts to single instrumentalists (with no percussion) and grouped them so that the strings were together on one microphone and the winds on another. I assumed there would be missing melodies on the subsequent tape which I could then assign to whatever instrument seemed appropriate. An unexpected result of the recording session was an introduction to the vast complexity of some of the *Robin Hood* orchestral parts, none of which was indicated in the piano score. Virtuoso woodwind parts and intricate string scoring proved to be a revelation to the musicians. Also, since these were master parts previously unplayed, numerous publishing mistakes and copyist errors turned up, forcing further difficulties for the musicians.

The replacement part writing proved to be quite manageable but somewhat time consuming. I had individual musicians play through the parts and add the appropriate bowing and phrasing indications. I thought this would complete the score preparations. Having shifted my attention to the promotion of the show, I left the insertion of revisions to the last two weeks before rehearsals, but soon discovered it would occupy nearly all of my waking hours. I had no idea of the complexity of adjusting the individual instrumental parts to the newly revised conductor's score, nor did I realize the time-consuming process of checking over everything for printer/copyist errors.

At that time I was also the tour organist with Abel Gance's reconstructed *Napoléon*. I spent the initial Chicago performances furiously writing in the pit while Carmine Coppola's music swirled about me. Imagine me with Walkman tape recorder in hand, headphones on, and scores and parts spread across the organ bench in the crowded orchestra pit at the Chicago Theatre. I quickly cleared off the bench whenever a new *Napoléon* organ cue came up and then went back to the *Robin Hood* score.

While on a solo tour in London the year before, I had chanced upon a copy of "Just an Old Love Song," credited as being the "theme song" for *Robin Hood*. Sid Grauman had set words to one of the minor Schertzinger themes which was not even played in its entirety in the score. The song provided an ideal prelude to the Ohio Theatre's screening, sung by a local tenor, Thom Gall, to my organ accompaniment. Since I was unable to locate a performance copy of the indicated G. Schirmer overture, "Songs from Shakespeare's Time," I created an orchestral overture by the "cut and paste" method of composition. This served as an introduction to the various film themes in a concert setting. The prologue of overture and theme song before the screening became a standard part of subsequent Ohio Theatre shows.

Don Juan (Warner Bros., 1926, with John Barrymore. Score by William Axt; orchestrations by Maurice Baron; synchronized by Axt, David Mendoza and Major Edward Bowes.) Presented at the Ohio Theatre on March 20, 1982.

After the resounding success of *Robin Hood* and the multiple sellout audiences for *Napoléon*, silent film revivals in Columbus became well established. I received authorization to proceed with what was to become the most difficult and expensive restoration production undertaken to date. I had seen *Don Juan* during my university days and was surprised then to find it to be a typical silent film with a recorded score and occasional sound effects. When I chanced upon the original score and parts in a film music collection, I decided *Don Juan* would be an ideal choice for the next Ohio Theatre film and set about creating the performance. I thought that what I had discovered were the complete score and parts, for there certainly was more than enough music paper to warrant such a conclusion based upon comparison with my earlier film score finds. Only after the theater was booked, the symphony contracted, and the show announced did I actually run a complete comparison of the score with a print of the film. The original score and parts were only 35% intact! Missing were major dance sections, several complete scene cues, and all of the repeats of the main thematic material which comprised the bulk of the second half of the score.

The new process of recording sound-on-film utilized in *Don Juan* gave the opportunity to create literal repeats of musical segments in the editing process. This possibility was confirmed by careful listening to the recorded soundtrack on the Vitaphone recording. The large gaps in the manuscript could be explained by the practice of compiling preexisting musical compositions into the score. Since the *Don Juan* score was not intended for live performances, the chosen works were simply played from separate manuscript and edited into the soundtrack. These pieces did not seem to be in the compositional style of the existing music, so I played the questionable portions for our local symphony conductor and other interested persons. Unfortunately no one recognized the music, so I was forced to transcribe the music from the soundtrack, with, of course, full orchestration. With only days before our performance but with transcriptions in hand, I determined the titles of two of the unknown segments, "Ballet Music" from *Le Cid* by Massenet and "Overture to Act II" of *Rienzi* by Wagner, after chance hearings on my car radio. My surprise was so great on hearing the Massenet that I nearly drove off the road.

The Vitaphone track was recorded by Henry Hadley, conducting the 107-piece New York Philharmonic Orchestra. Not being able to pay, much less place in the pit, such a large orchestra, we were forced to reduce the player complement to a more manageable size. By including all indicated wind parts and balancing them with strings, we arrived at a 48-piece ensemble.

The addition of the organ to the *Don Juan* score became quite a challenge, since the original orchestration was such a finely wrought effort. On viewing the film, I listened for sections that seemed to my ear to be most suited to the organ. I then culled these into sequences that offered the most relief for an orchestra performing the score live. I assigned the theme for the twisted and demented dwarf to the organ, for it was a most unusual theme (a la Strauss' Til Eulenspiegel's motive) and was a wonderful rest device for the orchestra. Hollywood filmmakers seem to favor twisted and demented organists as stock characters anyway, and I thought my choice was most appropriate. In addition, the low organ pedal tones proved to be most exciting for the scenes in the wizard's laboratory.

There was a series of lovely "hesitation" waltzes during the extended love scenes at the center of the film. These were well suited for orchestra/organ alternation and provided an opportunity for the lighter aspects of the theater organ registration to be displayed. An added plus was a welcomed rest for the orchestra preceding the lengthy suspense and chase sections shortly thereafter. The film score synchronization was no problem whatsoever, since the film was to run at modern sound speed of 24 fps and the score was already recorded. My only score modifications involved the above-mentioned addition of the organ. Still to be arranged was the live performance of the film's recorded sound effects.

There were three special effects: cathedral bells rung during the wedding of Adriana and Donati, the sound of a fist pounding on Juan's door, and the swords clanging together during the climactic duel. I assigned the bells to the organ—the Ohio's Robert-Morton theater organ is equipped with two large church bells in addition to its regular set of chimes. The effect of the sound coming from the walls of the theater, well away from the orchestra pit, gave an added performance dimension to the scene.

The dueling scenes required synchronized sounds of sabers clashing. After trying varying sizes of real swords and being quite disappointed with the resulting pathetic clink in the large theater, I discovered that the tube from a vacuum cleaner nozzle hit against the metal railing around the orchestra pit provided the ideal sound. The last effect was the knocking on the door. This was simulated by pounding a hammer on a large empty wooden box. We set the box behind the screen where the film could easily be viewed by the box-player (albeit, in reverse image). Garbed in dark clothes, the player remained invisible to the audience, and, most impressively, the door knock seemed to come directly from the image on the screen.

A visit to the Herrick Library at the Academy of Motion Picture Arts and Sciences provided an account of the West Coast premiere of *Don Juan* at Grauman's Chinese Theatre in Hollywood. I decided to recreate that performance in every possible detail. For the overture the orchestra performed a condensation of Rimsky-Korsakov's *Capriccio Espagnol*. The "Procession of Serenaders in the Twilight of Old Venice with Dancers of the 15th Century, Venetian Guardsmen,

Performing with Silent Films 77

Instrumentalists and other picturesque characters of the period" was recreated with dancers from Ohio State University appearing in front of a "Venetian" hanging drop and with onstage musicians playing authentic 15th-century music on replica period instruments. The theme song, "Don Juan" (originally sung by soprano Anna Case in the filmed Vitaphone prologue), was also located and performed.

Orphans of the Storm (United Artists, 1921, with Lillian and Dorothy Gish. Score by Louis F. Gottschalk and William Frederick Peters.) Presented at the Ohio Theatre on March 17, 1984.

After a Detroit performance of *Robin Hood* in 1982, I developed a close working relationship with the Ann Arbor Chamber Orchestra and conductor Carl Daehler. He is now my conductor for tour purposes, and I invited him to work with me on the *Orphans of the Storm* presentation for the annual Ohio Theatre series. He checked through the archive score and parts and found that they were intact, but that there were, as usual, unclear indications of precise sight cues.

As Carl recalled in our program: "Before viewing the film I catalogued all of the individual musical segments, noting if a cue was marked in the score, determining a metronome marking for the tempo, and listing the original instrumentation and the timing of a particular section of the music. The catalogue was prepared with the help of a personal computer which, in addition to keeping track of the above information, was programmed to play back on the computer's synthesizer the first thirty-two notes of each theme found in the musical segment. This was most helpful to pre-determine which themes recurred and to later assess the identification with certain characters or events. I then viewed the film, which was video taped from the original release print, and found it to be a nearly perfect match to the score. Exact timings for each scene were compared to the musical preparations and complete synchronization sight cues inserted. The instrumental parts were tailored for the Ohio Theatre performance, including extra string parts and insertion of the theater pipe organ part."

A particular surprise was the inclusion in the *Orphans* score of one of the great "Lucy" waltz themes from *Broken Blossoms*. This can probably be best explained by Edward Connor's statement: "Old scores, if they're good, never die; they just fade into subsequent films." The theme appears only once and is not assigned to any particular character or situation.

One of the most affecting stories to come out of our performance was when an elderly lady came up to me afterwards with a hint of tears in her eyes. She told me her father used to sing one of the film's themes to her as a child before she went to sleep. She was able to recite the complete lyric for me. A few days later I received a call from another woman expressing interest in the very same piece. She recalled the title: "Slumber Boat." There was no credit given in the score.

Reflections

Silent film is a performance medium. This concept was lost with the advent of sound-on-film. With it passed what is now seen as the single most necessary part of the silent film experience—the live performance. A certain excitement is felt when the viewer knows that live musicians are actually performing to the film. Even with the modern improvements in the reproduction of orchestral sound in the theater environment, the live element of silent film music performance cannot be ignored.

I have often wished for the ability to alter the film speed, sometimes even within the picture. At times certain scenes seem either too fast or too slow during the actual performance, even with the music thoroughly rehearsed and prepared. Whether this is a result of the internal emotions of the conductor, the interaction with the audience or the amount of attention and involvement of the orchestra players in a given performance is difficult to say. There is historical evidence for the possibility of altered film speeds as noted in surviving studio release instructions. In the *projectionist's* cue sheet for *Old Ironsides* (Paramount, 1926) there are specific instructions to vary the film speeds in performance to four different levels over a range of 20 fps to 25.33 fps.

The problem of intertitles must also be faced. There is frequently no indication of whether to begin music with the title, during the title, or with the action after the title. Another option is, of course, total silence during the titles. I once attended a European silent film performance with the silence approach and found it to be most distracting. Undue attention was called to the film music by its awkward absence (and subsequent resumption a few seconds later). In most cases, common sense dictates which practice to follow as judged by the evincible action, but there are the occasional moments when justification can be made for each of several approaches. In these cases, I record the segment and then choose the most appropriate version later.

Much of the charm of the original silent film scores lies in their orchestrations, which are remarkably similar to those used by Broadway pit orchestras of the same period. I have been quite dismayed at some modern "restorations" of silent film scores wherein the arranger has adapted the original music, ostensibly for modern ears, by altering the original musical harmonies. A sense of "period" setting, with the use of theatrical presentation elements such as songs, staged prologues and overtures, is vital. I have been told the addition of the organ makes my performances quite authentic for many who witnessed these scores in their initial presentation.

A lovely quotation, attributed to Mary Pickford, symbolizes all of my activity in the film and the near-evangelistic relish with which I proceed: "When films learned to talk, they took a giant step backward."

What Were Musicians Saying About Movie Music During the First Decade of Sound? A Symposium of Selected Writings

Fred Steiner

"New forms of art correspond to new physical means and new sociological circumstances."
(Carlos Chavez, *Toward a New Music*, p.167)

Film historians generally agree that, although motion pictures with synchronized sound had been known to the public since the early twenties, it was the phenomenal box office success of *The Jazz Singer*, which opened at the Warner Theater in New York City in October 1927, that gave the cinema world the first clear indication that the days of the silent film were numbered. Slightly more than thirty years had gone by since the motion picture had been more or less accidentally created, through the discoveries and ingenuity of Edison, Lumière, and others, yet it was already the most popular and widespread medium of entertainment the world had ever known.

However, despite its significant role in what was to be the surprisingly swift demise of the silent film (the last silents of any importance were produced in 1929), *The Jazz Singer* is little more than a silent film itself. Aside from a few lines of spoken dialogue and Al Jolson's singing, its sound "track" consists of only a rather conventional silent film score, compiled and arranged by Lou Silvers from Tchaikovsky, Lalo, Debussy, and Sibelius, as well as from Hebraic, popular, and folk melodies, all recorded on the discs of the then-new but soon-to-be-superseded Vitaphone system. During the next few chaotic years of trial-and-error, as the Hollywood studios were making the transition to sound, producers and directors had to find solutions to entirely new and often perplexing artistic and technical problems. Understandably, their primary concerns were how to write and record dialogue in a naturalistic way and how to make the most effective use of "noises" (as sound effects were often called in the beginning). The result was a spate of "all-talking" pictures, usually adaptations of Broadway plays or popular novels; there was also, for a brief time, a rage for "all-talking, all-singing, all-dancing" musical films. Neither of those new types of cinema had much need for incidental music or musical accompaniment of the dramatic kind, let alone original composition. It is fair to say, therefore, that the real history of music in sound films does not begin until the general acceptance of the sound-on-film method as the standard for the motion picture industry (after 1931, according to Knight 1978: 156). Indeed, it was the perfection of that method that made it possible for composers to develop and exploit the true emotional and dramatic latencies of music for motion pictures.

Although a few articles and handbooks relating to the topic of music in the movies had appeared in print during the days of the silent films, it was not until the arrival of the "talkies" that the aesthetic and theoretical aspects of film music began to be discussed in earnest. Articles by composers, music journalists, and film directors started to appear in music periodicals and cinema journals; books such as Sabaneev's *Music for the Films* (1935) and London's *Film Music* (1936) became available in English translations, and certain film theoreticians turned their attention to this important topic.

Admittedly the body of film music literature issued during the first decade of the sound era is not as large as it should be, certainly not in comparison to the vast amount of writing about other aspects of cinematic art that was published during the same period. Still there is enough for us to perceive how much interest was being shown in this new artistic medium, especially by musicians themselves. Among the composers contributing articles and film music reviews were such prominent names as George Antheil, Arthur Benjamin, Marc Blitzstein, Paul Bowles, Hanns Eisler, Maurice Jaubert, Walter Leigh, Darius Milhaud, Max Steiner, Herbert Stothart, Virgil Thomson, and Ernst Toch. Among the music journalists and historians were M.D.

Calvocoressi, Alfred Einstein, John Gutman, and Leonid Sabaneev. In addition, brief discussions or entire chapters devoted to film music were included in books on modern music by Carlos Chavez, Constant Lambert, Rollo Myers, Virgil Thomson, and others.

The principal outlet for articles was that excellent and much-missed journal, *Modern Music* (1924–46); a rough tabulation shows that almost thirty essays and reviews concerning film music appeared in its pages during the years 1930–39. Runners-up were the British film journals *Sight and Sound* and *World Film News*, with about half-a-dozen articles each. There was a sprinkling of articles in popular-type film and radio magazines, and I found a fair quantity of material in foreign-language sources, notably in the German modern music publication *Melos*. At the bottom of the list are the "learned" musicological journals such as *Music and Letters* and *Musical Times*, some with only one item in the entire decade; and, sad to say, in our own prestigious *Musical Quarterly*, I could find nothing at all.

Music had been an integral part of cinema from the very beginning, but the type of music used in motion picture theaters in the silent days offered very little opportunity to serious musicians. Because of the exigencies of motion picture production and distribution, almost all musical accompaniments to films were pastiches consisting of excerpts from the light "classical" and popular repertories, as well as pieces from certain standard published film music libraries. Depending on the size of the theater and the time of day, such accompaniments might be rendered by a single piano, theater organ, small ensembles of four to a dozen players, or the symphonic-sized orchestras of the great movie palaces. The music was frequently selected and strung together by the movie theater's conductor (or "fitter"), sometimes in rather haphazard fashion, sometimes by following suggestion sheets (also called cue sheets) issued by the producer. During the twenties, many such pastiche scores (some quite elaborate) were furnished for important pictures by musical entrepreneurs who selected the music and supplied complete scores and parts on a rental basis. In short, with few exceptions, the art of film music in the silent days was that of compilation, not composition.[1]

But with the advent of sound film, all this changed rather quickly. It soon became apparent that the role of music had to be different in the "talkies"; so different, in fact, that an entirely new field of endeavor might be opening up to "serious" or—to use a more accurate term—concert hall composers. It seemed to be a field which could offer them not only artistic stimulation, but, perhaps for the first time in more than a century, a means of earning a livelihood through composition alone. As more and more musicians began to explore the new medium, some of them were writing about the artistic and technical problems they had encountered.

This essay presents an overview of the most important film music literature that appeared during the years 1930-39.[2] Those writings covered almost all aspects of music for the movies, but the most frequently discussed topics were such things as the nature of film music and its integration with the other elements of cinema, problems of form and style, the status of the composer and his relationship with the film director, the attitudes of directors and producers toward music, the quality of current film scores, the opportunities for composers, and the pitfalls that might await them. To me, however, the most interesting and significant part of this corpus of literature is that which tells us how people from the musical world perceived the *functions* of music in the cinema, at the same time revealing some of their thoughts about the artistic principles to be observed by composers trying to create film scores that would successfully fulfill those functions: in other words, those writings that represented the first groping efforts toward the formulation of a theory of film music. Consequently, because the focus of this paper is mainly on functional and theoretical aspects, the following have been excluded from the survey: historical and biographical writings, discussions of composition methods or orchestration, special topics such as musicals and filmed opera, technical matters such as studio routine, recording and microphone technique, and, with a few exceptions, reviews of film scores.[3]

It is clear that even within such limitations, no survey can pretend to be complete. Nevertheless, I hope that the following brief symposium of writings by composers, critics, and music historians during the first decade of sound films will give readers some idea of (1) how those writers felt when such a seemingly miraculous technological marvel came into the world—a novel medium with untried and perhaps limitless possibilities for musical expression of an entirely new kind—

and (2) the corollary, problem-laden quest for theoretical and aesthetical principles of film music during those crucial formative years.

Movie Music in Transition

One of the first to write about the musical situation existing in the earliest days of the sound film, during that time when the changeover from silents was still in process, was the composer Darius Milhaud. He was one of the few who had written original scores for silent films and, being well acquainted with the difficulties encountered in the old medium, was quite enthusiastic about the new one:

> Sound movies are in their infancy, it is true, but their application has already become important. What was the condition formerly, when a composer wrote special music for a film? Only a few theatres had orchestras large enough to execute it. In the provinces any sort of accompaniment was used and the score disappeared without a trace. Thanks to talking pictures, the music will be recorded forever and will be heard everywhere, simultaneously with the view of the film. (Milhaud 1930: 12)

During this transitional period, many film producers, being uncertain how to use music in the new medium, often found it expedient to stick with the old ways. The complaint of this dissatisfied music critic probably originated from the fact that many of the synchronized scores for early sound pictures were compiled from conventional silent film music sources, resulting in much the same kind of musical accompaniments one would have heard before the arrival of sound:

> Up to now the sound film has given us only wretched results. Obviously no well defined formula has as yet been found. Producers have been content to record a musical adaptation which has been carefully made, not for musical reasons, but because, being finished once and for all, it must be therefore made decently. (Closson 1930: 18)

Some directors, especially those who were striving for "naturalism" in sound films, did manage to break away from the old established musical conventions, but in so doing, many went too far and tried to avoid the use of music altogether. One of our most famous film composers later explained this paradox, in an often-reprinted passage doubtless familiar to many readers:

> At this time [early days of sound] music for dramatic pictures was only used when it was actually required by the script. A constant fear prevailed among producers, directors and musicians, that they would be asked: Where does the music come from? Therefore they never used music unless it could be explained by the presence of a source like an orchestra, piano player, phonograph or radio, which was specified in the script. (Steiner 1937: 218)

The period of which Steiner spoke did not last very long; filmmakers soon learned how to handle sound in the new medium, and by the middle of the decade, music had been restored to its rightful place as an essential ingredient of cinema. In the meantime, as the search for an ideal film music style went on, one of the most frequent subjects of debate was that of musical illustration. This technique, denoting a style of film music that closely follows changes of scene or mood (sometimes to the extent of changing with every shot) or that attempts to imitate and synchronize with actions on the screen, was to become a frequent target for scorn in the coming decade and even beyond. In the earliest days of sound, however, it was regarded with considerable favor, according to the recollections of this composer:

> A film composer was considered clever and useful if he understood how to "illustrate" the happenings on the screen with music. If a machine was shown on the screen the music had to whirr, if a man was walking along a street the music had to walk, etc. This principle of illustration was supplemented by "sentimental" and "picturesque" music. The "sentimental" was used to make the sorrow of a lover still more sorrowful by means of adequate music. The "picturesque" were those horrible musical pieces which when green pastures were shown fell into detestable sobbing, or became angry to suggest the roaring sea. (Eisler 1936: 23)

But even if a composer abstained from musical illustration, preferring to express the overall mood or the underlying emotion of a scene, he might run the risk of overwhelming the picture by resorting to compositional styles more fit for a concert hall. Here, from the very beginning of the decade, is a surprisingly astute admonition to composers that they must evolve a different mode of musical expression, one suitable for the new medium:

> The music must always be appreciably secondary to the screened image. . . . It sometimes happens in the movies that the music suddenly asserts its rights, taking one away from the visual images into a blind world of sound. This of course is not permissible.
>
> The sound film relegates music to the inferior role of accompaniment, a sort of running bass that contributes merely a kind of emotional atmosphere. The composer writing specially for the "talkies" is in danger of falling back into the form of the symphonic poem and all the mistakes of program music, or, still worse, into a hazardous impressionism. (Closson 1930: 18)

There were many other pitfalls and snares lying in wait for those who were more accustomed to the concert hall than the film studio. For example, a pioneer British composer for documentary films had this to say about recording conditions in the early days of sound:

> The musician is at the mercy of a well-meaning body of sound-engineers who cannot yet reproduce the tone of a single violin adequately, let alone a mass of strings; whose idea of the characteristic tone of an oboe seems to be founded on tooth-comb and tissue-paper; and who, when criticised, think themselves unjustly abused because the banjo, the plucked string and the saxophone come off fairly well in recording. . . . There has as yet been no film recording of an orchestra, or even a part of one, to my knowledge which can stand comparison with the standard tone-quality of the best gramophone records. (Raybould 1933: 80–81)

Despite these problems and many more whose solutions would be sought in the years to come, there was optimism in the air. One important thing to many musicians was the possible opportunity for a new kind of artistic expression. This young American composer was guardedly sanguine about the future:

> And for that most unhappy of artists, the composer, is there not perhaps a fresh gleam of hope? For a public suckled on the love-strains of Tchaikowsky, who know the leitmotive of the Garbo by the inevitable melodic cue from Grieg, a public satiated with the theme songs of lovers dying on the desert to symphonic orchestral accompaniments, there is still the opportunity of hearing music actually requisite to the film and especially created for it. . . . If then the gods of this industry would bestow their lavish favors wisely on those chosen to do film accompaniments, what chance might a composer not have of doing interesting original work and, for the first time since the days of royal

patronage, with ample remuneration. The commercial theatre does it—why not the film? (Hammond 1931: 36–37)

As a whole, then, the situation in film music at the beginning of the thirties was typical of any transitional period: a mixture of good and bad, hope and gloom, certainty and confusion. In spite of the optimism of Milhaud, Hammond, and others, it was to be several years before enough concert hall composers and competent music writers took much interest in the phenomenon of sound film. Those who did soon began to realize that this new medium presented certain challenges quite different from any they had faced in their musical careers. And so started the slow process of searching for answers to some brand-new and extraordinary questions.

The Nature and Functions of Film Music

Most musicians rarely had to think about anything as anomalous as music performing duties. To them, music was an art which had its own inner workings and had always obeyed its own rules. Now, possibly for the first time since the invention of opera, they had to figure out what music was supposed to *do* for another medium of which it was a part. What are the functions of film music? What is it supposed to do for a picture? What is required of it? What is music's relation—physiological or psychological—to the other elements of cinema: photography, dialogue, sound effects? How does music support, reinforce, emphasize (or even neutralize) the dramatic and emotional impact of the visual images?[4]

We begin with a perceptive criticism from composer Virgil Thomson, who became one of the most articulate and respected writers on music and who created several fine film scores. The following statement is one of the earliest attempts to define the functions of music in a sound film:

> The trouble with most movie music is its lack of continuity. The cinema is naturally a discontinous medium. . . . Musical accompaniment should be an aid to continuity. It should establish and preserve an atmosphere, a tone of augmenting or unrolling drama. It should envelope and sustain a narrative, the cinematographic recounting of which is after all only a series of

very short incidents seen from different angles. To break the music with every shot or change of scene is an error and ineffective. (Thomson 1933: 188)

Some of the most stimulating thoughts on film music came from the pen of the British composer, Walter Leigh, who attracted attention with his innovative score for the British documentary film, *Song of Ceylon*. He noted with evident satisfaction an increasingly creative use of sound, *i.e.*, sound for emotional and dramatic effect, not just for literal illustration:

> Now that synchronized sound is no longer a novelty, there are signs of the development of a new technique in the use of sound, not merely as an explanation to the ear of what the eye is watching, or as a background to keep the ear pleasantly occupied while the eye devotes itself to the action, but as a part of the action itself, as expressive in its own way as the visuals, and a necessary complement to them. And it is in this field that the musician can prove of direct use in the making of a film, and take a more responsible part than hitherto. (Leigh 1934: 71)

Leigh even went so far as to suggest that the new responsibility of the musician should include the organization of the sound effects as well as the score, then added:

> He [the musician] will do well to abandon many musical conventions on which he was brought up, and attempt to approach this new problem of film-sound as a fresh art with many unexplored possibilities, which is only now starting to make its own conventions. (*ibid.*: 72)

The artistic progress of the new medium was observed by Constant Lambert, the British composer and conductor, whose book, *Music Ho!*, included a provocative essay entitled "Mechanical Music and the Cinema." He was another of those who hoped that the cinema would prove to be an important and satisfying outlet for the modern composer:

> In spite of its ephemeral nature it is the only art whose progress is not at the moment depressing to watch. . . . Films have the emotional impact for the twentieth century that operas had for the nineteenth. Pudovkin and Eisenstein are the true successors of Mussorgsky, D.W. Griffith is our Puccini, Cecil B. DeMille our Meyerbeer and René Clair our Offenbach. (Lambert 1934: 260)

It might have seemed strange to make such a comparison between cinema and opera, but in some ways the problems of the interrelation of music and drama are analogous in both media, as was noted by a well-known musicologist:

> It is in all respects the problem with which composers of operas and lyric dramas, from Monteverdi to the present time, have grappled in vain. Speech can achieve its dramatic or psychological purpose in a few seconds, music within the same short time very little indeed. (Calvocoressi 1935: 58)

The parallel was also discussed by composer George Antheil, one of the most prolific writers on film music, who recounted many of his cinematic experiences in the pages of *Modern Music*:

> Picture music is more closely allied to the dramatic forms than to the symphonic. By its very nature it must be loose in form and style. It is, quite simply, a kind of modern opera. And operatic music must certainly follow the emotional content of its drama and its accompanying poetry. Unless it does so, it will seem totally beside the point. This is just as true of picture music. (Antheil 1936a: 49)

The similitude was also noted by another well-known composer, but his inclusion of symphonic and instrumental considerations in the analogy would probably have been contested by Antheil, among others:

> If we look at the problem implied for the composer in conceiving a complex filmed music drama, we find that it is, in different manner and degree, the same problem presented in the case of an opera or a symphony: that of familiarizing himself with the instrumental means. (Chavez 1937: 168)

Nineteen thirty-five was a key year in the history of film music; several memorable, symphonic-style scores were composed, including Arthur Bliss's *Things to Come*, Erich Wolfgang Korngold's *Captain Blood*, and Max Steiner's *The Informer*. It was also the year that saw the issuance in English of the first comprehensive handbook on the practical and theoretical problems of music in sound pictures: Leonid Sabaneev's *Music for the Films*.[5] This pioneer effort to give practical advice and guidance to film musicians gives us many glimpses of the state of film music in those days. Unfortunately, the book is flawed by the author's rather cynical view of film composing as an art:

> As a rule, the cinema composer stands apart from his fellows, inasmuch as originality and novelty are not required of him; he is an arranger or transposer of the inspirations of others, rather than a creator. The ability to borrow wisely and opportunely, to

imitate good and suitable examples, is a valuable endowment in his case, though these qualifications by no means add lustre to the ordinary composer. (Sabaneev 1935: v)

Referring to the film composer as an arranger rather than a creator indicates that the old controversy over composition *vs.* compilation was still not completely settled, at least in Sabaneev's mind. But whether the music be original or derivative, the question still remained: what was its function in the picture? Sabaneev recollected that, in the silent era, music had supplied poetry and emotion, and had generally interpreted the happenings on the screen; and he believed that those important functions were still valid:

> With the arrival of the sound film the rôle of music was altered. . . . Whereas music was once the sole provider of sound for the cinema, it now has to share its functions with dramatic speech and various naturalistic noises. But its position has remained. Speech, pictures and noises constitute the purely photographic section of the cinema; music, whether with the silent or the sound films, supplies the romantic, irrational element illustrating emotion. (*ibid.*: 18)

But the fact that music was no longer the supreme provider of sound, that it now must "share" this duty with other cinematic elements, created an artistic dilemma that preoccupied Sabaneev. What became of musical values in this new physiological relationship? For instance, if music had to share a scene with dialogue, could it really continue to supply poetry and emotion? He seemed doubtful:

> It should always be remembered, as a first principle of the aesthetics of music in the cinema, that logic requires music to give way to dialogue. Even if the former is relegated entirely to the background and is barely audible, it still interferes to some extent with the dialogue, and, as it becomes vague and can hardly be heard, its aesthetic value is only second rate. (*ibid.*: 19–20)

Furthermore, Sabaneev contended that music connected with sound effects would usually be deprived "of any aesthetic significance," and therefore recommended that "music should cease or retire into the background when dialogues and noises are taking place. Except in rare instances it blends but poorly with them" (*ibid.*: 20).

Those statements of Sabaneev are worth noting on two counts: (1) as far as I can tell, they embody the earliest published specific recommendations to screen composers about the knotty problem of the presence of music vis-à-vis speech and noises on the sound track (a difficulty that has never ceased to trouble composers and directors); and (2), perhaps more importantly, because of Sabaneev's interesting choice of words in his contention that when music is mixed with dialog and sound effects it loses "aesthetic value" and "aesthetic significance." His use of those lofty sounding terms can best be accounted for if one remembers, as suggested earlier, that this was the first time musicians had to think seriously about music as a dichotomy. Given that its primary role in motion pictures is to follow and lend support to a series of images of specified lengths and varying content, at the same time it is subject to laws other than cinematic, *i.e.*, the laws of music, which every composer must obey—they certainly cannot be ignored.

> Music in the cinema . . . preserves a large measure of its individuality and its independent nature. It should possess a musical form of its own, in some way subordinated to the rhythm of the screen, but not destroyed by them [sic]. . . . Music in the cinema cannot sacrifice the principles governing its form: no matter what is happening on the screen, the music must have its melodic structure, its phrases and cadences. . . . (*ibid.*: 20–21)

In other words, music may play a secondary role in a film, but it cannot on that account be incoherent or amorphous. Its dual existence in the cinematic time-continuum means that it has both physiological and psychological relations with the picture, and this is what creates the artistic dilemma for the composer. In the first decade of sound film, musicians were trying to develop the necessary new styles and forms, yet it was hard to ignore the influence of the old. And in this quest for an appropriate musical language, one issue was constantly recurring:

> Another point long in question is whether or not moving picture music should follow the picture's action, or attempt its own individual symphonic expression. It must be plain to everyone that if the music *constantly* follows its picture's action, a spotty and choppy score will be the natural result. But . . . if motion picture music attempts a purely symphonic solution it will find itself in the same hot water as the symphonic music which has so misguidedly appeared in various modern operas of the past. (Antheil 1936a: 49)

Readers may recall that Virgil Thomson had already warned against losing continuity by breaking the music with every change of scene.[6] By the middle of the decade, everyone seemed to agree on this general principle. In particular, the old-fashioned type of musical "illustration" so detested by Eisler was pretty much a thing of the past, to be avoided as much as possible if musical integrity was to be preserved.

> When a composer strives to illustrate every moment of a film, his music almost invariably becomes jerky and scrappy if the pace is not to be inordinately retarded. (Calvocoressi 1935: 58)

> It [the music] expresses the general mood of the scene . . . and should not be required, except in a few instances . . . to follow the events in detail, otherwise it is untrue to its nature and becomes anti-musical. (Sabaneev 1935: 22)

Some of the most cogent statements on the nature and functions of music in films were made by Maurice Jaubert, who abandoned the legal profession for that of a composer and wrote the scores for some outstanding French films, including Jean Vigo's *Zéro de conduite* (1933). He was one of the first to urge musicians to abandon old symphonic forms and seek out a new, specifically cinematographic kind of music. Reminding them that one does not go to the movies to hear music, he asserted:

> We want music to give greater depth to our impressions of the visuals. We do not want it to explain the visuals, but to add to them *by differing from them*. In other words, it should not be *expressive*, in the sense of adding its quota to the sentiments expressed by the actors or the director, but *decorative* in the sense of adding its own design to that proper to the screen. (Jaubert 1936: 31)

The phrase "adding its own design"—in other words, music in equal partnership with the other elements of cinema—is a significant key to Jaubert's concept of film music's function:

> Music, like direction, set-design and cutting, must do its bit to bring clarity, logic and especially truth to the development of any film. If it can quietly add an extra element of poetry, so much the better. (*ibid.*)

Jaubert was much opposed to musical illustration (which he called synchronization) and once rebuked director John Ford for his use of that controversial procedure (curiously enough, without mentioning composer Max Steiner):

> In *The Informer*, where this technique [synchronization] is carried to its highest pitch of perfection, the music has actually to imitate

the noise of pieces of money falling on the ground, and even, by a roguish little arpeggio, the trickling of a glass of beer down a drinker's throat. Apart from its childishness, such a procedure displays a total lack of understanding of the very essence of film music. (Jaubert 1937: 108)

The second book on sound film music to be published in England was Kurt London's *Film Music*.[7] Although somewhat different from Sabaneev's little handbook, in many ways it was an improvement over that earlier work, for it contained much valuable historical material as well as musical examples—all lacking in the earlier work. From the standpoint of technological progress, London's book was already outdated when it was issued (he seemed to be completely unaware of developments in Hollywood), but most of his theoretical and aesthetic ideas were quite sound, and he gave us many valuable insights into prevailing conditions:

> The music which accompanies the film is still struggling for its place in the sun: the film people themselves almost invariably treat it very casually and are not quite clear in their own minds about its importance; musicians take it up more for the sake of fees than for art's sake, and he is a rare exception among them who shows any sympathy for its novel forms. . . . (London 1936: 11)

In one chapter of his historical survey, London revealed that the move away from illustrative music had already begun in the silent days—in some circles, anyway:

> Two theories of descriptive music are important for the film: the explicitly programmatic, or impressionistic, and the interpretative, or expressionistic. The former was more popular with the silent film owing to its greater effect on the audience. The second was preferred by modern musicians, who felt the determining factor for their musical accompaniment to be not so much purely illustrative considerations as the rhythm and basic psychology of the film. This point of view gained considerable ground later in connection with sound films. (*ibid*.: 74)

Which of the two theories London preferred was made quite clear when he joined the chorus of those opposed to using music merely to synchronize with the action on the screen:

> The dramatic possibilities of sound in present-day films and the uses and applications of music are numerous enough. Music as transition, music as the object of sound-events—yes, even as

entertainment or an element of good cheer—will still serve its purpose. But, if it is employed to strain after effects which the film itself cannot induce, then it degrades the film and itself. (*ibid*.: 125)

According to London, the new medium was too diverse for the old silent-film variety of illustration with its boundless descriptive passages:

> Each single bar must have its logical justification. In the sound-film, the music can say much more than in the silent film: that is the big chance offered it by technical progress. It should therefore penetrate to the depths of the plot which it accompanies. (*ibid*.: 156)

Perhaps it was Maurice Jaubert's legal training that enabled him to verbalize musical matters with more clarity than most, for example, his view of music's role in films and its relation to other cinematic elements:

> Into the raw materials of cinema—which acquire artistic meaning only from their relations to one another—music brings an *unreal* element which is bound to break the rules of objective realism. Is there no place for it in the film?
>
> Certainly there is. . . . The director sometimes [moves] away from the strict representation of reality in order to add to his work those touches of comment or poetry which give a film its individual quality. . . . Here the music has something to say: its presence will warn the spectator that the style of the film is changing temporarily for dramatic reasons. All its power of suggestion will serve to intensify and prolong that impression of strangeness, of departure from photographic truth, which the director is seeking. (Jaubert 1937: 109)

And here is his concept of the nature of film music, and how it should provide psychological support for the photographic images:

> I believe it to be essential for film music to evolve a style of its own. If it merely brings lazily to the screen its traditional interest in composition or expression, then, instead of entering as a partner into the world of images, it will set up alongside a separate world of sound obeying its own laws. . . . It will never have any point of contact with the visual world which it ought . . . to *serve*. It will live its own life, sufficient unto itself.
>
> Let film music . . . make physically perceptive to us the inner rhythm of the image, without struggling to provide a translation

of its content, whether this be emotional, dramatic or poetic. (*ibid.*: 111–12)

Jaubert felt that the image should be supported by a kind of impersonal musical texture of sound:

> Film music should never, so to speak, reveal its own musical nature. If the writing of it has pursued strictly musical ends, and if those ends have been achieved, thanks to the gifts of the composer, we shall be tempted to *listen to it*. And then it will detach itself from the image—a danger which increases in proportion to the inherent value of the music. (*ibid.*: 114)

Carlos Chavez's interest in the future of mechanical music led him naturally to an investigation of the artistic and sociological aspects of the sound film. Not unexpectedly, this great Mexican composer saw the role of music as an integral part of cinema, not as mere window dressing:

> The function of the true composer for the cinema is not that of superimposing music on the scenes to the order of the director of the production. He should have a conception of the cinematographic work as a whole, and of music's fulfilling an integral function within it. So that the artist may be capable of such conceptions, he must have a profound understanding of the potentialities of all the cinematographic instruments. (Chavez 1937: 169)

Certain music critics showed continuing interest in the functional and theoretical sides of film music, including the question which so preoccupied Jaubert and others—the evolution of a new compositional style.

> Music in its most profound use in the cinema must be in its rôle as an integral part of the cinematic scheme, in creating atmosphere and in developing emotional content. The success of this depends chiefly on the composer's willingness and initiative to throw overboard many of his orthodox methods of composition in the same way that the novelist-turned-scenarist might have to give up lengthy polemics and descriptive embellishments for the economic tempo of film. (Perkoff 1937: 41)

Paul Bowles was another composer who, like Lambert and Thomson, became as well known for literary as for musical accomplishments. In 1939 he took over the chores of film music critic for *Modern Music*.

As others had found an analogy between cinema and opera, he found an analogy with the dance:

> What music is to good choreography, the visual action of a film should be to its sound-track. Regardless of the music's form, the dance springing from it must have a recognizable pattern. And no matter what the vagaries of the film (including the restrictions imposed by the bugbear dialogue which is usually scattered haphazardly), the music created to give an extra dimension to the final impression must have a logical design and a sense of direction. . . . To ask that music be synchronized as exactly as sound-effects is the same thing as asking that the execution of the dancer's steps and gestures exist in some sort of fixed relation to the beat of the music, and not that they should merely come to pass during a given section of it. (Bowles 1939: 61)

It is interesting to discover from Bowles that the polemics against synchronized or "illustrative" music, which had begun during the infancy of the sound film, were still continuing at the end of the decade. This clearly indicates that the much-decried type of scoring was still being used in some quarters, despite the many declarations against it.

Taken as a whole, the writings we have seen thus far led to an incontrovertible conclusion: film music had to evolve a style of its own if it was ever to fulfill its destiny as an equal partner in the artistic demands of the new medium. What should the new style be like? How was it to be achieved? To begin with, as Leigh had suggested, the musician would first have to abandon many musical conventions on which he had been brought up. This sentiment was echoed by others who were convinced of the impracticality of most traditional procedures:

> Heard over the radio or in a sound film, many formal procedures seem antiquated—for example the principle of reprise, of development, in fact the whole sonata-form. (Eisler 1935: 184)

> As in the silent film, so in the sound-film, most of the traditional musical forms are useless. Yet it is much easier to have single detached pieces of music in the sound-film than in the silent film. (London 1936: 154)

What was wrong with the old forms? Why did certain traditional methods fail in sound films, although they may have worked in the silents? In his review of Jean Wiener's score for the French film, *Maria Chapdelaine*, American composer Marc Blitzstein complained that the music was too Wagnerian:

> It is symphonic music; it acts as overlay rather than support. . . . The big moments call too much attention to the music, so that when the music does subside the effect is of a wheezy and defective bellows; or worse, of a change in *distance*, as though the orchestra had gone mad in a body, and were crazily parading toward us and then away from us. (Blitzstein 1935: 132)

Several authors suggested that symphonic procedure in a sound film was wrong because it called attention to its own inner workings instead of supporting the image as an equal. Understatement was better, in most cases, because a little bit of music sometimes can have a potent effect:

> The composer approaching the film problem for the first time will be struck by one especially important fact, namely, that in film-music more than in any other kind of music the greatest virtue is economy. A phrase of five bars lasting twenty seconds . . . may express as much as a whole slow movement of a symphony. . . . The academic principles of leisurely formal development are therefore of little use in the composition of film-music, though they may well be employed in the construction of the whole film and its sound-score. (Leigh 1934: 72)

Although traditional devices such as development might be out of place, it might be feasible to use some of the short musical forms:

> A traditional musical form which might be taken over for the sound-film is the "Theme with variations." This old musicians' ideal, in free treatment, presents the film with extraordinary possibilities. (London 1936: 157)

We have seen that, as early as 1933, Virgil Thomson had pointed out the necessity for continuity in film music, decrying the custom of changing the music in every new scene. There was almost no disagreement on this issue, but old habits die slowly, even in such a rapidly changing art form as the cinema. The quest for ideal form would be hampered as long as music was used principally to synchronize with actions on the screen, or—as was many composers' wont—to imitate naturalistic sounds:

> The cinema has many means of accurately and photographically reproducing [*i.e.*, by means of the optical system] all the sounds of nature, and any attempts by music in this direction always seem naïve. . . . Music is essentially symbolical, and this rôle befits it. . . . (Sabaneev 1935: 24)

It is preferable that the music should give us an idea of the actor's hidden world of psychological emotions, rather than repeat (by translating it into the language of sounds) that which we have already seen on the screen without it—the gesture. (*ibid.*: 49)

This kind of musical synchronization came to be called "Mickey Mouse music," for obvious reasons. Admittedly, there were some instances when its use could be justified:

Complete rhythmical coincidence is more allowable when the subject of the film is gay and light-hearted than when it is tragic. (*ibid.*: 50)

In most applications, however, writers insisted that continuity was essential in order to establish and maintain the proper mood or atmosphere:

It is impossible . . . to achieve in music the equivalent of the "quick cutting" which is the basis of the Pudovkin-Eisenstein technique. There is no real equivalent in music even of the "wipe-dissolve" which leads the eye gently but quickly from one scene to another. (Lambert 1934: 263)

Of course there would always be certain cases wherein special types of scene changes might require the music to follow along somehow. But whatever the problem, continuity should still be the goal:

Musical punctuation plus some (a little) of Honegger's naturalism are likely to prove the best method. Given a competent composer, continuity can be maintained without going in for symphony writing, which muffs the whole function; the correct intensity-level can be set, the degree of the music's importance, which can be changed subtly for special commentary and the like; at the same time finickiness can be avoided, so that there need be no separate music for each closeup or long-shot. (Blitzstein 1935: 132)

Maurice Jaubert summarized the discussion with his customary Gallic precision:

Music is by nature continuous, organised rhythmically in time. If you compel it to follow slavishly events or gestures which are themselves discontinuous, not rhythmically ordered but the outcome simply of physiological or psychological reactions, you destroy in it the very quality by virtue of which it is music, reducing it to its primary condition of crude sound. Used for these purposes, music will never, I am convinced, prove to be a satisfactory substitute for natural sounds, justified by their authenticity. (Jaubert 1937: 108)

Judging from some of the comments that were made, even when a composer showed adherence to the principle of continuity by writing atmospheric or symbolic music, the mood he implanted might not always have been the correct one. A prominent British composer was among those who cautioned against this kind of mistake:

> Background-music . . . can be (indeed, it too often is) ridiculous. . . . It should be a rule that background-music should take the colouring either of the surroundings or the emotion of the scene. Concurrent with this one can superimpose orchestral noises. . . . Utmost care should be taken to ensure that the background be psychologically apt. (Benjamin 1937: 596)

In *Music for the Films*, Sabaneev devoted some thought to the question of what kind of music is best suited for lengthy dialogue scenes, particularly those with emotional and sentimental content, and suggested that it should not only remain stylistically consistent but also that it be kept at a constant dynamic level throughout:

> What is required is a continuous line in keeping with the lyrical mood of the scene. In any event, the composer will do well to arrange his accompaniment on the assumption that . . . it will be barely audible. Inexperienced musicians very frequently write lyrical, passionate, and strongly dynamic music, with the result that it has to be relegated to the background and the whole purpose of the composition comes to naught. (Sabaneev 1935: 40)

Choosing the wrong musical mood was not the only mistake that could be made by an inexperienced or thoughtless composer; the following writer may have had Hollywood in mind:

> Simplicity, clarity, and economy are virtues in all music, but doubly so in film-music. The worst thing a film composer can do is overload the microphone. The familiar type of hack orchestration, with its "doubling-up" and "filling-in" is useless for the film. (Leigh 1936: 40)

Composer Antheil's conclusion in the matter of proper mood and atmosphere in movie music contained a thought-provoking and useful idea:

> It must always have the sense of the picture at heart; after all it is picture music and not a demonstration of the composer's virtuosity in the various orchestral forms. This does not mean that music must only play *with* a picture; it can also play against it; in fact I believe that very often indeed it should play against it.

> But this "against" should be a definite and intended contrast, heightening the drama and the effect of the picture instead of merely drawing attention to the queer non-matching music. (Antheil 1938: 252)

In addition to pondering definitions of function, the search for musical style, and other theoretical matters, some composers were concerned with more practical, workaday aspects of movie music—for instance: how to get the "feel" of a picture, knowing where to place music, and how much of it there should be (albeit those are clearly interrelated with function and style). One of the very first sound film composers in England stressed the necessity for getting involved in the early stages of production:

> The musician must be given time and opportunity to get "into" the picture. He should be able to work out all his musical ideas step by step with the progress of the visual sequences and evolve from the tedious process of a mechanical measurement of feet and frames an accompaniment which will not only be an illumination of the camera's story but a musical entity in itself. (Raybould 1933: 80)

Regarding the composer's ability to get the "feel" of a picture, the following could have been written only by someone with lots of movie experience:

> The successful film-composer must have the gift of summing up the atmosphere of a scene quickly. He will then find that the rhythm of any scene will get into his subconscious memory, and so when the music is recorded, the rhythms fall to certain actions in the picture where, had he consciously tried, he would have failed. (Benjamin 1937: 596)

Having the feel of a picture includes knowing where to place music—the ability to sense the precise moment for the unreality of music to intrude into the illusion of reality created by the images:

> The break in sensory adjustment which is provoked in the spectator by the irruption of music into the film ought to be carefully prepared. . . . There are a thousand and one possible solutions to a problem which never twice presents itself in the same way. But it is precisely the function of the film musician to feel the exact moment when the image escapes from strict realism and calls for the poetic extension of music. (Jaubert 1937: 109-10)

The problem of correct placement of music is linked with something else of concern to film musicians then and now—the audience's awareness of the music. It is quite a dilemma: after all, composers do want their music to be heard; at the same time, most of them would agree that the spectators are not supposed to actually *listen* to it. Here is how one Hollywood composer viewed this quandary:

> The sincere musician in motion pictures does not mind the fact that the public does not realize his music's importance. On the contrary. If an audience is conscious of music where it should be conscious only of drama, then the musician has gone wrong. We can let the audience hear the music where music naturally would be heard, but in dramatic moments it must be subordinated. . . . Picture music has to appeal to eye and ear at the same time. Played without the picture being seen, it would lose much of its effect. But so would the picture, shown without the music. That is as it should be. (Stothart 1939: 143-44)

One of the few concert hall composers to find work in Hollywood during the thirties was Ernst Toch. He was also a sagacious writer about things musical and believed, as did Stothart, that sound film could bring good music to "the masses." Although seeming to agree with his confrere's view about the public's lack of awareness of film scores, Toch saw in that very passivity an opportunity for the composer (and the producer) to improve the state of things:

> There is no doubt that although the public accepts unfitting music indifferently or leniently it would be sure to notice and value the moving and enhancing power of appropriate music . . . . And . . . there is no doubt that if the people in charge would devote as much attention to the quality of the music as to the other items in a film they would deserve great credit. (Toch 1936: 18)

How much music should there be? It was not enough merely to say that it depended on the individual film; if a picture seemed to have too much music in it, it could mean that the composer (or director) lacked the ability to sense the right moment to start music—and when to stop it. There were a few complaints about excessive music in films, including this from a music critic who was probably referring to most Hollywood and many British films of the day:

> I do indeed believe that less music, or at least less background would be a very desirable slogan to be adopted by the musicians. Its effect when achieved should provide a pleasant relief for the

movie-lovers of five continents: and it certainly would mean a gain for the films as an art. In this respect . . . there is a lesson to be learned from the European, or rather from the French films. (Gutman 1938: 221)

It is evident that the search for an understanding of the nature and functions of film music was concerned mainly with two fundamental issues: the concept of music's role as a psychological and emotional element in the drama—coequal to other elements—and the necessity to evolve new form and style. In the final analysis, all the other matters that were discussed in the period under consideration—denial of the old illustration technique, continuity, uselessness of traditional musical forms and procedures, correct placement of music, etc.—were merely corollaries stemming from the challenge of the two basic problems. And, in reality, it could be said that there actually was only *one* fundamental question, for was not the necessity to evolve a new musical style prompted by the changing concept of music's relation to the film?

Many thoughts and opinions about the forms and functions of movie music have been scrutinized in these pages; some writers were succinct, others were verbose; some ideas reasonable, others impractical; some conclusions logical, others unconvincing. But if we wanted to educe from all these writings one single principle that would always be valid, incontrovertible, and applicable in every imaginable cinematic circumstance, I believe it would have to be the precept expressed so pithily by composer Arthur Benjamin in 1937: "Good film-music must never unduly obtrude, but should be missed if it were absent."

NOTES

[1] There is a thorough review of this phase of cinema music in London 1936: 33–96.

[2] For practical reasons, it has been necessary to confine the survey to sources in English.

³Many film score reviews of the era include useful comments on film music aesthetics, and should be consulted by anyone interested in pursuing this topic further.

⁴Questions posed in this essay originate not only from the writings themselves, but also from my own many years of experience as a composer and conductor of theatrical and television films.

⁵Sabaneev was a Russian journalist and critic who studied composition under Taneyev and graduated from Moscow University with a degree in mathematics. Before emigrating from Russia in 1926, he had already published a definitive book on Scriabin and a history of Russian music.

⁶See above, p. 88–89.

⁷London was a German musician and technician who had been active in film music, film criticism, and early experimental sound recording in Germany before emigrating in 1935. *Film Music* was the standard textbook on the subject all over the world until was superseded in 1957 by *The Technique of Film Music*, by Roger Manvell and John Huntley.

SOURCES

The following list comprises mainly sources cited in the text. Many others were examined but not included here.

Abbreviations: *MM* (*Modern Music*), *SS* (*Sight and Sound*), *WFN* (*World Film News*).

Antheil, George
- 1935 "Composers in Movieland," *MM*, 12/2: 62–68.
- 1936 "Good Russian Advice About Movies," *MM*, 13/4: 53–56.
- 1936a "On the Hollywood Front," *MM*, 14/1: 46–49.
- 1937 "Breaking Into the Movies," *MM*, 14/2: 82–86.
- 1937a "On the Hollywood Front," *MM*, 15/1: 48–51.
- 1938 "On the Hollywood Front," *MM*, 15/4: 251–254.

Benjamin, Arthur
- 1937 "Film Music," *Musical Times*, 78: 595–597.

Blitzstein, Marc
- 1935 "Theatre-Music in Paris," *MM*, 12/3: 128–134.

Bowles, Paul
- 1939 "On the Film Front," *MM*, 17/1: 60–62.

Calvocoressi, M.D.
- 1935 "Music and the Film," *SS*, 4/14: 57–58.

Chavez, Carlos
- 1937 *Toward a New Music: Music and Electricity*. Translated by Herbert Weinstock. New York: Norton.

Closson, Hermann
- 1930 "The Case Against *Gebrauchsmusik*," *MM*, 7/2: 15–19.

Eisler, Hanns
    1935   "Reflections on the Future of the Composer," *MM*, 12/4: 180–186.
    1936   "Music and Film: Illustration or Creation?" *WFN*, 1/2: 23.

Gutman, John A.
    1938   "Casting the Film Composer," *MM*, 15/4: 216–221.

Hammond, Richard
    1931   "Pioneers of Film Music," *MM*, 8/3: 35–38.

Jaubert, Maurice
    1936   "Music and Film," *WFN*, 1/4: 31.
    1937   "Music on the Screen," in *Footnotes to the Film*, edited by Charles Davey. New York: Oxford University Press. Pages 101–115.

Knight, Arthur
    1978   *The Liveliest Art: A Panoramic History of the Movies.* Rev. ed. New York: Macmillan.

Lambert, Constant
    1934   *Music Ho! A Study of Music in Decline.* New York: Scribner's.
    1936   "Foreword by Constant Lambert," in Kurt London, *Film Music*, q.v. Pages 7–9.

Leigh, Walter
    1934   "The Musician and the Film," *Cinema Quarterly*, 3/2: 70–74.
    1936   "Music and Microphones," *WFN*, 1/5: 40.

London, Kurt
    1936   *Film Music: A Summary of the Characteristic Features of Its History, Aesthetics, Technique; and Possible*

Developments. Translated by Eric S. Bensinger. With a foreword by Constant Lambert. London: Faber & Faber.

Milhaud, Darius
    1930   "Experimenting with Sound Films," *MM*, 7/2: 11–14.
    1937   "Wagner, Verdi and the Film," *WFN*, 2/4: 27.

Perkoff, Leslie
    1937   "Notes and Theories," *WFN*, 2/1: 41.

Raybould, Clarence
    1933   "Music and the Synchronized Film," *SS*, 2/7: 80–81.

Sabaneev, Leonid
    1934   "Music and the Sound Film," *Music and Letters*, 15: 147–152.
    1935   *Music for the Films: A Handbook for Composers and Conductors.* Translated by S. W. Pring. London: Pitman.

Steiner, Max
    1937   "Scoring the Film," in *We Make the Movies*, edited by Nancy Naumburg. New York: Norton. Pages 216–238.

Stothart, Herbert
    1939   "Film Music," in *Behind the Screen*, edited by Stephen Watts. London: Barker. Pages 139–144.

Thomson, Virgil
    1933   "A Little About Movie Music," *MM*, 10/4: 188–191.
    1939   *The State of Music.* New York: William Morrow.

Toch, Ernst
    1936   "Sound–Film and Music Theatre," *MM*, 13/2: 15–18.

Photograph of Stravinsky autographed to Herbert Stothart *(courtesy of the Herbert Stothart estate)*.

Stravinsky and MGM

William H. Rosar

There are a number of anecdotes about Stravinsky's flirtations with writing music for films and his notoriously unproductive negotiations with movie producers, but to date no systematic attempt has been made to document their factual basis with evidence from sources other than Stravinsky himself. Although having circulated in various versions for decades through the vast communications network of Hollywood gossip, most of these anecdotes can ultimately be traced back to Stravinsky himself and have been chronicled in the books he wrote in collaboration with Robert Craft. After Stravinsky's death in 1971, additional material about his interactions with the movie industry appeared with the publication of his letters, and after the death of his wife, published excerpts from her diaries.[1]

What follows is a historical account of the beginning of Stravinsky's encounters with the American film industry, occasioned by his first visit to Hollywood in 1935. What follows has been reconstructed as much as possible from sources in addition to Stravinsky's own published accounts.

On January 3, 1935, Stravinsky and violinist Samuel Dushkin arrived in New York from France aboard the Atlantic liner *S.S. Rex*, to embark on a three-month concert tour across the United States in which they were to make some thirty concert appearances featuring Stravinsky's music exclusively.[2] In addition to conducting his works in New York, Boston, Chicago, Detroit, and Minneapolis, Stravinsky was also to conduct them in San Francisco and Los Angeles, his first visit to California.[3] His coming to Los Angeles was at the invitation of Otto

Igor Stravinsky (seated at desk) with members of the MGM music department and guests, February 25, 1935. Others in the photograph are identified in the diagram on facing page. *(Photo courtesy of the Herbert Stothart estate.)*

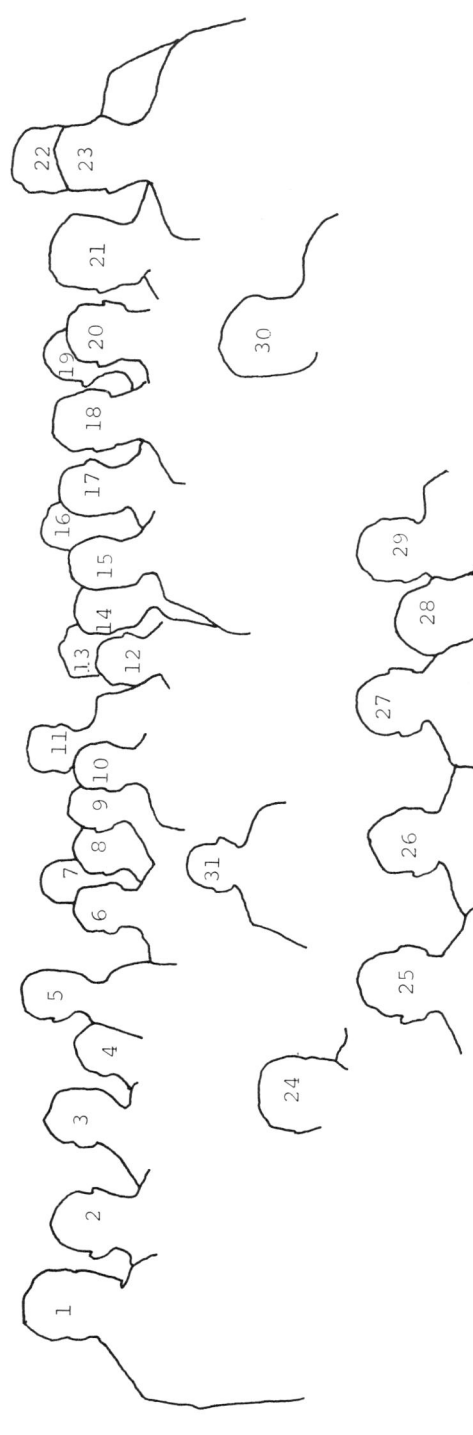

1) Nacio Herb Brown; 2) Arthur Freed; 3) Herbert Stothart; 4) Walter Donaldson; 5) Burton Lane; 6) Harold Adamson; 7) unidentified; 8) Leonid Raab; 9) Val Burton; 10) Victor Baravalle; 11) R. H. Bassett; 12) Jack Robbins; 13) Will Jason (?); 14) Ned Washington; 15) Walter Jurmann; 16) Charles Maxwell; 17) unidentified; 18) Alexander Merovich (?); 19) Harry Highsmith; 20) Ernest Klapholz; 21) George G. Schneider; 22) unidentified; 23) Milton Beecher; 24) unidentified; 25) Chris Schoenberg; 26) Oscar Radin; 27) Bronislau Kaper; 28) Gus Kahn; 29) unidentified; 30) Alexis Kall; 31) Igor Stravinsky.

Klemperer, then conductor of the Los Angeles Philharmonic, and was sponsored by Merle Armitage, who was a publisher and Los Angeles music patron.[4] During his two-week visit to Los Angeles, Stravinsky was to be the guest of Dr. Alexis Kall, who later became his personal secretary.[5] Stravinsky arrived in Los Angeles on February 17.[6] "As he stepped from the train, he was greeted by a delegation of musicians from the orchestra [the Los Angeles Philharmonic] and a group of local music lovers."[7]

On February 21 and 22, Stravinsky was to conduct the Los Angeles Philharmonic in a program featuring suites from his ballets *The Firebird* and *Pétrouchka* at the Philharmonic Auditorium in downtown Los Angeles.[8] Although it was announced that on February 28 Stravinsky would conduct the orchestra with Dushkin as soloist in his violin concerto (then new), apparently it was not performed, but instead, Stravinsky accompanied Dushkin at the keyboard in a recital featuring his *Suite italienne*, *Divertimento*, *Duo concertant*, and excerpts from *Le Rossignol*, *Pétrouchka*, and *The Firebird*.[9]

During his stay in the Movie Capital of the World, arrangements were made for Stravinsky to tour some of the movie studios; with one exception, it is not known which studios he actually visited. The studio he is known to have visited was Metro-Goldwyn-Mayer in Culver City, on February 25.

Stravinsky's arrival at the studio must have been an occasion met with mixed sentiments. Although it seems reasonable to assume that anybody working in the music world would know of Stravinsky as an *avant-garde* composer, who can say how a studio music department populated largely by Broadway song writers would receive him? A photograph commemorating Stravinsky's visit to the studio shows Stravinsky in the company of the MGM music department staff of song writers, lyricists, and composers and orchestrators. If one can judge from the expressions on their faces, reactions to his presence appeared to range from reverence to indifference.

Stravinsky was given a tour of the music department facilities by MGM's senior composer, Herbert Stothart, and arrangements were made to record Stravinsky making a brief speech for posterity. (Presumably this took place while he was being shown one of the recording stages, where the recording equipment would most likely have been located.) Alexander Merovich, a well-known artist's manager,[10] was present with

Stravinsky and MGM 113

Stravinsky and acted as his interpreter during a one-minute speech which the composer delivered in German, transcribed below:

> STOTHART: I had the pleasure the other night of listening to *Pétrouchka* for the first time—I heard it, I mean I heard it conducted for the first time, the way I felt it, wanted to hear it. I had the privilege of hearing it from the composer himself. It was the greatest thrill I've ever had in my life, Mr. Merovich, and I want you to express to Mr. Stravinsky the gratitude that all of we here in Southern California had, to him for coming to us and giving us this opportunity to hear his music the way we love to hear it. I want you to ask one or two questions regarding his impressions of Southern California.
> MEROVICH: I thank you, Mr. Stothart. Je veux demander à maître Stravinsky comment il a aimé la Californie et quelle impression que lui il y a.
> STRAVINSKY: Je repondre en français, oder im Deutsch?
> STOTHART: In Deutsch.
> MEROVICH: Im Deutsch.
> STRAVINSKY: Es ist sehr schwer in zwei worter ein grossen Eindruck zu aussprechen. Doch kanne ihnen sagen dass ich ein sehr grosse Freude hatte, nich nur in Amerika, diese heraus zu reisen und zu musizieren aber auch in California, dieses Land das ich noch nicht konnte, hat mir ein sehr grossen Eindruck gemacht. Ebenso, wie die Natur, die Musik und das Kunsterleben und ich bin sehr Froh hier bei Ihnen—wie sagt man in Deutsch *être reçu*?
> MEROVICH: Erfangen zu werden.
> STRAVINSKY: —Erfangen zu werden, ja, und ich bin sehr dankbar für alle diese interesanten Sache [inaudible] zeichen.
> [*English translation*: It is very difficult to express a great impression in merely two words. Yet, I can say to you that not only was it a great pleasure to travel and perform music just in America, but in California as well, a state of which I had not yet known, and which made a great impression on me, an impression of nature and of the artistic life style. I am very pleased to be here and to have been received by you. I am very grateful for all the interesting things which you are showing me.]
> STOTHART: Thank you, sir.
> STRAVINSKY: Danke vielmals [Many thanks].
> UNIDENTIFIED: Mr.—tell Mr. Stravinsky that in two days we'll give him a record of that so he can play it on his own phonograph. (*Laughter*.)[11]

After Stravinsky returned to Europe in April, the press there was most curious about his impressions of Hollywood, and in an Italian newspaper, Stravinsky gave a colorful account of his attempt to meet L.B. Mayer:

This past season I was in Hollywood, a very interesting place. I visited several film studios, each of which is a kind of principality, with its own borders, trenches, police, cannons, machine guns, as well as its ministers for the various technical and artistic operations. At Metro-Goldwyn-Mayer, I saw forty salaried composers, all working from morning to night to produce music. This way the directors avoid re-runs of music that already exists and do not have to pay royalties to the composers. . . . I wanted to meet the head of the company, Signor Mayer, and an interview was arranged. I was led through a grey corridor to a grey room crowded with others, waiting like myself. I remained there a long time, during which everyone talked about Mr. Mayer, though no one had seen him and he might have been a myth. But at long last a door opened and a little man with a large beak appeared, followed by two lieutenants. He approached me, nodded, said, "I am a man like others, with a lot to do," and with this, shook my hand and left. At least I can testify that Mr. Mayer is not a myth.[12]

In retrospect, the way Stravinsky characterized MGM and the other studios would almost seem to have been intended to appeal to the fascist, militaristic atmosphere of Mussolini's Italy!

There is another story of Stravinsky visiting Mayer, which Stravinsky related to Miklós Rózsa, which must have occurred after he moved to Hollywood in 1940:

In his first years in Hollywood, Stravinsky badly needed money.

The early works, registered in Tsarist Russia, were not protected by copyright and earned him no income; his inter-War compositions were not greatly performed. Eventually, Louis B. Mayer was persuaded to offer him employment.

"I hear you are the greatest composer in the world," said Mayer. Stravinsky bowed.

"Well, this is the greatest movie studio in the world." Stravinsky bowed again.

To prove his point, Mayer demonstrated the battery of technological wonders he had installed in his enormous desk.

"How much will you charge for a music score?" he finally asked.

"How long is it?" asked Stravinsky.

"Say 45 minutes."

Stravinsky did a mental calculation of the amount of work that had gone into *Petrushka* and *The Rite of Spring*, compositions of the desired length, and said, "$25,000."

"That's a lot of money, Mr. Stravinsky," said Mayer, "much more than we normally pay. But since you're the greatest

composer in the world, you shall have it. Now, when can I have the score?"
"In about one year," said Stravinsky.
Mayer stared at him in disbelief. "Good day, Mr. Stravinsky," he said.[13]

It is not unlikely that Stravinsky probably also felt a certain amount of animosity toward the American film industry during his visit in February 1935, because the previous year, Warner Bros. released a film using excerpts from his *Firebird*, and also bearing the same title, for which he sued and received little compensation.[14] In any case, a year after Stravinsky visited MGM, Herbert Stothart was quoted as saying that all Stravinsky needed was "but a spark" to start him on a film composing career. As Stothart put it, "An impressionistic ballet, perhaps a 'Petrouchka' would do it,"[15] as though it was the genre of the music that would have been Stravinsky's primary incentive, rather than financial gain as the following quip attributed to Stravinsky attests: "Film Music? That's monkey business, and for monkey business my price is too high."[16]

But perhaps even more important than financial concerns were matters of aesthetics. Only three years before his first visit to Los Angeles, Stravinsky had enunciated views in Europe which were completely at odds with the prevailing precepts of film scoring as it was being practiced, where the role of music was construed as being subordinate to the film as a whole:

> Not being a partisan of "Expressionism" in music, I think that the role of the latter is not to express the meaning of a piece or the meaning of its text, nor to create an "atmosphere" of the production. One might ask, then, according to what principle does a collaboration between the playing of music and the action of the scene operate? According to the principle of independence from each other, this is my response. Each true art is necessarily doctrinaire, possessing its own laws that rule and govern it. This principle applying to all theater, I do not find a single logical reason not to apply it equally to all cinema.[17]

This position, which Stravinsky expressed in 1932, was reiterated and elaborated by him in an article fourteen years later, indicating that his aesthetic convictions did not change in this regard.[18] Furthermore, Stravinsky's rejection of the "expression theory of music," alluded to in his remarks above, was voiced in 1936 with the publication of his *Chronicle of My Life*, where he wrote: "I consider that music, by its

Page from the Kalmus miniature score edition of *Pétrouchka* inscribed by Stravinsky to Herbert Stothart, 25 February 1935 *(courtesy of the Herbert Stothart estate)*. It is likely that this is the volume on the desk beneath Stravinsky's hands in the group photograph reproduced on page 110.

very nature, is essentially powerless to *express* anything at all, whether a feeling, an attitude of mind, a psychological mood, a phenomenon of nature, etc. . . . *Expression* has never been an inherent property of music."[19] No statement could be more diametrically opposed to the philosophy of film music!

In any event, if we accept Rózsa's account as being the final outcome of Stravinsky's negotiations with MGM, the composer and the studio were unable to come to terms with each other's requirements, a situation that was to repeat itself more than once in the future, when Stravinsky subsequently made his home in the Hollywood hills in 1940.[20]

NOTES

[1]*Stravinsky: Selected Correspondence, Vols. I–III*, edited and with commentaries by Robert Craft (New York: Alfred A. Knopf, 1982, 1984, 1985); *Dearest Bubushkin: Selected Letters and Diaries of Vera and Igor Stravinsky*, edited by Robert Craft (London: Thames and Hudson, 1985).

[2]"Stravinsky Here With New Music," *New York Times*, January 4, 1935, p. 26; Vera Stravinsky and Robert Craft, *Stravinsky in Pictures and Documents* (New York: Simon and Schuster, 1978), pp. 324–325.

[3]"Stravinsky Here With New Music," *loc. cit.*; "Stravinsky Will Conduct at Philharmonic," *Los Angeles Daily News*, February 19, 1935, p. 13.

[4]*Los Angeles Examiner*, August 4, 1934, Part I, p. 9; "Stravinsky to Appear Here: Own Compositions Program Feature," *Los Angeles Examiner*, September 2, 1934, Part V, p. 6. Armitage subsequently edited a volume of essays, *Igor Strawinsky* (New York: G. Schirmer, 1936).

[5]*Stravinsky: Selected Correspondence, Vol. I*, p. 440.

[6]Isabel Morse Jones, "Contemporary Composers Flocking to Los Angeles," *Los Angeles Times*, February 10, 1935, Part II, p. 6; "Stravinsky Will Conduct at Philharmonic," *loc. cit.*

[7]"Igor Stravinsky Arrives," *Los Angeles Examiner*, February 18, 1935, Part I, p. 4.

[8]In addition to the suites from the two ballets mentioned, the program included music from the ballet *Appolon musagète* (*Apollo,*

Leader of the Muses) and the *Little Suite* (Eight Little Pieces for orchestra). This information is from the Los Angeles Philharmonic concert program; the latter work is now known as Suites 1 and 2 for small orchestra.

[9]Isabel Morse Jones, *loc. cit.*; "Russian and Scottish Music Feature Weeks' Programs," *Los Angeles Times*, February 17, 1935, Part II, p. 6; "Condensation Essence of Stravinsky Compositions," *Los Angeles Times*, February 24, 1935, Part II, p. 6.

[10] It is unclear whether or not Merovich managed Stravinsky's American tour. According to Robert Craft, Richard Copley was Stravinsky's American concert agent after January 1935, having replaced Merovich. However, if this was the case, why was Merovich with Stravinsky at MGM? See *Stravinsky: Selected Correspondence, Vol. II*, pp. 304–307. For additional information on Merovich, see "Merovitch, 71, Dies; Managed Musicians," *New York Times*, August 9, 1965, p. 25.

[11]A transcription disc of this speech is the source of the text. The disc is identified with a printed label: "Sample Record Pressed by RCA Victor Company, Inc., Hollywood, California." Then, as today, the cost of all studio technical services had to be charged to a production. In this case, it was recorded as a "tech[nical] test" for the film *Public Enemy #2* (released in 1935 as *Baby Face Harrington*). On the label are marked in pencil the words "Stravinsky Speech" in Herbert Stothart's handwriting. The disc is in the possession of the Herbert Stothart estate, although a tape copy of it is in the Herbert Stothart Collection, Special Collections, Doheny Library, University of Southern California. The translation from the German was made by Ed Noelter.

[12]Vera Stravinsky and Robert Craft, *loc. cit.* (the original source was *La Gazetta del Popolo*, June 1[?], 1935). According to Craft, Stravinsky may have been somewhat sympathetic to the politics of Italy at that time: "[Stravinsky] was a frequent and welcome visitor of blackshirt Italy during the Ethiopian and Spanish wars, after all, and he conducted at the Maggio Fiorentino as late as 1939, by which time that festival had become a loudly pro-Axis celebration. He even inscribed a copy of his *Chroniques de ma vie* [*Chronicle of My Life*] for Mussolini." (Robert Craft, *Stravinsky: Chronicle of a Friendship 1948–1971* [New York: Alfred A. Knopf, 1972], p. 63.)

[13]Norman Lebrecht, *The Book of Musical Anecdotes* (New York: The Free Press, 1985), p. 309. Another telling by Rózsa of the same

anecdote may be found in Mark Evans, *Soundtrack: The Music of the Movies* (New York: Hopkinson and Blake, 1975), pp. 252–253:

> [Stravinsky] was receiving no royalties on his most frequently performed works, the three early ballets. Friends suggested that he could make a lot of money by writing a film score. So when Louis B. Mayer, then the all-powerful head of MGM, invited him to his office for an interview, the composer decided to accept.
>
> Stravinsky, ushered into the office, found the executive seated at an enormous desk. For the next half hour, Mayer talked about all the telephones on his desk, about how he could call every director or producer directly from it. Stravinsky was puzzled; he had come to talk about music, not desks. Then Mayer said, "I have been told that you are the greatest composer in the world." Stravinsky bowed. "How much money would you ask as a fee for composing a film score?" Stravinsky named a huge sum, equivalent to about $100,000 today. Mayer retorted without the slightest surprise, "If you are the greatest composer in the world, you're worth the money." Stravinsky again bowed. "Now, how long would it take for you to compose an hour of music?" Stravinsky paused for a moment, then replied, "One year." Mayer stood up and said, "Good-bye, Mr. Stravinsky."

MGM arranger Leo Arnaud recalled being present at a luncheon (or dinner) for Stravinsky held at MGM, which would have been some time after 1936, when Arnaud first came to America from France. Arnaud seemed to think that Stravinsky had been invited to the studio more than once (telephone interview by the author with Leo Arnaud, August 23, 1985). Stravinsky did subsequently become acquainted with Mayer, and even visited Mayer's home in 1942, to help in planning a benefit for Russian War Relief (Vera Stravinsky and Robert Craft, *loc. cit.*).

[14]*Stravinsky: Selected Correspondence, Vol. II*, pp. 250–252. Ironically, Bernhard Kaun, the composer whose job it was to adapt *The Firebird* for this purpose, once said that he had heard that Stravinsky thought him the most original of all the film composers! (Personal interview by the author with Bernhard Kaun, March 23, 1977.) Kaun (1899–1980), whose career as a film composer, arranger, and orchestrator spanned the years from 1925 to 1957, was the son of the distinguished German composer, Hugo Kaun (1863–1932).

[15]"The Future of Film Music as Seen by Mr. Stothart," *Milwaukee Journal*, April 26, 1936, p. 3. Interestingly, only a few years earlier, ballet sequences featuring the Albertina Rasch Dancers were incorporated into several of MGM's films as novelties. The music for

these was composed by another Russian—Dimitri Tiomkin, Rasch's husband. By 1935 the novelty of the ballet sequences apparently had worn off, at least at MGM.

[16] Alfred Frankenstein, "Stravinsky in Beverly Hills," *Modern Music*, 19, No. 3 (March-April 1942), pp. 178ff.

[17] Vera Stravinsky and Robert Craft, p. 358. The original source was the French review, *Candide*:

> N'étant pas partisan de l'expressionisme en musique je pense que le rôle de cette dernière n'est pas d'exprimer le sens d'une pièce ou le sens de son texte, ni de créer une "atmosphère" du spectacle. On demandera, alors, selon quel principe s'opére une collaboration entre le jeu de la musique et l'action du spectacle. Selon le principe de l'indépendence d'une de l'autre, voici ma réponse. Chaque vrai art est nécessairement canonique, possédant ses loix à lui qui le régissent et le gouvernent. Ce principe s'appliquant à tout spectacle de scène (theâtre) je ne trouve aucune raison logique de ne pas l'appliquer également à tout spectacle d'écran (cinéma).

[18] "Stravinsky on Film Music as Told to Ingolf Dahl," *Musical Digest*, 28, No. 1 (September 1946), 4ff.

[19] Igor Stravinsky, *Chronicle of My Life* (London: Victor Gollancz, 1936), p. 91.

[20] Stravinsky's encounters with filmmakers actually began in Europe. In 1919 he was approached to compose music for a film of *Don Quixote* (Vera Stravinsky and Robert Craft, p. 358). For accounts of Stravinsky's subsequent exploits with film producers and Hollywood celebrities, his aborted film music, and his opinions on film music, see Igor Stravinsky and Robert Craft, *Expositions and Developments* (Berkeley: University of California Press, 1959, pp. 77–79, 113, 129, 145–46); *Memories and Commentaries* (Garden City: Doubleday & Co., 1960, pp. 100-104); *Themes and Episodes* (New York: Alfred A. Knopf, 1966, pp. 15, 302-303); Vera Stravinsky and Robert Craft (pp. 357–58, 645); *Stravinsky: Selected Correspondence*, Volumes I–III (*passim*); *Dearest Bubushkin: Selected Letters and Diaries of Vera and Igor Stravinsky* (*passim*); and "Stravinsky on Film Music as Told to Ingolf Dahl" (*loc. cit.*). When the latter article was reprinted in *Cinema—The Magazine for Discriminating Movie-Goers* (1, No. 1 [June 1947], 7ff), film composer David Raksin, who had made the first arrangement (for band) of Stravinsky's "Circus Polka," wrote a reply entitled "Hollywood Strikes Back—Film Composer Attacks

Stravinsky's 'Cult of Inexpressiveness'" (*Musical Digest*, 30, No. 1 [January 1948], 5ff.)

By an interesting irony, although MGM was not successful in obtaining Stravinsky's services to compose music for its films, the studio derived the benefit of his music—or at least its influence—indirectly. Not three years later, an aspiring 27-year-old composer named Robert Wilson Stringer, who was a protégé of Stothart and, it happens, a devotee of Stravinsky's music, patterned part of a piece he wrote on the "Dance of the Nuns" from the fourth scene ("The Grand Carnival—Shrovetide Fair") of *Pétrouchka* for a sequence in *The Wizard of Oz* (1939). Entitled "The Spell," this impressionistic whirl in the orchestra provides a perfect musical setting to the action set in the pastel landscape where Dorothy (Judy Garland), the Scarecrow (Ray Bolger), the Tin Woodman (Jack Haley), and the Cowardly Lion (Bert Lahr) are seen scurrying through a field of poppies towards the gleaming Emerald City in search of the mysterious Wizard of Oz. Stringer was officially employed in the sound department as its music editor, although occasionally Stothart, who was Stringer's musical mentor, would give him the opportunity to compose music for a scene. This was the case with *The Wizard of Oz*. Stringer's cues were orchestrated by Murray Cutter and conducted by Stothart. Ironically, Stringer was composing more music for the concert hall in his spare time than were most of the composers working in the music department! (Telephone interview by the author with Robert W. Stringer, February 9, 1983.)

In another cue in *Wizard*, this one penned by Stothart and entitled "Delirious Escape," can be heard the trombone glissandi from *The Firebird* (suite) during the phantasmagoric montage depicting Dorothy's return to Kansas. As Stothart attests in the recorded speech, he too was an avid admirer of Stravinsky's music. Indeed, he owned many scores and recordings of Stravinsky's works. In fact, in Stothart's score for the silent film *The End of St. Petersburg*, his first film score which he wrote while still in New York in 1928, he interpolated part of *The Firebird* (evidence of this is to be found in the bound volume of Stothart's sketches for this film, in the possession of the Herbert Stothart estate). Leo Arnaud, who occasionally orchestrated parts of Stothart's scores at MGM, recalled Stothart requesting that a certain passage in one of his sketches be orchestrated with a strident trumpet à la *Pétrouchka* (Telephone interview by the author with Leo Arnaud, *loc.*

cit.) In one of Stothart's articles on the aesthetics and techniques of composing for films, he wrote: "We do not stress melodic themes as much as we seek musical effects that generate certain impressions. Stravinsky does it on the concert stage, and he has the ideal picture technique" (Herbert Stothart, "Film Music," in *Behind the Screen: How Films Are Made*, edited by Stephen Watts [New York: Dodge Publishing Co., 1938], p. 144). These words were published in 1938, again only three years after Stravinsky's visit to MGM. Perhaps further study of Stothart's musical output may reveal the influence of Stravinsky in other scores.

Apparently *Pétrouchka* was so well known by Hollywood composers by the late 1930s, that Oscar Levant wrote in his book *A Smattering of Ignorance* (New York: Doubleday, Doran, 1940) that "the orchestral pattern of all carousels, incidentally, is derived from Stravinsky's 'Petrouchka'" (p. 139). Those who would summarily dismiss all film music of this period as being "late Romantic" in style should thus be apprised of such interesting exceptions, where modern works were an influence.

Acknowledgments

The author expresses his gratitude to Herbert Stothart II for making available to him materials from the Herbert Stothart estate, and to the following individuals who helped in identifying the persons in the group photograph: George Bassman, Don Christlieb, Bronislau Kaper, Arthur Morton, Lawrence Morton, David Raksin, and Robert W. Stringer. The author would also like to thank Robert Craft for reading the manuscript and making several helpful suggestions and corrections.

Max Steiner and the Classical Hollywood Film Score: An Analysis of *The Informer*

Kathryn Kalinak

The development of the classical Hollywood film score parallels the early career of one of its most influential practitioners, and clearly its most prolific one, Max Steiner, whose series of successful scores in the formative years of sound empowered the musical practice he and others forged in the early thirties. Recent historical and theoretical studies have begun to delineate the methodologies and ideologies which constituted Hollywood's normative practice in the sound era.[1] It is my aim here to look in depth at the set of conventions that coalesced in the practice of film scoring through an analysis of Max Steiner's score for *The Informer* (RKO, 1935). Steiner had begun to establish his reputation with the scores for films like *Cimarron* (RKO, 1931), *King Kong* (RKO, 1933), and *The Lost Patrol* (RKO, 1934). With *The Informer* he consolidated his position as one of Hollywood's most important composers and won the first Academy Award for an originally composed score.

Regarded in its own day as a masterful example of film music, Steiner's score for *The Informer* consolidated practices which came to define a model. Its predominant characteristics include a selective use of non-diegetic music, correspondence between that music and the implied content of the narrative, a high degree of direct synchronization between music and narrative action, and the use of the *leitmotiv* as a structural framework. The score is also interesting for a practice Steiner himself came to exemplify: the exploitation of musical associations to provide the link between narrative content and accompaniment. Steiner's propensity for references both direct and indirect to popular and folk tunes as well as to the classical repertory became a personal stamp (a cry for recognition?) in a medium often oblivious to his contribution.

There was one way, however, in which Steiner's score for *The Informer* was somewhat atypical. A Hollywood composer usually worked in the post-production stage of a film's development, scoring completed footage in rough cut. This position was largely dictated by the studio system which defined the composer's contribution as incidental to the creation of the film. Usually Steiner would work this way by choice. Frustrated by composing music from a script that often bore little relationship to the final film, he avoided working from anything but the rough cut. "I never write from a script. I run a mile everytime I see one."[2] But for *The Informer* Steiner composed music before and during the shooting schedule.

The plot of *The Informer* turns on the betrayal of Frankie McPhillip, Irish rebel outlaw, by his friend, Gypo Nolan, for the sum of twenty pounds. John Ford's interest in *The Informer* began in 1933 when he acquired the rights to the Liam O'Flaherty novel. The major studios turned down the property as too risky, so in an effort to make the property more marketable, Ford and screenwriter Dudley Nichols agreed to work for a fraction of their usual salaries. Ford claims that it was Joseph P. Kennedy, then owner of a controlling interest at RKO, who gave him the go-ahead with his Irish picture until the studio could find a more appropriate vehicle (*i.e.*, a western). When Kennedy sold his share in the studio halfway through shooting, the new hierarchy, regarding the $200,000 production as small potatoes, let the filming continue, but moved the company to a backlot soundstage where the city of Dublin "was just painted canvas."[3]

Ford claims to have shot *The Informer* in less than three weeks and studio records substantiate at least the basis of that claim. *The Informer* was shot in twenty-seven days from February 11, 1935 to March 15th.[4] With that same speed, Ford and Nichols had produced the shooting script from January 1st to 11th at Mazatlan, Ford's Mexican retreat. By January 23rd Steiner was seeking copyright clearances on the Irish folk tunes he would incorporate into the score, including "The Wearing of the Green," "Rose of Tralee," "Would God I Were a Tender Apple Blossom" ("Danny Boy"), and "The Minstrel Boy." Typical of Hollywood practice he was also at work on six other RKO films.[5]

Regardless of his other obligations, Steiner finished *The Informer*'s score quickly and recorded most of the music on March 14, about the time Ford was finishing shooting. Thus Steiner had completed his job on *The Informer* at the point when he would usually be just beginning. Part of the consequence of Steiner's involvement in the film before and as it was being shot was the opportunity in certain scenes to reverse the usual practice of post-synchronizing the score to edited footage. Steiner composed music for several scenes before they were filmed and Ford actually shot them in synchronization with it. This practice not only facilitated direct synchronization in post-production, but it accorded Steiner a determining influence in the development of the film's protagonist, Gypo Nolan. Victor McLaglen, who played Gypo, was rehearsed to walk in the lumbering gait dictated by the accented rhythms Steiner had scored for his *leitmotiv*. Gypo's oafish quality, which is at least partially responsible for the sympathy his character elicits, is demonstrable in the walk Steiner created for him.

The score for *The Informer* begins with a main title that immediately binds music to narrative action. The titles in the film are unusual historically in that they initiate diegetic action behind the credits. The more usual practice was to use the simpler title cards. The score takes advantage of this opportunity to establish music's presence as a narrative agent through the practice of direct synchronization known as Mickey-Mousing. The credit sequence begins with the shadowy presence of Gypo in direct synchronization with the *leitmotiv* Steiner entitled "The Informer."

All of Gypo's brief appearances in the credits are directly synchronized to his *leitmotiv*. An extended example of his connection to this musical theme follows the opening intertitle as Gypo hulks down a Dublin street in synchronization with it.

Mickey-Mousing is a structural device that authorizes the non-diegetic presence of music as an emanation of the narrative itself. Its perfect synchrony with narrative action masks its presence so that the music can create certain effects on a semi-conscious level without disrupting narrative credibility on a conscious level. Mickey-Mousing also has a thematic function. In *The Informer*, for instance, the direct synchronization between Gypo's footsteps and the syncopation in his *leitmotiv* dictate his distinctive walk. Annotations in Steiner's own hand in the conductor's copy such as "heavily," "very heavily," and "*marcato*" suggest how deliberately Steiner created Gypo's gait.[6]

Finally, Mickey-Mousing can indicate extra-diegetic meaning. In a film as heavily laden with purpose as *The Informer*, Mickey-Mousing is put in service to the symbolic level of the narrative. The score has numerous examples of Mickey-Mousing which function on this level. One particularly pointed example occurs in the scene where Gypo tears down Frankie's wanted poster. Its crumpled remains dog him (it stops when he does), finally attaching to his leg before he realizes its presence and discards it. Music's mimetic capacity is here employed to simulate the wind that propels the paper along the street. (Steiner uses a harp with a celesta added for the last chord.) The point of this fatalistic gesture seems to be to foreshadow the irradicable guilt Gypo's betrayal of Frankie will engender, but the improbability of such a natural coincidence, and the music's emphasis of this improbability, seldom fail to raise a guffaw from an incredulous contemporary audience.

But Mickey-Mousing can be no more obvious or distracting than the often blatant and sometimes awkward attempts of the camera to force a symbolic reading. In *The Informer* the music may be synchronized to the footsteps of various characters, but the *mise en scène* privileges those feet by making them the focus of the frame. In a later scene, each of the four coins tossed on a table is accompanied by a note of a descending arpeggio, but the camera is there for a close-up. Mickey-Mousing has come to represent the worst excesses of the Hollywood film score. Still, it has a visual equivalent, and Mickey-Mousing has been made to bear the brunt of the criticism for a redundancy that it only partially creates.

The junction of narrative action and music in *The Informer* is largely achieved through a reliance on Mickey-Mousing. The Hollywood film score also developed conventions for correspondence between the implied content of the narrative and the music. One of the most important of these is use of music to define emotion. Classical Hollywood narrative film developed certain conventions for the representation of emotion based in the cinematic apparatus. Expressive acting was dependent upon the selective use of close-ups, specific patterns of lighting and *mise en scène*, and dramatic vocal intonation that positioned the spectator into an emotional ripeness. Music became the locus point of this process, its expressive power heightening and sometimes even defining the emotional response that the cinematic apparatus had prepared. The power of this process was such that it could create emotion in lieu of performance and frequently did.[7]

In *The Informer* the articulation of emotion through the cinematic apparatus is employed consistently in those sequences that require McLaglen to emote. In the opening sequence, for instance, the emotional upheaval Gypo experiences upon learning of the reward money offered for his friend Frankie McPhillip is created by a combination of the cinematic apparatus (specifically shot/reverse-shot editing) and musical accompaniment. During his nocturnal meanderings, Gypo discovers the wanted poster with a twenty-pound reward offered for information leading to Frankie's capture. As the camera dollies in for a close-up of the poster (an over-the-shoulder medium shot that includes the back of Gypo's head and Frankie's image on the poster), it is accompanied by a descending bass line in combination with a pedal point, a musical evocation of tension. Gypo's anxiety is set up by the dolly-in (a cinematic metaphor for deep thought) and articulated by the music; his face does not appear in the frame.

The poster dissolves into a superimposed flashback of Frankie and Gypo at a local pub, the Dunboy House. Steiner's use of the popular Irish ballad "The Wearing of the Green" which accompanies the flashback connects Gypo to Frankie as they sing in unison, while the associations of the popular tune evoke Ireland as the cause which binds them. The flashback dissolves back into the wanted poster followed by a straight cut to Gypo's face. In a medium close-up Gypo stares at the poster, rubbing his chin in contemplation. The look on Gypo's face is ambiguous. The shot/reverse-shot construction connects that look to the shot of the poster that precedes it and the close-up of "£20 Reward" that follows it, but what Gypo is feeling is still unclear. He mouths the words "Frankie McPhillip," but is he emoting hatred for the British, thinking about the reward money for himself, or simply absentmindedly staring?

Music here is crucial in delineating Gypo's response. During the close-up of his face, the first five notes of an ascending minor scale introduce a short fragment of the song "Rule! Britannia" which accompanies the next shot. Steiner has cast the quintessentially British melody into the unfamiliar minor, displacing its associations with British power and supremacy. These musical cues provide the key to Gypo's cryptic facial expression. I am suggesting here that the music operates in a way similar to and in support of the Kuleshov effect. Gypo's blank face quite literally "usurps" the meaning that the sinister associations of "Rule! Britannia" have constructed for it; hatred of the British becomes projected onto his face. A visual confirmation of this reading is offered immediately afterward when Gypo pokes Frankie's image in an gesture of camaraderie.

The next musical cue is diegetic, a street musician who sings "Rose of Tralee." Because the music is diegetic Steiner could expect his audience to be conscious of it and he exploits the opportunity by choosing "Rose of Tralee." Its lyrics tell the story of loss, of a boy far away from home who, cut off from his Irish heritage, comes to cherish its memory. This Irish ballad not only provides an authentic musical text for an Irish street singer but through its lyrics verbalizes the vague patriotic sentiment and Irish loyalty that Ford has been trying to establish. Other examples of diegetic music include "The Minstrel Boy," sung at Frankie's wake, and "Believe Me If All Those Endearing Young Charms," sung at a brothel. The film depends upon these standard ballads to evoke a mythic representation of Ireland which it has neither the budget nor the time to create visually.

Throughout these first few scenes, Gypo's centrality has been reinforced by position within the narrative, prominence accorded through placement in *mise en scène* and editing, and dominance of his *leitmotiv* in the musical score. The Hollywood film score was largely structured by the *leitmotiv*, which organized its discourse around the repetition of recognizable musical themes that could be developed or varied in response to the text. The *leitmotiv* served as both a point of identification and as an embodiment of that which it accompanied, delineating important narrative elements such as character or situation. In an interview with the *New York Times* Steiner explained it this way: "Every character should have a theme. In *The Informer* we used a theme to identify Victor McLaglen. A blind man could have sat in a theater and known when Gypo was on the screen."[8] A blind man would also have known something of Gypo's character. As discussed earlier, Gypo's *leitmotiv* reproduces his bulky clumsiness in its rhythmic structure. His theme also concludes with a quotation from "The Wearing of the Green," reinforcing his connection to the Irish cause.

The second major character, Gypo's girlfriend Katie, is introduced by a *leitmotiv* Steiner entitled "I Adore Him." Katie is a prostitute. Because of the strictures of the Production Code, prostitution could not be conveyed directly on the screen, and certain cinematic conventions evolved to convey the necessary information indirectly. The scene in which she first appears presents a clear visual metaphor for her trade. She poses under a streetlight with her head veiled in a shawl. As a well-dressed man passes by and gives her the eye, she dutifully lowers the shawl to expose her shoulders.

Like the Hollywood film itself which created an image of woman as the projection of its own (male) fear and desire, the Hollywood film score collaborated in the dominant ideology which punished women for their sexuality. The display of female sexuality was characterized by a nucleus of musical practices that carried indecent or shady implications through an association with so-called decadent forms such as jazz, the blues, and ragtime; a predominance of woodwinds and brasses, particularly saxophones and muted horns; the inclusion of unusual harmonies, chromaticism, and dissonance; the use of dotted rhythms and syncopation; and the use of portamento and blues notes.[9] Katie's theme dispels any possible ambiguity about her profession through a combination of those practices which connoted female promiscuity: jazzy rhythms, characterized by syncopation; brass instrumentation; chromatic harmonies, and portamento. Although the narrative clearly posits Katie's prostitution as a direct consequence of economic necessity (she sighs, "I'm hungry and I can't pay my room rent"), Katie retains the taint of promiscuity through a cinematic representation (unmistakable in its use of lighting, costume, and make-up) and a musical accompaniment which are unforgiving. In an interesting and not unconnected example later in the film, Steiner actually changed the instrumentation of Katie's motif to "make more sense." Gypo passes Katie the money he has earned for informing. Katie's motif had been scored by Steiner for the flute. This score page, however, was accompanied by a note, presumably from orchestrator Bernhard Kaun:

"Dear Max: Try it with solo sax. I think it will make more sense." The final version uses the saxophone.

On the other hand, the *leitmotiv* Steiner scored for Mary McPhillip, Frankie's sister and devoted girlfriend of rebel leader Dan Gallagher, embodies none of these pejorative musical conventions. Played initially by violins (and in one memorable reiteration a harp), her *leitmotiv* is accompanied by simple chords. Various musical markings used in conjunction with her motif suggests its intent: it is marked "*dolcissimo*," "*poco apassionata*," or simply "*legato*," culminating in the unequivocal direction "Heaven music" during her confrontation with Katie. Despite the fact that Mary inadvertently hinders her brother from escaping the British death squad and seems to do little else in an emergency than wring her hands, she is ennobled by her *leitmotiv* rather than judged by it.

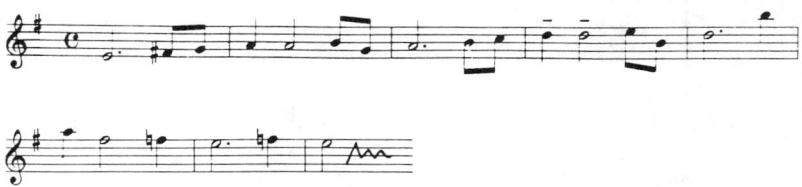

Up until and including the introduction of Katie the music has been continuous. By 1935 the length of the musical score was expanding significantly. Steiner's score for *Cimarron* in 1931 included only a few moments of non-diegetic music. In *The Informer*, by contrast, the first six minutes of the film have an unbroken musical accompaniment and music is used either diegetically or non-diegetically in almost every scene. (There are only two exceptions: a short street scene and Frankie's visit to his mother's house which culminates in his death.) This growing dependence of Hollywood practice on the presence of music is characteristically exhibited in the work of Steiner, whose score for *Gone with the Wind* in 1939 opened with nearly twenty-three minutes of continuous music.

This stress on musical continuity is demonstrated in the score's careful matching between musical selections. For instance, at that point in *The Informer* when "Rose of Tralee" is introduced into the score, the momentary disruption of music is covered by an aural match which masks it. The harp that accompanied the crumpled poster as it followed

Gypo down the street is replaced by a single violin accompanying the singer. The initial low dynamic level of the violin, and its similarity in sound to the harp, makes its entrance almost imperceptible and elides one scene to the next.

When Gypo meets Katie (and deals with her potential customer), he walks with her past a shop window with an advertisement for passage to America. The cost is ten pounds. This scene plants the seed in Gypo's mind of the possibility of a fresh start with Katie. The presence of "Yankee Doodle Dandy" on the soundtrack fleshes out the promise of opportunity that America embodied. ("Yankee Doodle" is a particularly interesting choice since that particular song is associated with the revolution in which America won its independence from Britain.) But the strikingly unfamiliar instrumentation (one variation for celesta and flute, one for bassoon) incorporates Katie's perception of the advertisement: "Look at that thing handing us the ha-ha." A descending tritone introduces a final reiteration of Katie's theme, accompanied by a descending chromatic line that reinforces her despondence.

Internal thought had always posed a problem in Hollywood's classical narrative model and a number of conventions developed to convey this process. First person voice-over was one solution, but this required structuring the film around a single character's point of view. Music was another of these conventions. In *The Informer* music functions as part of the cinematic apparatus that offers an analogue for Gypo's consciousness.

An extended example occurs during the sequence where Gypo decides to inform. The sequence begins in the Dunboy House, a local restaurant, where Frankie surprises Gypo. The process of thought is encoded in the film through a combination of focal distance (the close-up), facial expression (this generally emerges from McLaglen as a blank stare), and physical gestures appropriate to the act of thought (Gypo rubs his chin, wipes his forehead, or scratches his head). When Frankie appears, there is a cut to a medium close-up of Gypo rubbing his forehead and staring at him. The text offers an explication of what is transpiring in Gypo's mind through a superimposition of the reward money under the reverse-shot of Frankie's reaction.

As Frankie leaves, Gypo begins to ponder the opportunities Frankie's appearance has afforded him. Here music becomes part of the process that simulates thought. A series of ascending chords accompanies the reappearance of the superimposed image of Frankie's face with the twenty pounds reward money emblazoned beneath it. Gypo's ruminations continue after he leaves the restaurant and there is a cut to a scene outside the shop window which contains the advertisement for passage to America. In a medium close-up, Gypo stares at the poster rubbing his forehead. A shot/reverse-shot exchange focuses the content of Gypo's thoughts on that poster, but it is the music that provides information to help specify the nature of the decision-making process Gypo undergoes. A quotation from "Yankee Doodle Dandy" played on a muted trumpet represents one factor that figures in Gypo's decision: the promise of opportunity that America offers. The other is his love for Katie. Following "Yankee Doodle Dandy" is Katie's theme. Her centrality in Gypo's decision to inform is musically encoded in a series of upward modulations of her motif which culminates in Gypo's arrival at British headquarters. When the door closes behind him, Katie's theme is repeated once again.

The consequences of Gypo's betrayal are graphically demonstrated in the McPhillips' home, where Frankie's appearance takes his mother and his sister by surprise. Soon after his arrival, the British, tipped off by Gypo that Frankie will be going home, gun him down as he attempts to escape. This is followed by a direct cut to British headquarters where Gypo is paid his twenty pounds. The actual payment disgusts the British officer in charge, who lays the money on the table but leaves it to an underling to pass it along to Gypo with the tip of a cane. As the officer does so, Steiner introduces the *leitmotiv* entitled "The Money" against a pedal point, a theme composed of a descending tritone followed by an augmented chord arpeggiated downward.

The use of the tritone sets up an especially rich musical referent, the *diabolus in musica*, with its historical associations of evil. Steiner used the tritone in an earlier scene which contained the initial reference to the twenty pounds. In the money motif Steiner has found a musical analogue for the gesture of the British officer in a *leitmotiv* which symbolically incorporates the taint of evil attached to the money through the tritone and the tension associated with its acquisition through the unstable tonality of its harmonic base.

Gypo leaves the building by the back door accompanied by a musical passage which juxtaposes a 6/4 chord against the money motif. In Western harmonic practice this particular juxtaposition craves a strong resolution that a return to the tonic chord would provide. In this case, however, Steiner doesn't resolve it, setting up the spectator for the unexpected appearance of the blind man who materializes out of the fog. In place of that resolution the score offers another *leitmotiv*, that of the blind man who follows Gypo from the British headquarters. His musical accompaniment, entitled "The Blind Man," is initially orchestrated for an English horn and woodwinds and repeated by violins.

Ford creates a symbol of Gypo's conscience in the blind man who follows Gypo wherever he goes with the reminder of his guilt (the blind man is the only one who can connect Gypo to the British headquarters). Steiner's *leitmotiv* functions both on a representational level (as indication of the presence of the blind man) and a symbolic one (as manifestation of Gypo's guilty conscience).

Gypo will never realize the dream he thinks he buys with twenty pounds, and the remainder of the film chronicles his downfall. The successive stages of his destruction are signalled by a series of horn calls based on the opening motif of his theme. These include the opening five-note phrase of the motif itself (what I will call Variation I); a distillation of that phrase into its last two notes, the open fifth (Variation II); and a version which diminishes the last interval of the motif from an open fifth to a tritone (Variation III). Instrumentation (horns) and melodic contour (the attention on the intervals of the open fifth and the tritone) evoke the hunt, and this musical metaphor marks the trail of evidence Gypo leaves for his pursuers to follow.

The first of these horn calls occurs in the saloon where Gypo heads after being paid his twenty pounds. When he enters, Variation I is heard. Gypo orders a whiskey to ease his conscience, but in doing so he draws suspicion on himself and loses part of the money he needs for passage. When Gypo actually handles the notes themselves, the money motif is played low in the woodwinds' register against tremolo strings. As Gypo drinks his whiskey, Variation III is repeated twice. Its incorporation of the tritone is particularly telling, attaching its sinister connotations to Gypo himself while inextricably joining Gypo to the money motif through the shared use of that distinctive interval. Gypo's anxiety in the sequence is musically evoked through the use of several elements: the repetition of the money motif; the continued use of tremolo strings; the alternation of I and 6/4 chords; and the repetition of Gypo's theme in the unfamiliar instrumentation of the cello.

When Katie enters the pub, her theme returns reinforcing her connection to Frankie's death. Its instrumentation is particularly "bluesy": a saxophone, the quintessential blues instrument, takes the melody against an accompaniment of a string and harp pedal point. Steiner marks it in his score "*triste*" and "*doloroso*." Since Katie is now implicated in Gypo's guilt (she provides the motive, however unwittingly, for his crime), the music is harsher toward her, and her theme is played in the classic instrumentation of promiscuity. The implication of this instrumental change becomes explicitly stated a few moments later when Gypo says to her, "I did it for you." This is the first time the dialogue has verbalized the motivation that the music and the visual text have already suggested a number of times before.

The horn calls return a few sequences later during Gypo's interrogation by the commandant of the Irish rebel forces, Dan Gallagher, and his captain, Bartley Mulholland. A number of musical practices Steiner used earlier in the score reappear: the use of "The Wearing of the Green" (played "*mysterioso*") to provide a barometer for the magnitude of Gypo's crime against his country and heritage; the use of the money motif to reinforce Gypo's guilt in a scene in which he denies any responsibility for the crime; and the use of tremolo strings, pedal point, and dissonance to create tension. After Gypo is interrogated, Variation III can be heard in the background. When he is dismissed, Bartley shouts, "It's him, Dan." Steiner underscores Dan's response with variations of "The Wearing of the Green," and "Mary's Theme." Bartley will tail Gypo for the remainder of the night. The sequence ends with the repetition of Variation II, the open fifths creating anticipation, even anxiety, in the unresolved tonality of that interval.

The privileged aural discourse in the classical Hollywood model was the spoken word, and the film score developed a specific practice in relation to it. Music should not detract or distract from the dialogue, and this principle was reflected in the level of complexity and volume deemed acceptable for underscoring. This practice is particularly apparent in the previous interrogation scene. There is no music at all during the actual interrogation and when music is used, during the opening conversation between Dan and Bartley and during Dan's frenzied orders following Gypo's dismissal, it is at an appreciably low volume. In fact, Steiner has written in his score: "All of this sequence over dialogue—so be careful." This note suggests the care Steiner took in the recording session to preserve this relationship between music and dialogue.

Gypo's next stop is a fish and chips shop where he spends even more of his money buying food for the assembled crowd. This sequence is one of the most allegorical in the film and, like much of the rest of it, is overladen with religious symbolism which is not always consistent. An analogy is drawn between Gypo and Christ (suggested by his new title, "King" Gypo, his address as "m'lord," and his act of feeding the multitude with fishes). But he is also connected to Judas (who got thirty pieces of silver) through an attention to the money and to the apostle Peter (who betrayed Christ when the cock crowed three times) through his claim, "I'm going to be the cock of the walk around here." The melee that attends the serving of the food is intercut with a dolly-in to Bartley at the shop's window, accompanied by a variation of the blind man's *leitmotiv* associated with Gypo's guilty conscience. At the end of the sequence, Variation III returns to mark yet another bit of evidence Gypo leaves behind. This time it is the two pounds he has squandered on fish and chips.

Throughout the film Gypo has been desperately trying to avoid the consequences of his crime. The spectator, however, is frequently reminded of Gypo's guilt, visually through the insistent close-ups on the actual silver and aurally through repetitions of the *leitmotivs* of the money and the blind man. A crucial sequence follows that attempts to enter Gypo's consciousness. Like other sequences that reveal internal thought, this one relies heavily on music to suggest what is going through Gypo's mind. Gypo passes the shop window again and sees the advertisement that initially inspired him. The sequence begins with Gypo and his drinking companion pausing in front of the window. The shot/reverse-shot which structures it includes a medium two-shot of the back of their heads and the reverse angle that focuses on their faces. This time Gypo scratches his head with the same cryptic look McLaglen has produced before. Katie's theme scored for solo violin accompanies the gesture. Moments afterward, he verbalizes the thoughts that the music has implied when he tells his companion he wants to see Katie.

But before he can find her, Gypo is lured into Aunt Betty's. He will try one last time to ease his guilty conscience through a series of desperate acts: drunkenness; an attempt at social acceptance; an appeal to Irish loyalty; and finally, an effort at retribution. A honky-tonk piano, a musical convention equated with the bordello, establishes the nature of the saloon. Gypo spies a young blonde obviously out of place in her surroundings. That he imagines her to be Katie is prefigured by the music: Katie's theme is heard on the soundtrack before the dissolve that signals the blonde's visual metamorphosis into Katie herself. By this time Bartley has caught up with Gypo and enters Aunt Betty's to retrieve him. As Gypo leaves the brothel, he sees the young blonde once more. The film implies that she is being forced into prostitution. The fact that she cannot pay the rent ties her again to Katie. Gypo gives her the money she needs to return to her home in London. As Bartley adds up Gypo's tab, the money motif serves as a reminder of Gypo's inescapable guilt.

Intercut with this sequence is a scene between Dan Gallagher and Mary. Its placement draws a striking contrast between Gypo's retreat to the brothel and the chaste lovers' reconciliation. Mary's *leitmotiv* underscores their embrace but when the discussion turns to politics, specifically to Frankie's murder, it is replaced by other music. Dan questions Mary about her brother's death. When he tells her he is convinced Frankie's death was the work of an informer, Mary tells him that her brother mentioned seeing Gypo earlier that night. Gypo's theme plays in the background in a sinister instrumentation, a musical evocation of the implications of her statement. Gallagher begins to make the connection. The opening phrase of "The Wearing of the Green," repeated in rising modulations, provides a musical equivalent for the thought process that leads Gallagher to a knowledge of Gypo's guilt. What follows these modulations is Gypo's theme played on the cello.

Gypo is arrested and brought to the kangaroo court of the Irish rebels. His trial opens with a horn call of an open fifth (Variation II) played on a bugle. Personal testimonies reconstruct the night's events, weaving suspicion more and more tightly around Gypo. As is typical of Steiner's practice, visual references are "caught" with music, the appropriate *leitmotiv* responding to the visual text. The blind man's theme is heard when he gives his testimony; the money motif accompanies Bartley's accounting of Gypo's expenses; Gypo's theme, in the instrumentation of the horn calls, accompanies his testimony; and Mary's theme accompanies a close-up of her. When Gypo cries out in anguish, "Isn't there a man here who can tell me why I did it?," a variation of Katie's theme is heard in the background as if to answer the question. When a deviation occurs in Steiner's design, it is especially striking. Gypo's confession, quite unexpectedly, is accompanied by Mary's *leitmotiv* played by violins. This unusual coupling draws attention to the similarities between them, and the lyrical string instrumentation associated with Mary elicits sympathy for Gypo.

Imprisoned, Gypo must now await his execution. A dripping ceiling in Gypo's cell becomes the subject of direct synchronization between the drops of water, simulated by a plucked harp, and the money motif. Steiner himself describes the process.

> There was a sequence toward the end of the picture in which McLaglen is in a cell and water in dripping on him. This is just before he escapes and is killed. I had a certain musical effect I wanted to use for this. I wanted to catch each of these drops musically. The property man and I worked for days trying to regulate the water tank so it dripped in tempo and so I could accompany it. This took a great deal of time and thought because a dripping faucet doesn't always drip in the same rhythm. We finally mastered it, and I believe it was one of the things that won me the [Academy] award. People were fascinated trying to figure out how we managed to catch every drop.[10]

The conductor's copy includes two minutes and forty seconds of the musical figure that opens the money motif, but only at the beginning and the end is this musical figure actually synchronized to the drops of water. The majority of the scene is played out in the adjoining room where the rebels draw lots to determine who will execute Gypo. The continued repetitions function in several ways: as a chronometer, ticking away the final moments of Gypo's life; as a device to produce tension through the unstable harmonic base of the money motif; and as a referent to the off-screen drama of a frantic Gypo in the next room. Gypo is able to escape through his own brute strength. When his disappearance is discovered the horn call in Variation II returns.

Gypo barely escapes with his life and seeks the shelter and safety of Katie's room where he confesses what he has done. The horn call returns in the tritone (Variation III). Katie vows to lay down her life for him, and the purity of her motives is reflected in the reiteration of her theme, now played in a slow tempo in a string instrumentation with a harp adding texture in the background. Steiner wrote: "very light—strings and harp only, maybe Harp and cello in places (no W.W. [woodwinds] ever"). It is interesting to note how the change in orchestration ennobles Katie and how it does so at a moment in the narrative when Katie proclaims her love for Gypo.

Her devotion is reinforced by similar orchestration in the following scene at the McPhillips' home. Katie appeals to Dan and Mary to save Gypo's life. Her theme is heard in the string and harp accompaniment, usually reserved for Mary. Dan is immovable. But the connection between Mary and Katie that the music has suggested through their shared instrumentation is explicitly drawn in their confrontation. Katie reminds her: "I'm not the kind of girl you are. There was a time when I was. And I love Gypo no less for being what I am." A solo violin plays Katie's motif. Katie unwittingly betrays Gypo by telling Dan of his whereabouts in hopes of his clemency. The dialogue is accompanied by a dissonant passage played by tremolo violins marked "*furioso*" (an annotation in Steiner's score reads "Dissonance on purpose.") Bartley overhears and takes matters into his own hands.

As Gypo waits for Katie's return, repetitions of the money motif create a palpable musical tension. His brute strength allows him to escape the ambush at Katie's room only to be gunned down in the street by Bartley. Immediately before he is shot, the money motif is heard once more as he walks to the church. Dying, he seeks its refuge.

Gypo pauses at the iron gates which mark the church's entrance and spreads his arms in the crucifixion pose. He enters the church accompanied by a dramatic cymbal crash. Here he meets the mourning Mrs. McPhillip praying for the soul of Frankie. Gypo's motif, played on a solo violin, accompanies his painful walk down the aisle towards her as well as his tortured confession. Steiner's annotations in the score ("pathetic" and "*dolcissimo*") make explicit the intent of the music. Mrs. McPhillip's forgiveness is foreshadowed by the music. As she repeats the phrase, "You didn't know what you were doing," a choir (presumably non-diegetic) sings the "Ave Maria." Gypo calls out to

Frankie before he crumples to the ground in death. Rising chords herald his salvation. The choir's "Amen" is accompanied by the church bells.

There is one final characteristic of Steiner's work that is exhibited in this score: his appropriation of the classical repertory as thematic referents, a practice that allows him to draw extra-cinematic meaning into the score by incorporating established musical associations. Although the score was described by most critics as uniquely Irish,[11] its true debt lies more with nineteenth-century Romantic and post-Romantic composers than with Irish folk song. Perhaps the most far-reaching example is the motif Steiner composed as the Blind Man's motif, which draws upon Giacomo Puccini's opera *La Fanciulla del West*. Based on the play *The Girl of the Golden West* by David Belasco, *La Fanciulla del West* tells the story of an American frontier saloon keeper, Minnie, and her love for the bandit Ramerrez, alias Dick Johnson. Homesickness, love for one's family, loneliness, the quest for money and its consequences, and the redemptive love of a woman are all important thematic elements in this opera. In fact, many of the plot elements of *La Fanciulla del West* resemble those of *The Informer*: a man with a price on his head, a woman pleading for her condemned lover's life, a large sum of gold. Even structural elements resemble each other. *La Fanciulla del West* opens with the camp minstrel singing about homesickness. *The Informer* opens with a street singer intoning "Rose of Tralee" which embodies much the same sentiments.

Melodically, "The Blind Man" evokes the motif Puccini composed for Jake Wallace, the camp minstrel, whose distinguishing characteristic is his blindness.

Steiner: "The Blind Man"

Puccini: "Che faranno i vecchi miei"

The placement of this aria in the opera (the camp minstrel emerges from the chorus in the beginning of the first act) is similar to the placement of the song in *The Informer* (the camera passes a street musician who sings "Rose of Tralee"). Finally, the lyrics of both "Rose of Tralee" and "*Che faranno i vecchi miei*" detail the loneliness and homesickness of a boy cut off from his loved ones and country.

Later in the film, Steiner evokes *La Fanciulla del West* again. When Gypo is awaiting his execution, tension is produced both visually and musically by foregrounding dripping water, a chronometer that ticks away the final moments of his life. Steiner matches each drip of the water to the notes of the money motif. A similar scene occurs in *La Fanciulla del West* when Minnie, hiding Ramerrez in the loft of her cabin, plays cards with Sheriff Jack Rance for his life. Drops of Ramerrez's blood give him away, however, and as they drip onto the scene below, Puccini's score matches the drops.[12] It is not unlikely that Steiner was drawn to the similarities between *La Fanciulla del West* and *The Informer* and heightened them by borrowing musical ideas from the opera. In alluding to *La Fanciulla del West*, Steiner exploits extra-cinematic meaning that operates to universalize the personal tragedy of *The Informer* and its struggle for Irish independence into a larger human tragedy of loneliness, alienation, and their effect on the soul.

Another example of the score's harnessing of music's referential meaning occurs during the sequence played out in front of the America poster, where Gypo decides to betray Frankie. Steiner borrows a distinctive rhythm from the second movement of Antonin Dvořák's *New World Symphony*, later embodied in an American spiritual, "Goin' Home," based on Dvořák's melody. Both the lyrics of the spiritual and Dvořák's orchestration suggest displacement. Steiner uses its characteristic rhythmic motif to flesh out Gypo's motives for escape to America. When Gypo goes to the British police headquarters, this rhythmic motif is cast in a darker tonality with a clearer definition of a minor mode and, like the money motif, tarnishes the twenty pounds Gypo takes.

The theme Steiner entitled "Mary" is also strongly indebted to the classical repertory. This *leitmotiv* is used to underscore scenes between her and Dan Gallagher. The actual melody, with its highly chromatic line, is reminiscent of one of the most famous love themes in musical literature, the "*Liebestod*" from Richard Wagner's *Tristan und Isolde*. The reference to these legendary figures, whose passionate love consumed them both, is perhaps a little stretched in this context (Mary and Dan hardly seem the counterparts of their musical progenitors), but its evocation of passion is unmistakable. And Steiner's "The Money" has a clear antecedent in Giuseppe Verdi's *Requiem Mass*.

When *The Informer* was released it was dubbed "a brilliant work . . . a stirring and profoundly moving tragedy, certain to take its place as a clear-cut model in the future for film artisans who are intent on creating works of art as well as beguiling entertainments."[13] In large measure the score for *The Informer* fulfilled that legacy, drawing both attention and acclaim to the film score during a time when music was seldom noticed or commented upon and providing a model for the use of music in the Hollywood narrative film.

NOTES

[1] See, for instance, David Bordwell, Janet Staiger, and Kristen Thompson, *Classical Hollywood Film* (New York: Columbia University Press, 1985); Pam Cook, "The Classic Narrative System," in *The Cinema Book*, ed. by Pam Cook (New York: Pantheon, 1985), pp. 212–215; Nick Browne, "The Spectator in the Text: The Rhetoric of *Stagecoach*," *Film Quarterly*, 29, No. 2 (1975–1976), 26–38; and Stephen Neale, "New Hollywood Cinema," *Screen*, 17, No. 2 (Summer 1976), 117–122.

[2] Max Steiner, "The Music Director," in *The Real Tinsel*, ed. by Bernard Rosenberg and Harry Silverstein (New York: Macmillan, 1970), p. 392.

[3] Peter Bogdonavich, *John Ford* (Berkeley: University of California Press, 1968), p. 61.

[4] *The Informer*, Financial Records and Shooting Schedule, RKO General Pictures Archive, Los Angeles, California. All other RKO material is taken from this Archive unless otherwise noted. I wish to express my thanks to RKO for allowing me to consult this material and especially to John Hall for his help. [*Mr. Hall is now deceased.—Ed.*] For further information on the production history of *The Informer* see Emanuel Eisenberg, "John Ford: Fighting Irish," in *New Theatre*, April 1936, p. 42, and Andrew Sinclair, *John Ford* (New York: The Dial Press, 1979), p. 64.

[5] RKO Correspondence, Steiner to Hendee, January 23; February 9; February 14; February 18, 1935.

[6] Max Steiner, score for *The Informer*, composer's pencil sketches. I wish here to express my gratitude to the late Mrs. Max Steiner for allowing me to consult this material when it was in her possession. All future references to Steiner's score will be quoted from this copy. [*Now in the Max Steiner Collection, Arts and Communications Archives, Harold B. Lee Library, Brigham Young University, Provo, Utah.—Ed.*] Special thanks to Fred Steiner for his generous assistance. [*Fred Steiner and Max Steiner are not related.—Ed.*]

[7] Samuel Chell has been one of the first critics in English to undertake the articulation of a theory (based in psychoanalytical thought) of music and emotion. See Chell, "Music and Emotion in the Classical Hollywood Film Score: The Case of *The Best Years of Our Lives*," *Film Criticism*, 8, No. 2 (Winter 1984), 27–38. See also Charles Affron's work, *Cinema and Sentiment* (Chicago: University of Chicago Press, 1982).

[8] "Music in the Cinema," *New York Times*, September 29, 1935, Sec. 10, p. 4.

[9] For a discussion of female sexuality and the Hollywood film score see my "Musical Stereotyping in the Hollywood Film," *Film Reader*, 5 (1982), 76–82.

[10] Max Steiner, "Max Steiner on Film Music," in *Film Score: The View from the Podium*, ed. by Tony Thomas (South Brunswick, New Jersey: A. S. Barnes, 1979), p. 78.

[11] See *Los Angeles Herald Tribune* (September 1, 1935); and *Musical America* (August 1935).

[12] I am indebted to Charles Shattuck, University of Illinois at Urbana, for pointing this out to me.

[13] Review of *The Informer*, *Literary Digest*, May 25, 1935, p. 26.

The Music of *Flash Gordon* and *Buck Rogers*

Richard H. Bush

Between 1936 and 1940 Universal Pictures produced three Flash Gordon serials (and the similarly styled *Buck Rogers*). Their popularity seemingly inexhaustible, the films continue to find periodic revival on television. While perhaps not typical of the serial genre, Universal's "space" serials possess a charm and elan that continues to captivate new generations of children and adults alike.

Flash Gordon began as the brain-child of artist Alex Raymond of King Features Syndicate, first appearing in January of 1934 in the Hearst newspapers' Sunday comic supplement. The strip differed from others in that its drawings were done in a lavish style without the "cartoon" look that typified most other contemporary strips. Perhaps owing to its fantasy aspects, *Flash Gordon* became an immediate success and still appears in over three hundred newspapers in eleven countries.[1]

Flash Gordon chronicled the rocket flight by Flash Gordon, Dale Arden, and Dr. Zarkov to the planet Mongo to avert the Earth's imminent destruction. Their continuing battles against arch-villain Ming the Merciless and encounters with the alien life-forms and science of Mongo were followed by millions of readers.

Flash Gordon (1936)

Universal Pictures had previously produced two *Tailspin Tommy* serials (1934, 1935) based upon a popular newspaper strip. Seeking to repeat the success of a comic strip pre-sold to millions of readers, Universal optioned *Flash Gordon* in 1935.[2]

The film version was produced by Henry MacRae, Universal's serial ace, with scriptwriter Frederick Stephani making his directorial debut. Larry "Buster" Crabbe, an Olympic swimming champion turned actor, played Flash in what is probably his best-remembered role. Jean Rogers played his lady-love, Dale Arden, and Frank Shannon appeared as Dr. Zarkov. Character actor Charles Middleton, a veteran "heavy," was the arch villain, Ming.

The original 1936 serial follows the action of the adventure strip fairly closely. Flash, Dale, and Dr. Zarkov rocket to Mongo to avert the Earth's destruction. They find themselves adversaries of the fiendish Emperor Ming and his beautiful daughter, Princess Aura. The Earthlings spend the ensuing thirteen chapters outwitting Ming and the rulers of the undersea kingdom of Shark Men and the Sky City of the Hawkmen.

The production values of the serial were considerably above average, utilizing many standing sets and props built for previous Universal productions.[3] Curiously, while the *look* of *Flash Gordon* was superior to the average serials, the direction by scriptwriter Frederick Stephani was, even for a serial, uncommonly wooden. The serial was obviously aimed at an audience older than the typical Saturday matinee crowd. It has a highly charged eroticism throughout and ample displays of bare flesh, not only in the abbreviated costuming of the female leads but in an often bare-chested Buster Crabbe as well.

While unarguably many elements combined to give the Flash Gordon serials their lasting appeal, no small amount of credit must be attributed to their exciting and imaginative music, which added a distinction and sophistication lacking in most other serials.

The only original music composed specifically for these three serials, however, was the main title music for the 1936 original, all other music having been drawn from Universal's extensive library of music that had been composed originally for use in their feature films and previous serials.[4]

Universal's Flash Gordon serials benefited greatly from the practice of tracking library music. "Tracking" is film industry jargon for using previously recorded music tracks in a film instead of specially composed music. While economy was the foremost reason for tracking, it was not the only one. Ironically, the music is today more often associated with the serials in which it was re-used than with the films for which it was originally composed. In fact, since many of the original films are lost or no longer in circulation, the music can be heard only through its reuse in serials.

Unlike some film companies that employed a music editor to choose and lay the music tracks for their serials, Universal assigned several chapters each to three of four editors who worked under the direction of a supervising film editor.[5] The editors were then completely responsible for all editorial work in their respective chapters, including picture, sound effects, music, and any "rescue" work.

Usually the editors had a group conference in the music department to determine which music would be used to insure a thematic consistency from chapter to chapter. They auditioned hours of music from the library before deciding on appropriate material, then ordered up thousands of feet of optical positives. Sometimes the music tracks were assembled in an "A-B" system (an editorial system enabling smooth dissolves from cue to cue); more often the tracks were butt-end spliced, resulting in abrupt segues from cue to cue. The editors often used loud sound effects (explosions, rocket blasts) to mask key changes from the end of one cue to the beginning of a new piece of music. At other times the music was terminated before a cadence to smooth the transition from one piece to the next. Occasionally during the mixing session, if a piece was felt by the editing staff to have been "over-used," something fresher was quickly chosen from the library and substituted.

Clifford Vaughan[6] has the distinction of having written the only original music specifically composed for any of the Flash Gordon serials. Vaughan had gone to Universal in 1934 as an orchestrator for Edward Ward. Although he was never under contract to any studio during his career, he remained at Universal until late 1936, when he moved to MGM as Franz Waxman's orchestrator.[7] Vaughan did not remember who assigned him to write the *Flash Gordon* main title music, only that he composed and orchestrated, but did not conduct it.

Clifford Vaughan's main title for *Flash Gordon* impressively sets the tone for the original 1936 fantasy with an ascending brass fanfare echoed and developed by winds. In simple A-B-A form it leads to a languorous, romantic theme for winds and strings before returning to the opening theme. Later chapters, without the expanded cast credits of the first chapters, subsequently abbreviated the cue, eliminating the "B" theme. For the "Narrative," or résumé in succeeding chapters, Vaughan composed a haunting, exotic theme for saxophone which is picked up by full orchestra and rises to a stirring crescendo that recalls the opening fanfare. (Parts of Vaughan's Second Organ Symphony, written in 1948, echo the "Main Title" and "Narrative" of *Flash Gordon*.) Although the film's cue sheets list an "end title," this music is actually a portion of the main title that was tracked and then faded out.

The sequence of the Earthmen's flight and arrival upon the mysterious planet Mongo was underscored by music originally composed by W. Franke Harling[8] for *Destination Unknown* (1933). This score is heavily derivative of Wagner and liberally quotes the "Grail" theme from *Parsifal* as a *religioso*. Interwoven with this is a theme from Liszt's Hungarian Rhapsody No. 1.

If any one composer's style stamped the Flash Gordon trilogy it was that of Heinz Roemheld.[9] Roemheld had studied here and abroad, principally under Lisztian disciples, before embarking in 1925 as a pit orchestra conductor for Universal-owned theaters in the U.S. and Germany. His ability so impressed Universal's president, Carl Laemmle, that Roemheld was brought to Hollywood in late 1929 to work in the studio's music department, where he would subsequently become general music director in 1930.[10]

After Universal reduced its music department staff in 1931, Roemheld drifted out of film music for a short while before returning in 1933 to compose the brief but atmospheric score for James Whale's *The Invisible Man*. The airy main title for the classic horror thriller was given much mileage and was invariably used in the Flash Gordon serials whenever a rocketship took flight. The last-reel music of *The Invisible Man*, with its satiric tremolos and *pizzicati* strings, provided a perfect accompaniment to the suspenseful derring-do on Mongo.

Many of the scenes in Ming's palace in all three Flash Gordon serials made extensive use of Roemheld's score for *Bombay Mail* (1934), a train-bound mystery considerably less exciting than the exotic and Oriental score composed for it. Roemheld's score provides much of the martial-sounding music heard in *Flash Gordon*, played by brass and winds with snare drum punctuation. In Chapter Six, during a banquet in King Vultan's sky-city, a wild, bacchanalian dance ("March Bombay #3") with a queer, syncopated rhythm banged out by cymbals, low bass register, and piano (for doubling), effectively underscores Ballet Russe stock shots from *The Midnight Sun* (1926). Rhythmically, parts of the score are not unlike the "Scène Finale" from Act III of Tchaikovsky's *Swan Lake* ballet.

The tortuous music that accompanies Flash's enslavement in Vultan's furnace room was also composed for *Bombay Mail* and was obviously inspired by Tchaikovsky's "Marche Slav." The romantic "Shirley's Theme" from *Bombay Mail*, a typical sentimental Hollywood ballad of the period, was often used in all three Flash Gordon serials.

Roemheld's score for *The Black Cat* (1934), with its artful arrangements of and variations on classical themes, was employed often in *Flash Gordon* for both action and dramatic scenes. The score featured prominently the principal theme of Liszt's Sonata in B minor, as well as part of the symphonic poem *Tasso* and a curious paraphrase of Tchaikovsky's love theme from *Romeo and Juliet*.[11]

In 1931 Universal reissued *The Midnight Sun*, adding a music and effects track.[12] The bulk of the score was composed by Bernhard Kaun,[13] son of Hugo Kaun, one of Roemheld's teachers. Since no prints of either version of *The Midnight Sun* are known to be in circulation, the only music that can be heard from this film is through its reuse in subsequent Universal films. One cue, entitled "Orloff," used when Flash battles the Gocko in Chapter Two, is dated stylistically, being close to our present conception of silent movie music, but still contains a naïve charm.

Anyone familiar with *Werewolf of London* (1935) will immediately recognize the use of Karl Hajos' sinister muted trumpet motif signaling the werewolf. Hajos[14] composed a score based principally on two themes that were developed in different mood settings. The "Fight," a fairly long cue, was often used to accompany the cliff-hanger endings of *Flash Gordon* and other serials. The "Finale," a soaring *maestoso* with religious overtones, was used in several chapters.

Flash Gordon's Trip to Mars (1938)

Following the success of *Flash Gordon*, Universal produced a somewhat padded 15-chapter sequel, released in February 1938. *Flash Gordon's Trip to Mars* begins with the earth again in peril, this time by a deadly ray from Mars. Flash, Dale, and Zarkov, accompanied by comic-relief newsman "Happy" Hapgood (Donald Kerr), find themselves again battling Ming, who has allied himself with Azura, Queen of the Martians (Beatrice Roberts). Following the precepts of the original, *Trip to Mars* featured an underground kingdom of Clay Men and the forest kingdom of the barbaric Fire People. The sequel was produced by Barney Sarecky on a smaller budget than the original and does not match its production values. The direction by Ford Beebe and Robert Hill was far more competent, however.

While the original serial used music only to set tone and atmosphere, *Trip to Mars* employed music in a somewhat more sophisticated manner. Certain themes were used for character identification or scene locale in the manner of Wagnerian *leitmotivs*. For example, Tarnak, Ming's underling, is often underscored with Roemheld's "March Bombay." The Clay People and Fire People also have their own related themes.

While the second serial used much of the same music as the original, it also featured some significant additions and deletions. Chief among these was the inclusion of many sections of Franz Waxman's fanciful score for *Bride of Frankenstein* (1935). Waxman[15] composed an original and brilliant score for that horror classic, although the film was revised extensively after previews and partial and entire scenes—and the accompanying music—were cut from the final release print. Ironically, the practice of tracking affords the opportunity to hear many of these sequences (such as "Processional March" and "Graveyard") in their original unabridged form.

Trip to Mars made heavy use of other *Bride* music such as the "Chase" to underscore action; the Grand Guignol "Dance Macabre"[16] as a *leitmotiv* for the eerie Clay People; the bizarre "Pretorius" theme for the Fire People; and the scintillating "Creation" for scenes in Emperor Ming's laboratory.

Roemheld's last major film of the thirties for Universal, *Dracula's Daughter* (1936), which itself completed Universal's first horror cycle, contained a brooding score with ominous overtones. Two of its sequences, "Transylvania" and "Croydon Airport," were often used in *Flash Gordon's Trip to Mars*. "Croydon Airport" sounds remarkably similar to the second and third bars of the "Montagu and Capulet" section of Tchaikovsky's *Romeo and Juliet*.

Although music for *East of Java* (1935) was tracked in many of Universal's serials, only one sequence was used in *Trip to Mars*—and it was not written by any of the above composers. The music was "Orgy of the Spirits" by the Russian composer, Alexander Ilyinsky.[17] This furious agitato, the final section of an eight-part suite entitled *Noure et Anitra* (Op. 13), is somewhat reminiscent of Mussorgsky's "A Night on Bald Mountain." It had been frequently used in silent films to underscore storm scenes with its pulsingly dynamic ethnic Russian sound. Carl Fischer Music published its own arrangement (by Charles J. Roberts) for theater orchestra, which was used in *East of Java* to underscore a typhoon. Although in that film the music was overpowered by the sound effects, "Orgy" was reused dozens of times in serials such as *Tim Tyler's Luck* (1937) and appeared occasionally in *Trip to Mars*.

One section of Edward Ward's[18] score for *Great Expectations* (1934) turns up in *Trip to Mars*. "A Gentleman" is a rather wistful, lachrymose melody that fit in nicely whenever a particularly sentimental feeling was needed.

Eliminated from the second serial was any use of Kaun's cue "Orloff," and Harling's music from *Destination Unknown* was used only sporadically.

Nineteen thirty-eight saw a labor dispute which was to materially alter film music in Hollywood. Thousands of musicians had found themselves out of work with the advent of sound films and the dissolution of the theater pit orchestras that had played the musical accompaniments to silent films. The American Federation of Musicians had been trying for years to put musicians back to work, and one way to increase employment was to eliminate the practice of tracking. In April 1938 the Musicians' Union, helped by the powerful International Alliance of Theatrical and Stage Employees, signed an agreement with the major studios that would end the practice of using tracked music in theatrical films.[19]

Because of this new contract with the musicians, beginning in 1939 all library music used by Universal was newly recorded. Previously an editor might pull any one of several hundred cues he felt appropriate. Now, to economize on an expensive turn in production, the film editors would decide what music cues were needed and requisition the music department to re-record them. These recordings could then be used throughout the production. As a result, the new serials displayed a musically homogeneous sound that no longer exhibited the eclectic diversity of the earlier films.

The original orchestrations of the music were used with certain modifications. Generally omitted from these new recordings were organ and piano parts, used in earlier scores for doubling purposes to add "body" to the sound of the music. In some cases ("Dance Macabre" and "You'll Need a Coat" from *Bride of Frankenstein*) xylophone highlighting was substituted for the organ and string parts.[20] Most of this re-recorded music has a more "modern" sound, but whether from the different instrumental components or due to the advances in sound recording techniques in the intervening years it is difficult to say. The music certainly has a sparer, leaner sound than the original versions.

Although the music was initially re-recorded, it appears that subsequent re-recordings were often junked and tracked music used anyway![21]

Flash Gordon Conquers the Universe (1940)

The final and weakest entry of the Flash Gordon trilogy, *Flash Gordon Conquers the Universe*, relied on many of the pieces used previously, including *Bombay Mail, The Invisible Man,* and *Bride of Frankenstein.* Inexplicably, it also used large portions of *Les Preludes*, even though Liszt's symphonic poem has the distinct stamp of a classical work and often seems oddly out of place in the serial. Its use may have been the handiwork of Charles Previn.[22] Previn had been a conductor of Broadway shows, the Radio City Music Hall orchestra, and the radio program, "Real Silk," before becoming Universal's music director in 1936.

Aside from *Les Preludes, Conquers the Universe* reflected the changing of the guard at Universal.[23] Sections of the scores for *Son of Frankenstein, The Sun Never Sets,* and *Tower of London* (all 1939) by Frank Skinner[24] were used in the third serial. Yet the film harked back to the very beginning of the sound era by using a short piece, "Oriental Dance," from Universal's first part-sound serial, *Tarzan the Tiger* (1929), that had been composed by Sam Perry.[25]

The third entry in the series also made good use of Heinz Roemheld's pioneering score for *The White Hell of Pitz Palu* (1930). Originally a German silent picture typical of the mountaineering films then in vogue in Germany, it starred Leni Riefenstahl and was co-directed by G.W. Pabst and Dr. Arnold Fanck. Universal acquired the rights to it and released it as a hybrid sound film. A foreign version (the only one apparently surviving today) employed intertitles and sound effects.[26] Both versions had virtual wall-to-wall scores. For the film, Roemheld composed an extensive classically styled score that made use of the full battery of film music techniques. In fact, Roemheld was proud to recall that MGM's Jack Chertok arranged for a music department staff screening of the film as an example of a model film score.[27]

The most memorable part of *Pitz Palu*'s score is Roemheld's "March of the Torches," a beguiling, insistent march heard most prominently in *Conquers the Universe* during the snow scenes in Frigia (which, coincidentally, made extensive use of stock shots from *Pitz Palu* as well). The "Snowstorm Theme" is a swirling capriccio which Roemheld often imitated stylistically in later films (including the "Atlanta Fire" sequence in *Gone with the Wind* which he ghost-wrote for Max Steiner).

Buck Rogers (1939)

During the interim between the release of the second and third Flash Gordon serials, Universal produced *Buck Rogers* in 1939. The 12-chapter serial was based upon the Phil Nowlan-Dick Calkins comic strip syndicated by the John F. Dille Co., and in no way is related to *Flash Gordon*, which it predated, having appeared in daily strips in 1929.[28] The film version of *Buck Rogers* is so similarly styled to the Flash Gordon serials, even starring Buster Crabbe, that film buffs often consider the four serials collectively as a quartet.

Buck Rogers, however, was nominally science fiction, without the fantasy elements that helped make *Flash Gordon* so appealing. It details a 20th century Rip Van Winkle (Crabbe) who through suspended animation awakens in the 25th century. Finding Earth dominated by a vicious dictator, Killer Kane (played by Anthony Warde), Buck allies himself with a rebel group to eventually overthrow the villains. The film was briskly co-directed by Ford Beebe and Saul Goodkind.[29]

Buck Rogers employed the stand-by scores that had become a staple of the Flash Gordon serials, although newly recorded with a few interesting changes. Parts of "Creation Pt. II" from *Bride of Frankenstein* were repositioned. From the same score, the ending of the

"Chase" was tacked onto "Monster Breaks Out" to form a new piece. In "You'll Need a Coat," *pizzicati* strings were supplanted by a xylophone to create a totally new-sounding composition. The organ which had supplied Waxman's score with so much of its timbre was omitted. Tempi and dynamics were liberally changed. Essentially, however, the orchestrations of the many scores involved retained their original character except for the alterations noted.

It is not known who arranged the music for these recordings, but most probably the modifications were the result of a need to economize on orchestra size as well as add freshness to music used so heavily in preceding years.[30]

Buck Rogers' main title was a re-recording of Roemheld's main title music for *The Great Impersonation* (1935), a sweeping, grandiose melody, coupled with Roemheld's tragic appassionata from *Dracula's Daughter* (1936). *Buck Rogers* also made frequent use of a sprightly scherzo from *The White Hell of Pitz Palu* as well as the mournful "Erotic Theme" and the elegiac "Lyrical Suspense."

Feature Versions

Mention should be made of the feature versions of the Flash Gordon serials that Universal produced. In November 1936, a 72-minute film was edited from *Flash Gordon* and released under that title. A new music track was prepared from the library which was different from the serial's. The film also used music not heard in any of the Flash Gordon serials, including some cues originally composed in 1930, such as "Furioso" by Roemheld (from *Lightning Express*) and "Cavalcade" by Sam Perry (from *The Indians Are Coming*), and other cues as yet unidentified.[31] In addition, music from *Bride of Frankenstein, Dracula's Daughter*, and other cues used later in *Flash Gordon's Trip to Mars* are heard. Unlike *Trip to Mars*, however, at times the music in the feature *Flash Gordon* seems hilariously inappropriate, actually burlesquing the screen action.

In April 1938 a feature version of *Flash Gordon's Trip to Mars* was prepared. The 67-minute film, *Mars Attacks the World*,[32] is understandably a hash in view of the task involved in condensing the serial's five-hour running time to feature length. Generally, the music closely follows the selections tracked in the serial, although some

The Music of Flash Gordon *and* Buck Rogers

Vaughan and Waxman cues originally composed for *Sutter's Gold* (1936) were added.

A feature version of *Buck Rogers* was released in 1939 entitled *Buck Rogers vs. the Planet Outlaws*.[33] Other feature condensations such as *Spaceship to the Unknown, Deadly Ray from Mars, Purple Death from Outer Space,* and *Destination Saturn* are simply cut-downs edited from the composite prints for distribution to television.

Flash Gordon Conquers the Universe brought to a close Universal's "space" serials. Subsequent serials became progressively cheaper, using Western and contemporary backgrounds for economy. Quality diminished steadily. In 1946 Universal announced a merger with International Pictures and a new policy of "A"-only productions. The serial unit (along with the horror-film and shorts units) were summarily shut down.[34]

But it remains a source of amazement that the Flash Gordon serials, periodically finding new audiences among children and adults, have placed the indelible stamp of their music on those who normally take no special notice of film music. The imagination and vigor of these tracked library scores has in large measure contributed to the lasting charm and classic status of these serials.

Appendix I

The Cue Sheets

Universal prepared cue sheets through a numbering system. According to Joseph Gluck (note 5), each negative optical music track was marked with reference numbers that would print through onto positive film. This enabled an assistant to compare the numbers against music department files to record the title and composer of each cue. This explains why repeats are almost never listed in the early cue sheets. Unless a splice or reel change was observed, it would not be evident that a given strip of film might contain the same cue repeated more than once, or even that different cues from a single "take" might be spliced together out of sequence.

It is entirely possible that whoever assembled the cue sheets for *Flash Gordon* used an abbreviated music department reference file that identified a cue by *film*, but not by *title*. This would explain why most of the cue titles in the ASCAP cue sheets are inaccurate (although the composer and the film of origin are generally correct).

To rectify this the author systematically listened to the serials and identified each cue. Without the aid of a conductor part or sketches to follow, such an attempt can be risky, since the suspicion exists that the cue sheets for the feature films from which the cues were tracked may themselves be incorrect or incomplete. For example, the climactic finale music from *The Invisible Man* contains one long, continuous musical sequence, possibly even recorded as one take; yet the cue sheets list fifteen separate cue titles. *Bombay Mail*, on the other hand, contains cues that seem to encompass two or more sections of music. In this case, the author relied on the logic of the cue titles, their sequencing, and their use in other films for which cue sheets were available.

If public domain music was used, the arranger is listed after the composer, *e.g.*, Liszt/R[oemheld]. In the case of Liszt's *Les Preludes* as used in *Flash Gordon Conquers the Universe*, since it is not clear whether the piece was recorded specifically for the serial or used in the 1940 Universal feature, *Zanzibar*, no "source" film is given.

Although the author prepared new, corrected cue sheets for all four serials, it has been impractical to reproduce them here because of their

The Music of Flash Gordon and Buck Rogers

length. The following condensation provides the essential information from the cue sheets in a manageable form. The films for which the musical cues were originally written appear in the first column, together with the titles of the cues. The composer of each cue appears in the second column. The remaining columns identify the serials in which the cues were used and the number of such uses.

FG	*Flash Gordon*
FGTM	*Flash Gordon's Trip to Mars*
FGCU	*Flash Gordon Conquers the Universe*
BR	*Buck Rogers*

FILM/CUE TITLES	COMPOSER	FG	FGTM	FGCU	BR
All Quiet on the Western Front (non-dialogue version, 1930)					
Western Front March	Perry	-	1	-	-
The Black Cat (1934)					
Allegro Appassionato	Roemheld	9	3	-	-
Cat Interlude	Roemheld	13	15	-	-
Cat Love Theme	Roemheld	4	21	-	-
Cat Neutral	Roemheld	1	-	-	-
Cat Threat	Roemheld	-	3	-	-
Main Title	Roemheld	7	16	-	-
Prelude	Chopin/R	1	-	-	-
Les Preludes	Liszt/R	17	-	-	-
Rakoczy March	Liszt/R	1	-	-	-
Rhapsody	Brahms/R	7	3	-	-
Sonata in B Minor	Liszt/R	31	23	-	-
Bombay Mail (1934)					
Bombay Tension	Roemheld	2	5	-	9
Calcutta Suspense	Roemheld	12	3	-	6
East Indian Skirmish	Roemheld	6	1	-	-
Emergency Brake	Roemheld	3	-	-	-
Fight in Bombay	Roemheld	5	2	-	-
Governor's March	Roemheld	-	6	-	7
Inspector Interlude #1	Roemheld	4	8	2	1
Inspector Interlude #2	Roemheld	5	6	-	-

Inspector Theme #1	Roemheld	3	2	4	9
Inspector Theme #2	Roemheld	8	1	3	12
Main Title	Roemheld	4	8	4	12
March Bombay #1	Roemheld	4	5	-	-
March Bombay #2	Roemheld	11	3	-	-
March Bombay #3	Roemheld	7	2	-	-
Shirley's Theme #1	Roemheld	-	-	-	12
Shirley's Theme #2	Roemheld	4	6	-	1
Shirley's Theme #3	Roemheld	-	1	4	3
Sinister Foreboding	Roemheld	-	1	1	7
Station Bombay	Roemheld	-	-	9	4
Whistling Drunk	Roemheld	-	1	-	-
Xavier	Roemheld	12	5	-	-

Bride of Frankenstein (1935)

Chase	Waxman	-	16	-	-
Creation Pt. I	Waxman	-	6	-	-
Creation Pt. II	Waxman	-	24	3	26
Crucifixion	Waxman	-	9	26	-
Dance Macabre	Waxman	-	17	-	-
Female Monster Music	Waxman	-	10	4	4
Graveyard	Waxman	-	3	-	-
Main Title	Waxman	-	1	-	-
Monster Breaks Out	Waxman	-	-	-	20
Monster Enters #2	Waxman	-	4	-	-
Pastorale	Waxman	-	18	-	-
Pretorius Entrance	Waxman	-	32	9	18
Processional March	Waxman	-	2	-	3
A Strange Apparition	Waxman	-	1	-	-
Village	Waxman	-	24	-	-
You'll Need a Coat	Waxman	-	6	-	15

Destination Unknown (1933)

Bellamy with Lantern	Harling	1	-	-	-
Christ Motive	Harling	2	-	-	-
Reel 6A	Harling	-	4	-	-
Storm Scene	Harling	8	-	-	-
Sun Streaming	Harling	4	-	-	-
You Can't Get Away with It	Harling	11	2	-	-
unidentified cue	Harling	1	-	-	-

The Music of Flash Gordon and Buck Rogers

Dracula's Daughter (1936)					
Croydon Airport	Roemheld	-	14	-	-
Main Title	Roemheld	-	-	-	13
Transylvania	Roemheld	-	14	-	9
Village Festival	Roemheld	-	1	-	-
Flash Gordon (serial, 1936)					
Main Title	Vaughan	25	-	-	-
Narrative	Vaughan	12	-	-	-
Great Expectations (1934)					
London Arrival	Ward	-	-	-	8
The Great Impersonation (1935)					
The Chase	Roemheld	-	-	-	9
Knife Scene	Vaughan	-	5	-	-
Main Title	Roemheld	-	-	1	13
The Invisible Man (1933)					
Chase	Roemheld	5	-	-	-
Exterior of Farm	Roemheld	4	1	-	-
Exterior Snow	Roemheld	4	-	-	-
Farmer Enters	Roemheld	7	3	-	-
Farmer Enters Police Office	Roemheld	1	2	-	-
Fire	Roemheld	8	1	-	-
Interior of Barn	Roemheld	8	1	-	-
Invisible Man Awakes	Roemheld	2	-	-	-
Main Title	Roemheld	49	43	37	58
Men Approach	Roemheld	8	-	-	-
Men Run	Roemheld	6	1	-	-
Police Captain's Orders	Roemheld	1	1	-	-
Police Office	Roemheld	6	1	-	-
Shot	Roemheld	5	-	-	-
Shots	Roemheld	3	-	-	-
Steps	Roemheld	4	1	-	-
The Midnight Sun (non-dialogue re-release, 1931)					
Orloff	Kaun	4	-	-	-
Mystery of Edwin Drood (1935)					
Death Storm	Ward	-	-	-	12

The Raven (1935)					
Adagio Dance	Vaughan	1	-	-	-
Son of Frankenstein (1939)					
Monster on Rampage	Skinner	-	-	3	-
Spell of the Circus (serial, 1930)					
Main Title	Perry	-	1	-	-
The Sun Never Sets (1939)					
War	Skinner	-	-	40	-
Sutter's Gold (1936)					
The Cattle	Vaughan	-	1	-	-
Tarzan the Tiger (serial, 1929)					
Oriental Dance	Perry	-	-	3	-
Tower of London (1939)					
Anne Neville Montage	Skinner	-	-	27	-
Torture Scene	Skinner	-	-	7	-
Tower Conspiracy	Skinner	-	-	8	-
Werewolf of London (1935)					
Appassionato	Hajos	3	-	-	-
The Fight	Hajos	30	4	-	7
Finale	Hajos	3	1	-	26
First Murder	Hajos	11	-	-	-
First Sign	Hajos	9	3	-	-
In Despair	Hajos	1	-	-	-
The Lost Soul	Hajos	16	-	-	-
Main Title	Hajos	3	1	-	3
The Menace	Hajos	1	-	-	-
The Old Tale	Hajos	-	5	-	-
The Prowling Monster	Hajos	4	7	-	-
Second Murder	Hajos	2	-	-	-
The Two Werewolves	Hajos	3	4	-	-
Werewolf Theme	Hajos	1	6	-	-
White Hell of Pitz Palu (1930)					
Alpine March	Roemheld	-	1	-	-
Erotic Theme	Roemheld	-	-	7	-
Lyrical Suspense	Roemheld	-	-	2	11
March of the Torches	Roemheld	-	-	11	-
Night Theme	Roemheld	-	-	8	-
Scherzo	Roemheld	-	-	1	9

Snowstorm Theme	Roemheld	-	-	8	-
Tristamente	Roemheld	-	3	-	-
Classical and miscellaneous					
Allegretto Grazioso	?	-	-	2	-
Entrance of the Duchess	?	-	-	1	-
Fanfare	D. Klatzkin	2	-	-	-
Fanfare	Perry	1	-	-	-
I Mourn the Day	?	-	-	1	-
King's Theme	?	-	-	1	-
Orgy of the Spirits	Ilyinsky	-	8	-	-
Les Preludes	Liszt	-	-	78	-
La Rhumba	Previn-Skinner	-	-	1	-
Spagnoletta	?	-	-	2	-
Tribulation	Perry	-	-	4	-

Appendix II

Music Manuscript

The first copyright entries of Universal music were recorded in November 1929, for Sam Perry's compositions for *Tarzan the Tiger*. Until early 1931, over 200 cues and a few complete scores were registered with the Copyright Office. No orchestrations were deposited, only three- to four-stave "conductor" parts.

None of Universal's music was again registered as copyrighted properties until 1937. At this time someone in Universal's music department possibly realized that none of the music composed between 1931 and 1936 had been protected by copyright, and this music was belatedly registered for its re-use in subsequent films (for example, the "Main Title" to *The Black Cat* was copyrighted for its use in *Flash Gordon's Trip to Mars*).

Another example is Karl Hajos' "Main Title" for *Werewolf of London*, used seven times in the Flash Gordon and Buck Rogers serials. Although composed in 1935, it was not copyrighted until 1937. As reproduced here, it was used in the Universal feature *Reported Missing* (1937).

These later entries are sometimes very sketchy—in some cases consisting of a one-stave lead sheet, and often containing only the barest information on dynamics or orchestration. In many cases new titles were invented (many of the *Bombay Mail* entries, for example, contain titles bearing no relation to the original film).

While the original 1930 entries were never renewed and have fallen into public domain, the later entries were assigned to Loew's, then Robbins Music, and are now controlled by CBS Songs—which can find no record of them!

The only extant manuscript materials used in any of these films appear to be Franz Waxman's sketches for *Bride of Frankenstein*, in the possession of his son, John Waxman.

Music Recordings

Universal seems not to have had a policy during the 1930s of producing transcription discs for composers' use, or else few of the composers working there at that time had any interest in acquiring them. Universal today has no idea where, or even whether, any optical music tracks from that period survive.

Partial recordings on 33-rpm acetates for Waxman's *Bride of Frankenstein*, and for *Sutter's Gold* (including some Vaughan and Roemheld cues), are in the George Arents Research Library at Syracuse University.

As to the other composers, a search of their estates, university collections, and Universal Pictures proved fruitless; no private or studio recordings from this period are known to exist.

NOTES

[1] Information from King Features Syndicate, New York City.

[2] Rudy Behlmer, "The Saga of Flash Gordon," *Screen Facts*, 2, No. 4 [whole no. 10] (1965), p. 53.

[3] George Turner, "Making the Flash Gordon Serials," *American Cinematographer*, 64, No. 6 (June 1983), p. 56. The most comprehensive article on the subject to date. Turner's occasional errors of fact regarding the music are silently corrected in the present article.

[4] Much of the information pertaining to the composer credits derives from ASCAP and ERPI cue sheets, *The United States Copyright Catalogues* of 1930 and 1936-40, and rigorous screening and cross-checking by the author of the films involved that were available for screening.

[5] Information pertaining to the post-production editorial work and music tracking was related to the author in recorded telephone interviews with Joseph Gluck, July 1 and July 23, 1984. Gluck was an editor at Universal in the serial unit from 1933-35 and 1937-43.

[6] Born Bridgeton, New Jersey, September 23, 1893; died Arcadia, California, November 23, 1987. Biographical information about him and other composers is from the *ASCAP Biographical Dictionary* (various editions), and from William H. Rosar, "Music for the Monsters," *The Quarterly Journal of the Library of Congress*, 40, No. 4

(Fall 1983), an important article on Universal's horror film scores of the 'thirties.

[7] Letter to the author from Clifford Vaughan, February 10, 1985.

[8] Born London, England, January 18, 1887; died Sierra Madre, California, November 22, 1958.

[9] Born Milwaukee, Wisconsin, May 1, 1901; died Huntington Beach, California, February 11, 1985.

[10] Interview with Heinz Roemheld by the author, September, 1970.

[11] Roemheld freely admitted that the "Cat Love Theme" in the main title to *The Black Cat* was modeled on the love theme in Tchaikovsky's *Romeo and Juliet*, done to avoid possible copyright infringement (see Rosar, "Music for the Monsters," p. 404).

[12] "Synch Old Pics as Foreign Fillers," *Variety*, April 29, 1931. Since early 1930 Universal had supplied its foreign markets with "non-dialogue" versions of its films. These were inter-titled, non-talking versions with soundtracks containing only music and sound effects. Much of the music composed at Universal during this period was for these non-dialogue films and was subsequently tracked in other productions.

[13] Born Milwaukee, Wisconsin, April 5, 1899; died Baden-Baden, Germany, January 3, 1980.

[14] Born Budapest, Hungary, January 28, 1889; died Los Angeles, California, February 1, 1950.

[15] Born Königshütte, Germany, December 24, 1906; died Los Angeles, California, February 24, 1967.

[16] Waxman's cue "Dance Macabre" should not be confused with the Saint-Saëns composition, although Waxman drew obvious inspiration from it.

[17] Born Tsarskoye Selo, Russia, January 24, 1859; died Moscow, February 23, 1920.

[18] Born St. Louis, Missouri, April 3, 1897; died September 26, 1971.

[19] "Pic Sound Track Redubbing Ruled Out . . .," *Variety*, April 20, 1938, p. 7. It was estimated that the change would result in increased employment of 25-30% (approximately 200 more musicians would have work). The pact was formally ratified during the summer of 1938 to avert a threatened strike.

[20] In re-recording, only the "Female Monster Music" portion of "Dance Macabre" was used, the first part being a veritable concertino for

organ and strings which would have become senseless musically without the organ part.

[21] Hans J. Salter, who composed and orchestrated for Universal, stated that the quality of playing in the re-recordings was often so poor that they were often scrapped in favor of better, previous re-recordings. In effect, this was tracking, but since musicians were employed in a new recording session (despite which tracks were ultimately used) it was condoned (unpublished interview with Hans J. Salter by William H. Rosar, December 16, 1974). Joseph Gluck also remembered that although new recordings were made, these were often done as a formality to comply with musicians union requirements and then junked. Salter recalled that the Union would make occasional checks of the emulsion numbers on the edge of the music tracks in an attempt to ascertain whether or not the studio was using new recordings as it was bound to do by the new AFM contract. According to Salter, musicians were hired on a quota basis, regardless of their playing ability. Although this practice was challenged (and subsequently overturned) in court, presumably the Union continued to supply musicians on a "call" basis.

[22] Born Brooklyn, New York, January 11, 1888; died New York City, September 22, 1973.

[23] In 1936 a new management acquired control of Universal from Carl Laemmle, who had founded the company in 1912. Frank Skinner was hired and became Universal's principal composer.

[24] Born Meredosia, Illinois, December 31, 1897; died Los Angeles, California, October 9, 1968. Cue sheets list Ralph Freed as co-composer of *Tower of London*. In Rosar's interview with Salter, Salter stated that Freed was a song writer who had a unique arrangement with Universal in that he received co-composition credit for an entire score when one of his songs was written for a film.

[25] Born Russia, March 28, 1884; died Los Angeles, California, November 1, 1936.

[26] From the Universal press book (distributed to theater exhibitors to publicize a film company's product).

[27] Interview with Heinz Roemheld by the author, September, 1970.

[28] Maurice Horn, ed., *World Encyclopedia of Comics* (New York: Chelsea House, 1976), p. 137.

[29] Goodkind normally was supervising film editor of the serial unit.

[30] Although the main title of *Buck Rogers* lists Charles Previn as musical director, in a telephone conversation with the author (*ca.* 1966) Previn stated that Universaloften credited department heads for work done by the staff, and that he had no recollection of having worked on the film. Salter stated that Previn conducted most of the studio's recordings except for scores by Salter and Skinner. Joseph Gluck remembers that both Previn and Skinner conducted re-recordings.

[31] Cue sheets for the feature version of *Flash Gordon* have not been located.

[32] The original title was *Rocketship*. Joseph Gluck explained that he proposed editing a feature version of *Flash Gordon's Trip to Mars* to obtain a few extra weeks' work during a general studio shutdown at Universal. The edited feature version entitled *Rocketship* was released in April 1938. After the notorious Orson Welles "War of the Worlds" radio broadcast in October 1938, Universal rushed the film into re-release, cannily retitling it *Mars Attacks the World*. Confusion exists because Universal subsequently assigned the title *Rocketship* to the feature version of the original 1936 *Flash Gordon*. The films are currently distributed to television under the later titles and are so referred to in this article.

[33] Although *Buck Rogers vs. the Planet Outlaws* was unavailable to the author for screening, there is no reason to believe that it used any music other than that recorded for the serial version.

[34] "Universal to Drop 4 B-Film Units," *New York Times*, July 26, 1946, p. 16; see also "Two Movie Producers Announce Merger," *New York Times*, July 31, 1946, p. 22.

Holding a Nineteenth Century Pedal at Twentieth Century-Fox*

David Raksin

In 1938, largely as a result of a flaw of character that made it difficult for me to agree with opinions less astute than my own, I was not exactly overwhelmed with work. Despite my efforts to be cool about that, my dear friend Herbert Spencer, who was under contract at "20th," saw through my amateur stoicism and landed me a job there.

At that time, all but the top ("A") features at that studio were flogged through the post-production process (after completion of principal photography) at a killing pace. The music department had developed a kind of assembly line to cope with the pressure imposed upon it by executives in charge of inventing schedules that made few concessions to the limits of human endurance.

Presiding over this process as Musical Director was Louis Silvers, a veteran of Broadway musicals; as a songwriter he also had at least two important hits: "April Showers" and "Mother of Mine." Silvers had begun his film career in the silent picture days, with a score for D.W. Griffith's *Way Down East*, which was arranged and composed with William Frederick Peters. In 1927 Silvers acted as musical director of one of the first "talkies," *The Jazz Singer*, directed by Alan Crosland and starring Al Jolson; and in 1934 he won an Academy Award for musical direction on *One Night of Love*. (The title song was composed by the film's director, Victor Schertzinger.)

---

*This title is borrowed from my colleague, Hugo Friedhofer; it refers to the musical practice of sustaining one pitch—usually called a pedal point—while other chords or voices move through varying harmonies, related or unrelated.

Lou Silvers was the personification of the no-nonsense boss; generally considered a journeyman conductor, he often behaved as though wary and suspicious of those who worked for him. Grateful to be employed again, I wanted very much to feel warmly toward him, but he seems to have been one of those studio politicians who generates problems because he is driven by insecurity. And among the matters he considered "nonsense," and therefore neglected, were the very ones I thought of as the heart of our profession. I think he tried to be a good guy, but his crude pragmatism got in the way. Nevertheless, most of the music department fellows got along with him most of the time, probably because he knew enough to value what we could do.

It could hardly have been otherwise, because that department included some talented people: composers David Buttolph and Cyril Mockridge, Arthur Lange (who always seemed to work for autonomous production units), and Samuel Kaylin (who scored the output of the "B" picture unit of Sol Wurtzel). Among the arranger/orchestrators were Herb Spencer, Gene Rose, and Walter Scharf; Paul van Loan and Jack Virgil were fine band arrangers; Charles Maxwell and that excellent composer, Ernst Toch, were sometimes called in to assist.

David Buttolph (who deserves an article of his own) was a thoroughly schooled composer and conductor who had lived and studied in Europe; his facility and speed were such that we had a standard joke about him: "Buttolph had a bad week—he scored only three pictures!" Cy Mockridge, British to the core, had studied at the Royal College of Music in London and was a master of the quiet pastoral music of his native land. Herb Spencer was, well, Herb Spencer: born in Chile and having completed his education in the United States, he was (and *is*) one of the great, world-class orchestrators and arrangers. A natural aristocrat, his elegant style won him a nickname: "the Sash"—as in those wide red ribbons worn diagonally by Latin American diplomats. Gene Rose was about as odd as they come; friendly but peculiar: one minute outgoing, the next phlegmatic; a good arranger who used to sit up all night in the "office" next to mine, drumming away at his muted upright piano and swigging a concoction called "rhubarb and soda" in a vain attempt to assuage his ulcers, which he claimed to have earned. Because of his abstracted manner—he seemed to lapse into a trance while dreaming up his outrageously swinging arrangements—he was referred to as "the Swami." In his honor, I wrote a parody lyric to a

Louis Silvers, about 1939

Stephen Foster melody, which I called "Way Down Upon the Swami's Liver."

As for me, the new boy, after an initial period during which it was established that I was a "pro," I was accepted as an insider, although I doubt that Silvers ever quite figured out what to make of me. With Spencer's help, I managed to avoid the political undertow in the department. A list of films on which I labored during the stewardship of Lou Silvers at 20th includes several that I can't recall having worked on—which is just as well, since I am easily disconcerted by evidence that at one time I was less than perfect.

In addition to orchestrating for Buttolph and Mockridge, I also arranged a number of endless "routines" for some of the extravagant musicals produced at 20th, including several that featured the Olympic skating star, Sonja Henie. The studio had built her an enormous sound stage, with a large ice rink—Stage 15, a source of much parochial studio pride. One day I appeared at the Tennessee Avenue studio gate, which was the favored entrance of departments such as ours, which were down at that end of the "lot." The gatekeeper that day was a particularly obstreperous policeman, who was showing off to a group of would-be visitors, regaling them with statistics about the facilities as though they were his private domain. Although he saw me there almost every day, when I attempted to walk through he said, "Where do you think *you're* going?" The onlookers were pleased by this demonstration of his power over the lesser orders—but I was annoyed. Without trying to match his peremptory tone, I said, "I've come for Stage 15." He deflated.

When the department was informed that a new routine was ready on Stage 15, one of us would go over to see the number and to confer with the choreographer. The job was, more or less, to convert some defenseless 32-bar tune into a "skating ballet," to decorate the virtuoso gyrations of Miss Henie with appropriate musical flourishes and to glamorize her performance with the opulence of a symphonic orchestra. This meant a lot of notes and a lot of work. I remember arriving at the studio one day with a particularly large bundle of score pages. Seeing this, Lou Silvers hefted the manuscript as though he was the appraiser in a fish market, and pronounced it "a regular sea bass!" So much for sows' ears, silk purses, similes, and the art of the arranger.

There were, of course, certain redeeming aspects of studio life. For one thing, we music people were conveniently located so that we could not reach the music copying offices without passing the small, Romanesque courtyard-building where newly acquired "starlets" were given instruction in such essentials as walking and talking at the same time. Our pleasure at this proximity is perhaps best expressed by our name for it: The Happy Hunting Ground. And we never insulted Fate by doing less than justice to this lucky circumstance. The mother superior of this house of beauty and plumage was a young and charming woman named Geneva Sawyer, a dancer and assistant choreographer whose job it was to teach the new girls style and grace. We were especially fond of her, since she seemed to understand that our interest in her charges was founded in a sincere wish to expand their cultural horizons. One morning, when the wind from Santa Monica Bay was whipping the foliage about and the sky was overcast, Herb Spencer spied Geneva walking through the courtyard on her way to the rehearsal room, all huddled over from the chill. "Hey, Jenny," said he, "are you freezing?" She straightened up and gave him a long glance. "This is the kind of morning," she said, "when I'd like to crawl back into bed and pull a nice, warm man over me."

After I had been working at 20th for a while, Silvers asked me to come up with something for a scene in a picture called *Suez*. As I recall, it was a sequence in which Tyrone Power and his intrepid comrades find themselves in an African village, so whatever I devised would have to work with the ambient sound effects. The following day I brought in some old recordings that would have delighted the 78-rpm soul of a dedicated researcher; I had remembered that many years ago an expedition led by Armand Denis and Leila Roosevelt had recorded the music of some African tribes in the Belgian Congo. Lou listened; in fact, he gave the music his full partial attention, after which he stared at me with his baleful approximation of paternal incredulity. "Are you *nuts*?" he asked. "All that goddam drumming—it sounds like Duke Ellington!" And he wasn't altogether wrong; Sonny Greer, who sat behind the cymbals in the Duke's band, would have been envious. So I had to invent some ersatz "native" music, and Silvers was so pleased by this reaffirmation of Gresham's Law (in this case: the spurious drives out the genuine) that the next time they needed help in a crowded schedule he called upon me again. And in time that led to more composing—and less of the other.

One of the procedures employed to deal with the implausible time schedules was "team composition." On the day when a new film was turned over to the music department for scoring, the staff gathered in the projection room of our headquarters, the Lasky Building. This was a small, movie-set-quaint structure in the southwest corner of the Fox lot; it had been built to house the "unit" of film pioneer Jesse Lasky, whose career spanned the history of moving pictures from *The Squaw Man* (1914), produced with his brother-in-law, Samuel Goldwyn,* to *Rhapsody in Blue* (1945) and beyond.

Present at these departmental film "runnings" would be Silvers, with his chief assistant and all-around nice man, Rudy Schrager; the composers, David Buttolph, Cy Mockridge and me; orchestrators—Herb Spencer and Gene Rose, or one of the freelance fellows; Cliff Ransom, head of the music editors ("cutters"), with his colleagues, Carroll Knudson, George Adams and Earl Dearth—the latter dubbed "a Dearth of good cutters."

We usually ran the picture one reel at a time, stopping at the end of each 1000-ft. reel to determine where music was indicated and to give the necessary instructions to our music cutters: where the scoring sequences would begin, where they would end, and which specific actions, dialogue, sound effects ("Fx"), particular shots or moves of the camera should be noted in the "breakdowns"—the timing-sheets that would display all this information, accounted for in seconds and fractions thereof, by which we would coordinate our music with the precise footage of the film. Sometimes these discussions tended to drag out, and those of us in danger of going stir-crazy from confinement would head for a ping-pong table that some kind soul had installed in the middle of the projection room, and compete our way back to sanity while the arguments waxed hot and heavy. When the scoring layout for each reel was complete, one of the cutters would leave for the music editing rooms to begin work on the timing-sheets for that reel.

By lunch time we had almost always "broken down" the film into sequences adjudged to need music and decided what kind of thematic material would be required. After lunch, while the music cutters prepared the timing-sheets which we would use to synchronize our

---

*At that time, Goldwyn went by his original name, which was Goldfish. The name by which he is now known was contrived from the first syllable of this patronym and the second syllable of his former partner's, (Arch) Selwyn. When I learned this, I pointed out to my friend, Friedhofer, that if Goldwyn had reversed the order of borrowing, his new name would have been Sam Selfish.

music with the film footage, Buttolph, Mockridge and I retired to our own studios to compose whatever specific material we had assigned ourselves. We would presently reconvene, usually with several versions of each proposed theme, to decide which ones would best serve our purposes—which were well understood, although they were rarely articulated. In retrospect, it seems remarkable that this process, which might have been complicated by rivalries, went so smoothly, and that the essential agreements were so easily achieved. The themes chosen would then be photostated, and a set was given to each of the composers. By then the timing-sheets were ready, so Buttolph, Mockridge and I divided up the reels to be scored more or less evenly among ourselves, and each man headed home to compose his third (not to be confused with Beethoven's).

Occasionally there was time to orchestrate my own sequences; as the junior member of the trio, not as fast a composer as the others, I would often have fewer cues to write than they did. But the rush was usually so great that by the next morning we were already feeding our sketches (short scores) to the orchestrators, and by noon they would have many pages of full score ready for the copyists.

On the morning of the fourth day the recording sessions would begin, with Lou Silvers, or sometimes Dave Buttolph, conducting. The studio had a good orchestra of about forty-five musicians under contract, with more available when necessary. The film scores of these second-string pictures were from twenty-five to forty minutes in length, often including "chases" at very fast tempi—which means lots of notes to cover long, open spaces, and slows down the pace of composing considerably. Even with the skill and speed of all involved, it was quite likely that while we were recording a sequence the orchestra parts of the next were being copied.

Recording completed, on the fifth day the re-recording would commence, in which the various tracks—dialogue, music, and sound effects—were "mixed" together for the preview, or sometimes for the final print. After that, there might be a brief respite; then the process would go into high gear again. In this way I worked with Dave Buttolph and Cy Mockridge, and sometimes with other composers, on quite a few films at 20th Century-Fox.

It is sometimes said that this policy of using teams of composers on the three-day marathons of scoring differed from that of other studios at that time. Not so. While the better films were usually handed to a single composer, very often scores were done by teams—even when there was no particular hurry. I myself worked in this way at nearly every studio in town. The common misconception seems to arise from the unreliability of reference books and from the fact that often the screen credit was given to the musical director at the studio where the film was made.

With several composers working on one film score, it would seem inevitable that disparity of styles would be a problem. True; yet it is surprising to recall how well, despite the unfavorable odds, we managed to accommodate to one another. With little or no time to consult among ourselves, we sought to minimize differences. To some extent this was accomplished by the use of thematic material agreed upon by members of the team. However, in the case of *Stanley and Livingstone* (Henry King, 1939), Cliff McCarty finds my music and that of Rex Bassett "as different as can be." Very likely; I do remember Bassett as a good musician, with a number of complete scores of his own, but I cannot recall having encountered him while we were working on that film. I was brought in to provide "native" music for another African village (as a result of my triumph on *Suez*, I was now an expert!) and to compose music for a montage narrated by Spencer Tracy, which appears in the conductor book under the title, "Dear Diary." In such instances, where there was no opportunity to refer to what the other composers were writing, disparity of styles was what we would have called a fivegone conclusion. Disparate or not, it was this one narrative cue that elevated me to the status of composer at 20th Century-Fox.

The movie-score-by-relay system was also in flower when I worked at Universal in 1936 and 1937. And during the same period I also spent many weekends composing for Leo Forbstein, head of the music department at the Warner Bros. studio. If I was not needed at Universal, I would show up at Warners on Friday afternoons. There I would view only the sequences I would be writing; I doubt that I saw any other parts of these films or that I ran any of them all the way through (meaning that in most cases I was unaware of the rest of the story); nor did I know who was composing the rest of the score. For Warners I seem to have written mostly main titles, fights, chases, and montages. I showed the music of one montage to Leopold Stokowski, with whom I was working at Universal. He asked me to re-orchestrate it for symphonic forces, and a few months later he performed it with the Philadelphia Orchestra; in the program it is called "Montage." (In fact, he played it twice, probably because of its excessive length, which was fifty-eight seconds!)

At 20th, and for that matter 'most everywhere in the studios, we composers and arrangers got along very well; such symbiotic relationships thrive upon mutual respect. Some of us left it at that when we were not working together; but others, particularly Herb Spencer and I, were very good friends, and often saw one another socially. Questions are sometimes raised concerning the "seriousness" with which we approached and carried out our work. For all the offhandedness and the "nothing to it" style that we affected in the face of our implausible tasks, I doubt that even the most prosaic fellows among us did less than their best. Despite the fact that certain of our brethren whose wits had been pickled by frustrations and long hours referred to their studio alma maters as "sausage factories," few of us really condescended toward our work. (The characteristic griping and complaining, justified though they may have been, should be understood as safety-valves on overworked organisms.) I *will* say that when Al Newman took over at 20th-Fox the standards in the music department took a large and most welcome upward turn. But even under Silvers, there was a certain *esprit de corps*: colleagues whom one would not let down. And one reason why we put in the incredible hours we did was to make sure that we were not compelled by the pressure of time to produce shoddy work.

One of my favorite music editors at 20th Century-Fox was Carroll Knudson, with whom I worked many twenty-hour days. At that time, the first digital computers, EDVAC and ENIAC, had been invented at my alma mater, the University of Pennsylvania, in the Moore School of Engineering, where I had worked as an assistant for a semester or two. I told Carroll about the magic machines, and explained that some day they would make it possible to circumvent the laborious process of calculating and collating click-track charts. (A click-track is a film-timing device, analogous to a metronomic beat, which is used to achieve exact synchronization of music and image.) I went on to say that with instructions from paper tapes, the computers would print out the detailed charts in a fraction of the time it then took. That was in 1938. It was not until 1965 that, with the assistance of a subsequent generation of electronic computers, Carroll was able to accomplish this, and I bought the first saleable copy of *Project Tempo* from him. A few days later I was surprised by a visit from my brother Ruby, who brought me the first copy of his own click-track book, on which he had been laboring in secret for several years, unaware that Carroll was also trying to solve the problem. My brother's *Technical Handbook of Mathematics for Motion Picture Music Synchronization* displays click-track information in graphic form, while Carroll Knudson's book uses charts of numbers. The initial shock of coincidence to both Carroll and Ruby was eventually alleviated when the Academy of Motion Picture Arts and Sciences awarded "technical" Oscars to them for their work. Both books are still widely used today.

From time to time, artists encounter—usually among theorists, aestheticians and critics—a certain uninformed speculation about the intellectual aspects of our work. Many, though not all, of our colleagues are quite capable of abstract thinking; but I believe we did what we did with a blessed lack of self-consciousness. If the attitude of "it's all in the day's work" was an obvious affectation, I doubt that many were deceived by it. We were young men enjoying our charmed lives to the hilt, but there was a true purposefulness when we sat at our drawing tables with music manuscript before us. As I remember it, we theorized very little; we would have said that we left the theorizing to those who had nothing better to do.

I don't mean to suggest that we never discussed our work, or that we made no effort to understand the effect of the imposition of music upon the film image. Some of us read the little film magazines in which academics and aficionados outdid one another in driving intellectual wedges between the intentions of filmmakers and their films. (You haven't lived until you have waded through one of those "interpretations" of your work according to some arcane theory that leaves you wondering where you were while the music that bears your name was being composed.) But more likely, when we were together we talked about music, of all kinds; and we read scores and played recordings. Herb Spencer, Eddie Powell, Hugo Friedhofer and I would gather to listen to the latest recordings and to borrow contemporary scores from one another; I think we often had the new music before most people on the eastern seaboard were aware of it. I don't believe we delved into the aesthetics of our medium. When I am asked whether we thought seriously about adding "another dimension" to the films we scored, I reply that we assumed that if we dealt effectively with action and mood—the meaning of the story and of specific scenes—when another dimension was called for we would generate that. The validity

Holding a Nineteenth Century Pedal at Twentieth Century-Fox 177

of this assumption can be tested by looking at and listening to what we did.

My first round of employment at 20th Century-Fox ended rather abruptly on a serio-comic note; at the time it seemed more serio than comic. The arrangement under which I worked for Silvers was that I had a modest retainer—enough for me to indulge my taste for immoderation and not much more. But when I composed or arranged or orchestrated, my earnings were computed according to prevailing rates and union minimums, so that in a week I could earn many times the amount of the retainer. As part of this deal, when I was not needed at 20th I was free to accept work elsewhere, and I did. Mostly I worked for Al Newman, then musical director for Sam Goldwyn at United Artists studio. (For a tale of arranging prowess at United Artists—which is literally true!—see Appendage.)

At lunch one day a member of the 20th staff who knew I had composed some music for Newman over the weekend asked me why I wasn't at United Artists for the recording. At that, Lou Silvers, who knew very well that I often worked "on the outside," suddenly burst forth with a tirade in which he accused me of just about everything from personal disloyalty to sabotaging the Hindenburg. When he finished this outburst, everyone at the music table sat there stunned; and when I tried to say that such work was within the terms of my agreement and that he had known about it for nearly two years, he refused to listen. He went so far as to say, "I picked you up and ironed out the wrinkles in your stomach" (an allusion to my previous unemployment, somewhat exaggerated) "and you repaid me with this . . . !" and added that he knew my type, that I was "nigger rich"—an appalling allusion to the notion that when a black person gets a few dollars they are quickly squandered.

We were all horrified, unable to imagine what had precipitated this diatribe. Spencer advised me not to quit, saying that something must have gone wrong for Lou, and that it would probably blow over. It was a bad afternoon. When I had completed my work, I went up to the studio cashier to pick up my check. I had a standing arrangement there that every week $100 of my earnings would go direct to the studio's credit union—my way of saving. This time I noticed that the usual deduction had not been made, and said that I wanted it done. The reply was a beauty: "Even if it's your last check?" That was how I learned that I had been fired.

I began this memoir with a sardonic reference to "a flaw of character," and I end it with another. For some reason, I could not get up the steam to hate Lou Silvers, even when, a few days later, somebody explained what it was really about. No one was aware at the time that Darryl Zanuck had just activated what seems to have been a long-standing plan to bring his admired friend, Al Newman, to 20th to take over the music department. What was sad was that Lou apparently believed I knew about this well-kept secret and was trying to ingratiate myself with the new boss. I was struck, and not altogether favorably, with my inability to feel resentful toward Silvers; it was the passivity of my response that troubled me. But perhaps I was thinking how it must have hurt to be thus humiliated; he too had been fired, and from a far more exposed position.

What I found more difficult to understand and to forgive was what happened next. I learned that a colleague at 20th had immediately relayed the news to Al Newman that I had been fired for incompetence. It seems odd that Newman, who had just conducted the music which had precipitated the incident, and which should have told him something about my competence, appeared willing to let it go at that—without further investigation. Sensing this, I could not bring myself to call him and argue something that should have been self-evident. But fortunately, someone else, probably Spencer or Powell, perhaps both, intervened, and must have asked Al whether he didn't think it strange that it had taken Silvers nearly two years to discover my "incompetence." The outcome was that shortly after Newman settled into his new position at 20th I was rehired, with a far more substantial salary; and I remained there until I decided it was time to go out on my own.

Appendage

When composers and arrangers get together, the stories of exploits often suggest what Homer might be writing these days if he worked for *Down Beat*. A typical tale concerns Eddie Powell, Hugo Friedhofer and me.

In 1937 Sam Goldwyn was producing *The Goldwyn Follies*. He had a script by Ben Hecht, George Marshall to direct, Alfred Newman as musical director, and the choreographer was George Balanchine; the songs were by George and Ira Gershwin, and included two ballads that

David Raksin, June 1940

have since become standards, "Love Walked In" and "Our Love Is Here to Stay." But George became seriously ill, and one Sunday morning, while I was working at United Artists on some music for Newman, his pianist and assistant, Urban Thielmann, came into my studio and told me that George had died.

The effect this tragedy had upon those of us who knew him and thought him the personification of life and musical talent was like a gasp of pain that stays with you and doesn't go away. At such a time, when you can't bear to face your work, it is, paradoxically, that work which sustains you and makes it possible to go on. And a picture in production is like a juggernaut. So *The Goldwyn Follies* kept rolling; Vernon Duke was brought in to write one more song that was needed and to compose two ballets that would feature Vera Zorina.

During this period I was freelancing, and one day I had a call from Newman's incomparable orchestrator, Eddie Powell, who was the arranger on the Goldwyn film. He said that Duke had completed the first ballet, which was not scheduled to go into production for a while; but for some reason plans had suddenly changed, and the dates moved up. In order to make the new schedule and to get the music tracks to Balanchine in time for him to be ready, the ballet had to be pre-recorded *the next day*. Was I available?

"Tomorrow . . . ?!?"

"Yes." (Laughter on the other end of the line.)

"Come on, Eddie—how long is this thing?"

"About eight minutes or so," he said, "and for full orchestra. You ought to know—this is the one George has been working on."

That was Powell's way of telling me he knew I was spending most of my free time at Balanchine's rehearsal hall with one of the ladies of the ballet. But there was more to it than that; both Balanchine and Vernon Duke, who, under his real name, Vladimir Dukelsky, was a formidable composer, were old friends of ours, and this was a fine opportunity to be with them.

That evening, Eddie, Hugo Friedhofer and I met for dinner at a favorite restaurant in Hollywood. Powell had three copies of the ballet music, duplicated in a process called Ditto, which produced copies in a lurid purple-pink that would have been more appropriate to a ballet about Bluebeard than to this one, which was called "Ondine." He told us that the scenario was about a water nymph, who would be portrayed by Vera Zorina; at the thought of that beautiful girl in that role the atmosphere, which had been a mite apprehensive, took a turn for the better. But there were pages and pages of music—written for piano, without any indications of orchestral color! Trying to avoid decorating the music with gravy stains, we set about dividing the score into fairly brief sections; Eddie took the first, Hugo the second and I the third, and continued in this order until we had parceled out the entire manuscript.

An hour later we were under way, sequestered in three studios at United Artists, communicating only by telephone. The instrumentation lists showed that while the first-chair woodwind players were symphony men, the second and third positions were filled by "doublers." These were highly skilled performers, usually saxophone players who doubled on various other woodwinds: flutes, oboes, clarinets, and bassoons. This presented a problem: there was no way of knowing what the configurations in the woodwinds would be when the transitions from Eddie's first section to Hugo's, and Hugo's to mine (and so on) were made; none of us could tell in advance which woodwinds the doublers would be playing. Our solution was to leave the woodwind staves open for the first few bars of each section, until we got the telephone call informing us which player was playing which instrument. The other problem was getting enough coffee.

By the time the copyists came in, shortly after midnight, to begin extracting the individual parts, we had several sections ready for them. And when the day-workers at the studio began to filter in we were nearly finished, except for checking to see that the transitions had been properly managed. The recording would soon start, but not before we three miserable looking specimens, Eddie, Hugo and I, had a chance to clean up a bit. We knew that Balanchine would bring Zorina and the *corps de ballet* over to the recording stage, and that they were all aware that what they were about to hear had not existed the previous evening. It was therefore important to appear no more disheveled than necessary, if we were to play the roles of heroes of the moment to the hilt. As in the movies, so in the studios: being a hero has its rewards. I still have one of mine. It is a Technicolor 35mm frame from *The Goldwyn Follies*, in which Vera Zorina is seen emerging from a pool of water— her first appearance in the ballet "Ondine." She is wearing a gold lamé tunic and a small tiara, and she looks ravishing.

Miklós Rózsa's *Ben-Hur*: The Musical-Dramatic Function of the Hollywood *Leitmotiv*

Steven D. Wescott

A certain uniquely Hollywoodian aura of reverence so quickly engulfs any mention of Miklós Rózsa's score for the film classic *Ben-Hur*, it seems altogether natural to assume that every nuance of the score might by now have undergone the closest scrutiny and critical assessment. Except for the shower of superlatives (and otherwise watery adjectives) that one might expect to rain down on any Academy Award winning score, it is somewhat surprising to discover, then, that Rózsa's worthy effort has in fact received little critical attention in print.[1] Now, twenty-nine years after the film's release, there still exists no straightforward cue-by-cue explication of the way in which Rózsa's highly praised music actually fits the film. More importantly, we still lack a simple elucidation of the basic musical materials and methods he employed in meeting its complex challenges, both musical and dramaturgical.

Although the former prospect looms beyond the reasonable scope of this brief article, the latter, by revealing Rózsa's adept use of the *leitmotiv* in response to the very particular requirements of the film itself, has the potential to inform a broader and more vital question of film scoring methodology. To be sure, any well-formed evaluation of how the music *itself* was designed to function within the dramatic context, as an integral part of the cinematic experience of *Ben-Hur*, must necessarily seek to interpret Rózsa's use of this sometimes maligned and often misused musical device. At the same time, such an analysis serves to confirm *Ben-Hur* as a singularly appropriate application of that compositional strategy, expanding our appreciation of this truly monumental score.

Ben-Hur is, above everything else, an *immense* film, and any analysis, simple or otherwise, must begin with that important fact. Rózsa's pre-production discussions with producer Sam Zimbalist and director William Wyler, early in 1958, must certainly have focused upon the problems posed by the sheer enormity of the project. Undoubtedly, every aspect of the production, and every artistic and creative dilemma encountered in its realization, were significantly magnified by the extended length, the heroic dimension, and the intricately interwoven plot-lines of the screenplay itself.

From the outset, then, two overriding musical concerns must have commanded the attention of the collaborators. The first was a need to adequately portray the panorama and spectacle of the film. Rózsa had, of course, many times demonstrated his ability to meet such a challenge, and even to provide, when necessary, a suitably grand façade for the occasional big-budget Hollywood production. His thirty-two previous films for MGM had included several "historical" features and had more than introduced him to the peculiar problems of the "epic" film through his work on *Julius Caesar* and the scrupulously researched *Quo Vadis*.[2]

A second concern must have focused on the need to provide, despite its great length, a *coherent* musical score, one that might serve to clarify and lend cohesiveness to the inherent cinematographic complexity of the film itself. In order to respond to this challenge, Rózsa chose to employ a so-called *leitmotivic* approach in scoring the film. This method, which he had often used in earlier films (occasionally with less success, and generally with less necessity than in this case), makes use of a number of readily identifiable "basic themes" (or *leitmotivs*), each consistently associated with the appearance of a particular character, situation, emotion, or event on the screen. In its most effective application, this technique allows the composer to comment on and respond meaningfully to the action, conveying a heightened sense of the drama and lending a certain musical-dramatic interplay to enhance and unify the film. At the same time, it allows the drama itself to impart a justifiable logic and a coherent, more-or-less parallel structure to the musical score.[3]

Actual composition of the *Ben-Hur* score began on location in Rome, early in the summer of 1958. Several scenes required musical cues even before they could be filmed. Source music was needed, for example, to accompany the dancers at Arrius's party in Rome, and a curiously deceptive rhythm-track had to be laid down to measure the accelerating cadence of the famous "Rowing Scene."

Returning again to Rome just before Christmas 1958, Rózsa began to compose and record the quasi-source music which, together with Wyler's majestic visual images of Imperial Rome, would both capture and help to create the spectacle of *Ben-Hur*. This "Roman music" included four important marches and several march fragments and fanfares used to accompany the paraded power and glitter of the Roman legions. At regular intervals throughout the film, these scenes recur as a dramaturgical reminder of the omnipresent Roman force. They also return, almost *a la rondo*, to reassert their peculiar musical character in bold contrast with the rest of Rózsa's score.

The "Roman music" is characterized by strong and regular beats, dotted rhythms, and a not unexpected emphasis on the use of percussion, winds, and brass. Confirmed by the symmetrical regularity of melodic periods and easily perceived A B A structures, this "Roman music" (Ex. 1 and 2) seems almost propelled by its unrelenting martial "squareness." Through his use of "uncolored" modal melodies, consistently harmonized with parallel P5ths and 8-5 sonorities, Rózsa achieves a certain harshly primitive sound that effectively reverberates a peculiar tenor of the immutability of Roman dominance which functions, in fact, as a culpable antagonist in the film. At the same time, this almost banal "brutishness" seems somehow remarkably effective in obviating most questions of musical/historical authenticity.

Ex. 1

Ex. 2

Indeed, Rózsa states that in seeking to create a "specialized pseudo-archaic style" for *Ben-Hur*, he "simply developed the 'Roman' style... already established in *Quo Vadis*."[4] In that film, "Roman music" was specifically distinguished from that which he had designed to re-create an authentic musical sense of the first century (to the limited extent that such music can, in fact, be known or even suggested). In *Ben-Hur*, however, Rózsa's musical challenge was more in the nature of an attempt to dramaturgically encompass the epic than to musically define its historical setting, and his musical solution so adeptly confronts the cinematic challenge that it must surely mollify all but the most delicate of musicological sensitivities.

In any event, *Ben-Hur*'s "Roman music" establishes one primary pole of musical focus for the film and stands in direct and easily perceptible stylistic opposition to the rest of the music in the film. Furthermore, the Roman marches, being in themselves a group of set pieces, also create a formal contrast to the rest of the score, whose structure is primarily dictated by the dramatic requirements of the action by means of the parallel employment of the "basic themes" (the so-called *leitmotivs*). In the music, as in the drama itself, however, melodic features, motivic fragments, and even orchestrations characteristic of the "Roman music" continue their pervasive influence throughout the film. They recur as accompanimental figures, momentary interjections, and obligati, and on occasion serve even to color the "basic themes" themselves.

Most of these "basic themes" are drawn, however, from an opposing musical pole which, for want of a better term, may be called the "Judean music." The contrasting character of this music is most clearly demonstrated just after the "Title Music" early in the film, as Rózsa juxtaposes the "Marcia Romana" (Ex. 2) with a theme consistently associated with the people and the land of Judea:

Ex. 3

Many contrasts are immediately apparent. The "Roman music," for example, is almost awkwardly "square," symmetrical, and overridingly rhythmic; the "Judean," fluid, lyric, and quickly "spinning off" into the kind of endless, "rest"-less melody so familiar to devotees of Rózsa's concert music and *film noir* scores. (Any generalization of Rózsa's compositional style must necessarily include an observation that his melodies seldom *end*, but instead *evolve* into something else.) The dotted rhythms of Rome give way, in this style, to flowing, languid, seemingly improvisatory melodic ornaments—hinting of folk music origins, or at least a closer kinship with the "heart" of a people—in contrast with the martial façade of the Roman presence. The homophony of Rome also yields here to a more characteristic Rózsa-esque polyphony. This is not so much counterpoint as it is countermelody in flowing dialogue over a broad chordal foundation. The result, however, is an overriding impression of the supremacy of melody.

Interestingly, and perhaps symbolically, the "basic themes" that exhibit these "Judean" elements in their purest form are also the two principal "love themes" in the film. One portrays the unassailable and enduring bond between Judah Ben-Hur and his mother, Miriam, in a musical cue aptly entitled "Mother's Love":

Ex. 4

The other is an exquisite and enchanting "Love Theme" for Judah and Esther. This well-known and compellingly beautiful melody also, of course, provided the film with a successful and perhaps compulsory commercial "theme song":

Ex. 5

The inherent strength and apparent inevitability of these themes reflect, in some ways, Rózsa's essentially linear approach to musical composition. It is his characteristic use of modal "scales" in the construction of melodies and counter-melodies heard throughout, however, which imbues the score with a certain exotic charm and a particularly Rózsa-esque warmth and depth of color. If it were possible, in fact, to meaningfully generalize Rózsa's use of tonality or modality in *Ben-Hur* (and any analysis of Rózsa's music in this regard presents a monumental challenge to even the most capable musical theorist), it might be noted that the Roman marches and themes tend to favor the more strident Phrygian and Mixolydian modes. Their modal colors are also, perhaps, more clearly evident to the listener since the simple phrase structures and A B A designs of the "Roman themes" require the establishment of a more-or-less functional tonal center and, at the same time, allow few modulations. The "Judean music" leans, however, toward the warmer Dorian and Aeolian modes, as in the examples just cited. Modulations within the melodic phrase are more frequent, and thus these melodies often imply derivation from far more complex folk-music scales. Most are quite clearly and significantly drawn from pentatonic scales. Nevertheless, while tonal "focus" in Rózsa's music is often elusive and at times remarkably transient, it is seldom wholly absent. His music generally reveals, in fact, a supreme devotion to the principles of functional harmony.

This is clearly evident in the case of two "basic themes" that appear prominently in the film's "Prologue." The first, entitled "The Star of Bethlehem," attempts to paint a broad scenic panorama of the quiet little town on the star-lit night of Jesus' birth. While the apparent dramatic function and the overall musical design of this melody otherwise group it with the "Judean" themes, it instead presents an exception to the prescriptions noted above, fulfilling its musical and cinematographic mission in the Mixolydian mode. At the same time, however, the harmonic accompaniment, plentifully scattered with functional leading tones (c#'s), juxtaposes an essentially *major* foundation below:

Ex. 6

In the same scene, this cue becomes intertwined with a second, more recalcitrant theme, "The Adoration of the Magi" (Ex. 7), as the camera moves closer to reveal an interior setting of the Nativity scene. Originally heard with an orchestration "celestially" dominated by a chorus of women's voices, this melody recurs with varied instrumentation throughout the film, always associated with the character of Balthazar. Ostensibly a part of the "Judean music," the most salient feature of this theme is, in fact, its undisturbed predictability and "songfulness." Its almost unbroken step-wise motion, coupled with the lack of any truly distinctive rhythmic feature, and its regular and repetitive phrase structure, impart a certain harmless innocence to the theme. At the same time, despite the insistent intrusion of a flat-6 scale degree in the accompaniment, it is also unquestionably, though somewhat benignly, *major*—the *only* principal theme in the film set in a major key.

Indeed, while Rózsa may have wished to avoid any reference to Roman or Judean influence in his musical portraiture of Balthazar, or perhaps to provide a symbolic allusion to the newborn child, this rather innocuous musical idea suggests less of the character of a foreign personage, or even a starry night, than the quiet essence of an English carol or a country garden dance:[5]

Ex. 7

Nevertheless, the melody eventually elides with the "Star of Bethlehem" material, which provides a cadential figure, effecting the completion of the musical structure and the close of the scene itself. It gives way to an onscreen call of the ram's horn, not only proclaiming the fulfillment of the prophecy, but also announcing the start of the film's "titles"-sequence.

Despite these somewhat aberrant "later" additions to the score, Rózsa had nevertheless certainly established the basic parametric contrasts that distinguish the Roman and Judean "poles," in general terms, at least, long before he returned to Hollywood, early in 1959, to begin the real task of providing a musical framework for the twenty-four reels (nearly four hours) of *Ben-Hur*. Over the next nine months,[6] working with supervising editor Margaret Booth,[7] Rózsa composed, recorded, and assembled the fifty-seven musical cues for the film. He created a remarkable two hours of music for the final edited version, including an "Overture" and "Entr'acte," and undoubtedly a good deal more which ended up on the cutting room floor.

In attempting to create a sense of musical coherence and cinematic logic within this over-sized, yet "atomized" structure, Rózsa composed approximately twenty easily recognizable "basic themes" and a number of smaller musical motives and "gestures" which would serve as fundamental building blocks for his score. Furthermore, he carefully designed these materials to reflect a sense of familial interconnectedness, through the common use of prominent melodic contours and intervals,[8] and many shared melodic and rhythmic motives which also serve to generate accompanimental figures and transitional material throughout.

Related, at times, by a sense of implied melodic variation, these materials also, in fact, *evolve* in a few cases, one from another, during the course of the drama.

Whether or not these subtle interrelationships reflect at all times a deliberate and conscious design, they unquestionably demonstrate an innate and masterful sense of musical construction. Indeed, Rózsa's adept manipulation of these carefully interrelated musical materials resulted, in this case, in the creation of a score almost totally devoid of the sort of disjointed musical dysfunction and dramaturgical redundancy which so often plagues *leitmotivic* scores. The "basic themes," along with the smaller musical materials which they generate, not only serve as an effective means for the unification of Rózsa's score, but also function as a powerfully cohesive element within the broader cinematic context of the film itself.

Exercising care to avoid a temptation to dramaturgically over-interpret or to attach unintended extra-musical meaning to Rózsa's interpolation and manipulation of these musical materials, let us briefly consider the "basic melodies" and how they function within the dramatic context of the film. Setting aside the more straightforward and generally predictable applications of these themes, it is perhaps more beneficial here to observe the more complex "thematic groupings" in order to better demonstrate Rózsa's inventive approach to the use of *leitmotivic* technique in scoring the film.

The first of these groupings involves the primary branch of *Ben-Hur*'s interwoven plot that relates the story of Ben-Hur and Messala. Several "basic themes" are required to adequately portray the complex and ever-changing relationship between them. Judah Ben-Hur, of course, has his own theme:

Ex. 8

Like the character himself, the theme is inherently confident and heroic but must undergo the many trials and changes forced upon it by the demands of the drama. Through the use of varied accompaniments, textures, orchestrations, tempi, etc., Rózsa is able to describe the many emotional responses and dramatic confrontations that define the character, ranging from a certain pensive helplessness to an almost swashbuckling optimism.

Messala, on the other hand, does not entirely command an independent theme of his own. Instead, *two* "primary themes" are employed to describe his relationship with the title character. The first is a warm and ever-"reposing" melody entitled "Friendship" (see Ex. 24). The second, however, is a determined, brooding, and even sinister portrait of their shattered brotherhood. This "Messala" theme, or more accurately, "Messala in opposition to Ben-Hur" theme, develops almost subliminally until, at last, it is heard full-force in the cue entitled "Messala's Revenge":

Ex. 9

The "Ben-Hur" theme, and this "Messala" motive, both prominently display features of the Roman *and* the Judean music. Their Roman character undoubtedly stems from the fact that both were first composed during the early stages of Rózsa's involvement in the project as a part of the Roman march "Parade of the Charioteers." For that cue, Rózsa was called upon to blatantly oppose the two themes as a prelude to the characters' ultimate confrontation in the chariot race at the Circus in Jerusalem. Recalling, however, that Ben-Hur, a Jew, and Messala, the son of a Roman tribune, grew up as inseparable friends in Jerusalem, it is not altogether out of line to speculate that, in developing these "basic themes," Rózsa sought equally to portray the common (though dual) heritage and basic similarity of the characters. Only by the force of circumstance do they come to stand against each other, each the paragon of his own intransigent people.

Their rise, or fall, to this point is carefully echoed by Rózsa's subtle manipulation and interpolation of the many additional themes that surround and influence them, both musically and dramatically, throughout the film. In the important scene which first marks the rift in their relationship, for example, we hear first a "basic theme," derived from the original "Judean theme" (see Ex. 3), describing Ben-Hur's boyhood home in Jerusalem:

Ex. 10

A common melodic feature of both themes, (a.), slightly modified in this new context, serves both as an accompanimental figure and as a perceptible musical reminiscence, recalling both melodies throughout the scene. Continually interjecting its presence against the "Friendship" theme (Ex. 24), this melodic fragment in fact provides a link to the initial presentation of the "Messala" theme (Ex. 9).

Later, in fact, as Ben-Hur returns from Rome, himself a respected and honored Roman "son," he thoughtfully anticipates his homecoming in Judea as Rózsa sounds the following melody:

Ex. 11

The expected recapitulation of the "Judean theme" (Ex. 3) at this point in the drama, seemingly confirmed by the melodic feature (a.), is in fact replaced by an altogether transformed but unmistakable variation of the theme of "Messala's Revenge." Does this musical interjection thus imply Ben-Hur's own inheritance, now transformed by the impress of his sojourn in Rome? Does he long, then, to return to his Judean homeland or to his lost friendship with Messala? Or does he somehow foresee, or dread, or perhaps now savor, his ultimate act of revenge? In a quiet and subtle fashion, Rózsa's music serves to effectively underscore not only the scene, but the dramatic question as well.

A similar, but wider-ranging sort of motivic and thematic evolution involves a "family" of "basic themes" which Rózsa employs to describe scenes of personal confrontation between the individual characters in the film and the sheer military force that confines and restrains them. Although the musical ideas associated with these dramatic and often violent encounters continue to display characteristics of the "Judean" and "Roman" polarity already established, Rózsa now draws them together in closer proximity, setting one against another, even within the same musical measure.

At the same time, he interjects new musical materials, not only to help effect this more immediate juxtaposition, but also to ascribe a particular musical character and *leitmotivic* representation to the opposition itself. In this way, he paints an effective musical picture of the oppression and despair brought about by the dominance of the Roman regime.

Most of this new material is distinctively *chromatic*, and all of its essential character and expressive potential are first revealed in a cue entitled "The Burning Desert." In this scene, a procession of Judean prisoners, including the newly conscripted Ben-Hur, is herded through the Judean desert to slavery in the awaiting Roman galleys:

Ex. 12

This is, in essence, a new "Roman" march, though its accompanimental colors reverberate the inescapable fate of the prisoners through the mournful sounds of a solemn dirge. The ebullient, tympanic V-I of the Roman march is here overcome by a ponderous ostinato, pitting a minor subdominant against tonic. (If a tonal center must be identified here, it is certainly A-flat, on the off-beat.) At the same time, the formerly triumphant dotted rhythms of Rome now confront a chromatic "Judean" triplet to create a sort of falling, almost stumbling gesture. Clearly downcast, and laden with despair, this entire melody is harmonized with parallel tritones (diminished 5ths and augmented 4ths).

Another new motivic idea introduced here is a shimmering chromatic fragment (b.), undoubtedly intended to portray the heat of the desert. This important gesture descends chromatically through the interval of an M3rd, but borrowing the B-flat from two octaves below may be seen more accurately to encompass the interval of a tritone. Often modified, but always dramatically reminiscent of this first appearance, this simple descending motive recurs throughout the score, generally providing accompanimental and transitional material, and enabling, to some extent at least, the evolution of the "basic themes" associated with this *leitmotivic* family.

It appears later in the same cue, still emphasizing the important influence of the tritone, as an accompanimental figure surrounding the "Ben-Hur" theme itself (Ex. 13), and near the end of the film, it provides a significant reminiscence of this event in the scene of Jesus' "Procession to Calvary" (Ex. 14).

Ex. 13

Ex. 14

The melodic and harmonic use of the tritone, especially in boldly descending gestures and often colored by chromatic ornamentation, represents the most salient feature of this group of themes. (Without need for further interpretation, it may in fact depict the traditional *diabolus in musica*, here working its symbolic musical evil in the drama of *Ben-Hur*.) This powerful and dissonant prescription pervades many of the most tragic scenes in the film, including those which involve Ben-Hur's imprisoned mother and sister, and is especially evident in the music associated with the "Lepers" (Ex. 15). In this context, it may also be insightful to recall the boldly descending tritone in the cue "Messala's Revenge" (see Ex. 9).

Ex. 15

In another example drawn from the cue "The Burning Desert," just a few measures after the example cited earlier, Rózsa's imposing ostinato now also reveals a repetitive and unsettling tritone (as in the "Lepers" cue) as its essential foundation:

Ex. 16

Above, however, he exposes still another new thematic idea, though it is perhaps more a musical symbol than a melody in the true sense. Here, trumpets and strings insistently and rhythmically hammer out a single pitch in harmonic opposition to the immovable ostinato below, incessantly driving to a brief but accented instant of "melodic escape," momentarily free, but immediately falling back into the captivity of the original opposition. This extremely important and pervasive musical conception, heard here in its earliest manifestation in the score, is often magnified by the use of melodic and harmonic sequence and recurs throughout in scenes of explosive tension, unendurable restraint, and impending violence. Related to Rózsa's technique of compositional "additionalism" discussed below, this idea is yet another vital feature of this thematic "family."

It appears most boldly as a theme in the famous "Rowing Scene," set once again against an imposing ostinato heavily burdened with tritones and coupled as well with a descending chromatic fragment:

Ex. 17

In an altogether different rhythmic configuration, this melodic idea reappears in the cue describing the "Leper's Search for Christ" (Ex. 18), and it is even condensed into a concise two-note motive in the "Procession to Calvary" (Ex. 19).

Ex. 18

Ex. 19

Its impact may also be noted in much of the music of the "Naval Battle" sequence, infecting even the fanfare which trumpets the start of the conflict.[9]

Ex. 20

Finally, this gesture of "melodic escape" is clearly evident in an important theme which Rózsa reserves to parallel and enhance one of the most effectively drawn of the many dramatic visual symbols that appear in the film: the symbol of *water*. First heard in the desert scene, as a cup of water given to Ben-Hur by Jesus is kicked away by a Roman soldier, this moving theme returns in the "Procession to Calvary," as Ben-Hur struggles in vain to hand a cup of water to the suffering Christ:

Ex. 21

It is significant to note once again the pervasive influence of the tritone in this cue. The melody itself encompasses the range of a diminished 5th, as do the accented fragments in measures 4 and 5, and the entire theme is set in canon, its bitonal echo "dislocated," in fact, at the interval of a tritone.

As the procession continues to the scene of the Crucifixion, the ultimate and most tragic testament to political intransigence and inescapable servitude, the plodding ostinato once again impels the action with unparalleled strength and oppressive despair.

It is important to consider still one more "family of basic themes," perhaps the most significant and readily perceptible thematic group in the film. This is the music which Rózsa designed to inveigh the spirit of Christ himself. Not a single "basic melody" but a group of *four* melodic motives, the "Christ music" dramatically and musically pervades much of the score. The first two fragments appear as the opening nine measures of the "Overture" (or in the version of the film which omits the "Overture," the music that accompanies the MGM logo):

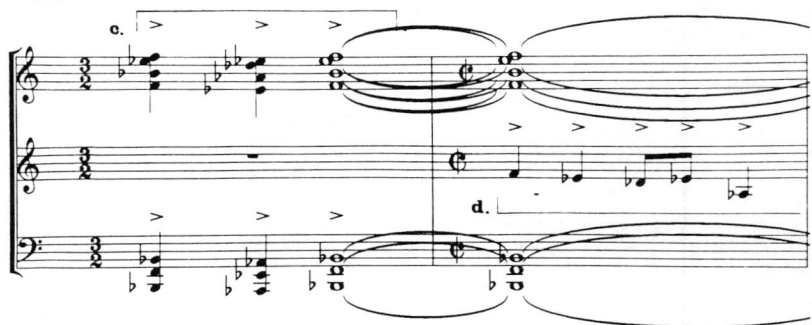

Ex. 22

The opening fanfare presents a simple M2nd lower neighbor figure (c.) which will echo throughout the film as a prominent melodic motive and accompanimental figure. It appears melodically, for example, in many of the themes, including the "water" motive just cited and the "Procession to Calvary." As an accompanimental feature, it appears in parts of the "Burning Desert" and "Leper's Search for Christ" music, slightly modified in the Nativity music (see Ex. 6), and is even prominent in the "Love Theme" (see Ex. 5).

Apart from the characteristic answer (d.), almost a signature of Rózsa's style, it is important to note the technique of melodic construction which Rózsa employs here. The three-note fanfare is immediately repeated, but with an additional note (flat 6) and a larger interval. Again it is repeated, now with an additional note (flat 7) and a still larger interval.[10] This kind of melodic and rhythmic "additionalism," ever expanding, yet focused upon a single repeated pitch, is a fundamental compositional procedure which Rózsa employs throughout to construct, unify, and in fact to energize many of the "basic themes" in *Ben-Hur*. (Look again, for example, at measures 3–7 and 7–11 of the "Ben-Hur" theme (Ex. 8). The "Friendship" theme (Ex. 24) and nearly all of the Roman marches exhibit a similar construction, together with many of the themes that reflect the "escape" gesture noted earlier, including the "Rowing" theme (Ex. 17). Furthermore, Rózsa employs this compositional "additionalism" as a device for modifying themes and developing transitional material throughout the score.

Two more parts of the "Christ music," including the "Christ theme" itself (e.), appear as the opening measures of the "Title Music." This section also employs the same technique of "additional" construction and displays once again the M2nd lower neighbor figure. Rózsa's initial answer (d. in Ex. 22), a "diatonic" pentatonic idea, is here transformed, however, to incorporate a distinctively dissonant sharp-4 scale degree (f.):

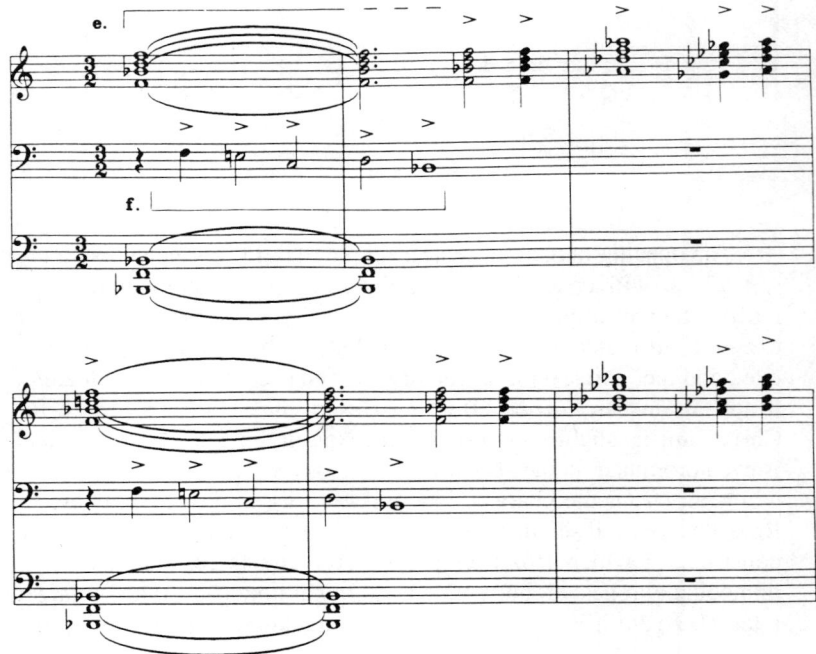

Miklós Rózsa's Ben-Hur

Ex. 23

The original fanfare (c. in Ex. 22), harmonized by the use of parallel quartal sonorities, here gives way to the bold use of parallel major triads (e.). The resulting M2nd and chromatic third harmonic relationships impart the theme with a sense of uplifting introspection and towering majesty. Belying Rózsa's more characteristically delicate and highly inventive application of this harmonic technique, this juxtaposition of major triads, consistently combined with pianissimo, non-vibrato string harmonics and the sound of an organ,[11] creates an effect guaranteed to impress even the most inattentive listener as nothing less than "celestial."

This musical, if not altogether psychological effect envelops every reference to Christ and every appearance of the holy personage on screen, recurring again and again, almost as counterpoint to the ever-present Roman marches.

A similar musical process, which also involves the use of parallel major triads and the now characteristic "question and answer" type of musical dialogue, serves to infuse the "Friendship" theme of Ben-Hur and Messala with a similarly heightened relevance:

Ex. 24

Invoking much of the character of the "Christ theme" itself, this important idea recurs only sparingly after the break in their relationship—as a quiet reminiscence of their lost brotherhood. As an ultimate symbol of reconciliation, however, it becomes the first musical phrase to comment upon the death of Christ.

Further instances of this sort of well-constructed interdependence of action and "message," dramatic inspiration and concomitant musical interplay, abound in Rózsa's score for *Ben-Hur*. His clear vision of the programmatic potential inherent in the interweaving of complex dramatic and musical ideas, coupled with his imaginative conception and design of every aspect of the score, here provides, in fact, a compendium of truly viable and effective techniques for the application of *leitmotivs* in film scoring. Much more than having merely dealt with the many challenging problems and pitfalls of the method itself, Rózsa has instead established a model and a standard for its competent use.

His composition of the score began, in fact, as it artistically should, with a perceptive assessment of the musical potential of this method as a cogently justified response to the particular challenges posed by the immense proportion and complexity of the film itself. The compositional method thus finding necessity in these cinematographic requirements, the ultimate success of the score rested upon Rózsa's own imagination and artfulness and, of course, his consummate compositional skill.

While the examples quoted here may serve to guide the interested listener to some of the essential features that distinguish the score, they only begin to suggest the remarkable inventiveness demonstrated throughout in Rózsa's adept application of the techniques of *leitmotivic* scoring to musical and visual relationships only fully perceivable through the experience of the film itself.[12]

NOTES

[1]Though brief references appear throughout the Rózsa literature, only one full-length article is entirely devoted to the subject: Mark Koldys' "Miklós Rózsa and 'Ben-Hur'" in *Pro Musica Sana*, 3, No. 3 (Fall 1974), 3–20.

[2]See Rózsa's articles, "The Music in *Quo Vadis*," *Film Music*, 11, No. 2 (Nov.–Dec. 1951), 4–10, and "*Julius Caesar*," *Film Music*, 13, No. 1 (Sept.–Oct. 1953), 7–13.

[3]The use of the *leitmotiv* as a film scoring device has, however, inspired considerable critical debate over the years. Dismissed by Leonid Sabaneev as an essentially commercial device, useful only for the "plugging" of popular tunes (*Music for the Films*, London: Pitman, 1935, p. 38), the method was panned in the strongest possible terms by Hanns Eisler and Theodor Adorno in their highly perceptive but controversial analysis of film music, *Composing for the Films* (New York: Oxford, 1947). Denouncing it as a mere compositional expedient, artistically inappropriate for the unique demands of film, they observed: "The effective technique of the past [*i.e.*, in Wagnerian opera] . . . becomes mere duplication, ineffective and uneconomical . . . Since it cannot be developed to its full musical significance in the motion picture, its use leads to extreme poverty of composition [p. 6]. . . . The composer can quote where he otherwise would have to invent [p. 4]."

[4]In *Double Life: The Autobiography of Miklós Rózsa* (New York: Hippocrene Books, 1982), p. 177.

[5]Rózsa relates (again in *Double Life*, p. 177) that Wyler wanted a certain undeniably "Christmas-y" musical background to accompany this scene, suggesting the use of the 18th-century tune "Adeste

Fideles." It was apparently only the inherent simplicity and tunefulness of Rózsa's alternative (Ex. 7) that eventually sufficed to change the director's mind. Rózsa must be credited, therefore, with preserving the stylistic integrity of his score, at least to the extent that his persistent objections prevented this nearly catastrophic intrusion.

[6]Rózsa's one-and-a-half-year involvement with *Ben-Hur* would seem a leisurely schedule for a film composer. Two other works were also completed during this period, however: one, a film score for *The World, the Flesh and the Devil*, the other, his *Sinfonia Concertante*, Op. 29 (for Piatigorsky).

[7]Booth also won an Oscar for her work on *Ben-Hur*.

[8]Note especially the use of melodic skips of an octave or P5th (or P4th) prominent in almost every important theme heard throughout the score.

[9]Incidentally, of the literally thousands of notes Rózsa penned to accompany the lengthy "Naval Battle" (nearly eight minutes in all), only a few are actually perceptible over the din of battle itself. The low-level music track was likely prepared simply as insurance against any dull moment in the action and, except for the theme noted above and some compositionally skillful "working out" of the "Ben-Hur" theme and the "Rowing motive" (Ex. 17), serves only to underplay the scene with a rather nondescript musical program of chromatic riffs and percussive sallies.

More significantly, however, Rózsa and Wyler agreed early in their collaboration that any underscoring of the famous "Chariot Race" would only detract from the visual power of the onscreen duel. This decision is much to their credit, of course, though Rózsa has, in fact, consistently displayed an intelligent sensitivity to the use of *silence* as an effective musical element in all of his films.

[10]Rather than attempting to impress upon this music any analysis in the Phrygian mode, it is better to interpret Rózsa's "modality," in this case, within the context of a free use of flat 6, flat 7, flat 2, and even sharp 4—an inheritance from the tradition of Hungarian folk music which so pervades and distinguishes the great majority of his film and concert music.

[11]Rózsa apparently balked at early suggestions that he use the Theremin as an instrumental signature for the "Christ theme." Nonetheless, the exceedingly tremulant sound that unfortunately appears on most recordings, including the soundtrack itself, seems ultimately

not far removed from that of its electronic predecessor and greatly diminishes the potentially thrilling effect which Rózsa envisioned and, in fact, notated in his manuscripts.

[12]The complete orchestral manuscripts for *Ben-Hur* now reside at the University of Wyoming. This score, together with the laserdisc recording of the film, will certainly facilitate and encourage, I hope, further study and appreciation of this important work.

Information for the present article, however, was culled from a collection of closed scores and pencil sketches, among them the scores which Rózsa prepared for the 1960 recordings by MGM (Symphony Orchestra of Rome) and Lion (North Frankenland State Symphony). I express sincere appreciation to Carolyn Davis and her staff at the George Arents Research Library in Syracuse, New York, for their efforts in making this valuable material available for my use.

A Conversation with Bernard Herrmann

Leslie T. Zador and Gregory Rose

 Bernard Herrmann was interviewed for the Los Angeles Free Press *by Leslie Zador and Gregory Rose in Herrmann's North Hollywood home in September of 1970. About two months earlier Herrmann had declined an interview, telling Zador that he had said everything there was to say and suggesting that he interview someone else. Subsequently, however, Zador received a telephone call from Norma Herrmann, the composer's wife, who said that Herrmann's producer for London Phase 4 Records, Tony D'Amato, thought that an interview in the* Free Press *would be worthwhile, and Herrmann had relented.*
 The Herrmanns soon were to be flying to London, and there was a problem concerning the care of their dogs during their absence. The taped interview is interrupted several times by telephone conversations between Norma and her veterinarian and the ensuing discussions with her husband. Herrmann's concern was such that he begged his wife not to be upset, when actually it was he who was upset to the point of tears, while she was rather matter-of-fact about the situation. These interruptions have been omitted from the transcript, although one exchange is perhaps worth preserving. Norma explains to Zador and Rose that "this man's animals are the most important things in the world." Retorts Herrmann, "What do you think, film music is?"
 Except for these domestic intervals, the conversation is printed virtually verbatim. No attempt has been made to smooth the transcript of hesitations and false starts—a process that often gives published interviews an unnatural formality. In a further effort to capture Herrmann's personality, I have also retained his syntax and his occasional (and intentional) poor grammar. He usually spoke in a low,

growlish voice, and his pronunciation and accent were those of a man born and raised in New York City.

At the time of the interview, Gregory Rose was employed at KFAC, a Los Angeles radio station that specializes in playing recordings of classical music. Leslie Zador is the son of the noted composer, Eugene Zador.—Ed.

HERRMANN: How's your dad?

ZADOR: He's pretty good. He's written a new piece, *Sketches for Orchestra*, which he's kind of excited about. How did you get my phone number?

HERRMANN: Out of the phone book.

NORMA: I rang the *Free Press*, and they said they didn't know anything, but then they gave me a number where somebody might.

ZADOR: Right. I don't work at the *Free Press* per se. I work for a typesetting shop as a typesetter. We just do the *Free Press*.

NORMA: You know, when I said he didn't know what the *Free Press* was, he didn't quite. In a review of his Hitchcock record somebody once wrote he knew how to create the "psychedelic" experience, and he said to me, "What's this word mean?" [*She laughs; then, to her husband:*] You still don't know, do you?

HERRMANN: No. Why?

NORMA: I just find it interesting that somebody doesn't know all this stuff that everybody else knows.

HERRMANN: Oh. [*To Zador:*] So your father's in good shape. That's good.

ZADOR: Yeah, he's pretty good for a guy who's about 75 years old.

HERRMANN: Well, that's not old.

A Conversation with Bernard Herrmann

ZADOR: Your wife, over the telephone, seemed concerned about other interviews that you've had where you didn't quite get what you wanted across, where they censored some of your comments.

HERRMANN: Well, no. They didn't censor my comments. They went off and got other guys' opinions, but they didn't say who they were. And they said I was a liar. And I just told them to get the hell out of my life. I mean, I'm not interested in that. You ask me, and then you go behind my back to some guy who says I don't know what I'm talking about. Why don't you print his name? Tell me who says I don't know what I'm talking about so I can answer him back. But they do it all the time. So I don't really give interviews for that reason. In this town particularly they'll say, "Well, a colleague says . . ." or "another composer says . . ." So I called them and asked, "Who the hell is he? Why didn't you go interview him instead of me?"

ZADOR: Would this be another composer who'd be discussing your work?

HERRMANN: No. I make a statement about something, and they'd refute what I said by quoting somebody else; but they never say who it was. I must say that's one of the real reasons I don't give any interviews. I mean, uh, this town . . . these guys they all come to see me, Kevin Thomas or whatever his name is, the fellow at the *Times*, they ask you and then they quote just the opposite of what you say. So who needs it? I don't need that.

ZADOR: You won't get that from me. Don't worry about that. I'd like to start by asking you what you're doing at present?

HERRMANN: Well, what's the subject you want to cover? Then I'll be able to tell you.

ZADOR: Well, I'd like to cover both your career as a symphonic composer and as a composer for films.

HERRMANN: There's no difference between being a composer for one thing and the other. You just have a career as a composer. Whether you write occasionally for television, for films, or for symphony, I don't

Bernard Herrmann with his dog Twi at Big Bear Lake, California, about 1970 (*photo courtesy of Steven Smith*).

A Conversation with Bernard Herrmann

see that there's any difference. It's all part of the life of being a composer. I mean, I don't think that even a great man like Mozart, a great genius like that, thought he was not being a composer when he wrote some ballroom music or when he was writing a symphony. That's part of being a composer. I mean, I think the reason you asked that question is most people in this town who say they're film composers are not composers at all. They just farm the music out to ghost-writers. They can't write. They couldn't write four bars on their own, or orchestrate it, or write down the notes even.

ZADOR: I suppose it would be libelous if we wanted to mention any of the names in print.

HERRMANN: Well, there's nothing that you have to mention them by name. It's common knowledge. It's been written about. I get telephone calls all the time from people who want me to ghost-write for them. This town is full of . . . I think there're more ghost-writers here in music or in scripts than there are . . . it's the great unsung profession.

ZADOR: I remember my father telling me that he went to the premiere of a film called *Raintree County*, which was supposedly scored by Johnny Green, and during the intermission he was introduced to Reel #1, Reel #2, Reel #3, 4, and so forth. How does a composer with a big name get to a position where he can farm his music out?

HERRMANN: Because they have contempt for what they're doing. They feel that pictures are just a lot of crap, and that's all. Why should they bother? The producers are just buying the composer's name, a name that will sell. The producers don't care what the composers give them.

ZADOR: But how do the composers get to such an elaborate position in the first place?

HERRMANN: Well, it has got to do with the fact that some fellow wrote one little tune that somebody liked or became a good seller, or was a friend of somebody, or he was "it" for four seconds. And then he maintains he gets so much work he couldn't do it . . . he got other people to do it, and uses it.

ZADOR: My father did that for a few people also, by the way.

HERRMANN: Well, there you are. So you should really ask him. He knows more about the subject than I do. The reason that those kind of people might say that you can be a composer for this and only a film composer for that . . . you know what I mean?

ZADOR: You're talking about the people who ghost-write scores now?

HERRMANN: No. I mean these composers that seem to think writing a film and writing something else is different. It isn't different. It's all the same. But to them it's not the same because they're not composers at all.

ZADOR: In the last six or seven years, film music has become pretty awful. The new crop of composers . . . their music doesn't enhance, it detracts from the film.

HERRMANN: Crappy films with crappy music for a crappy audience. For Christ's sake. That's why it's what it is; it's what they want. Water finds its level. If you have an audience standard, who care more, you have better music. You have better pictures. Today, every half-wit's a director of films. The less he knows, the more "original" he is.

ZADOR: But once we had scores like *North by Northwest* and *Vertigo*; before that we had *Citizen Kane* and *The Devil and Daniel Webster*.

HERRMANN: There were a lot of good scores written, because there were interesting films. But today, what are they?

ZADOR: I heard one this year that was pretty good: Jerry Goldsmith's score for *Patton*. That's about the only one.

ROSE: He seems to be the only serious composer writing for films now. You haven't done a score since *Twisted Nerve*.

A Conversation with Bernard Herrmann 215

HERRMANN: I did one called *The Battle of Neretva*. It isn't out yet. It's a Yugoslav film.

ROSE: But you say that your concert music comes first?

HERRMANN: I didn't say that at all. I mean I'm a composer. You write what you're writing, that's all. It doesn't make any difference. Concert music isn't any more sacred than any other music. You just write music as you want to write it. What makes concert music so great? You live in this city . . . how often does the orchestra here play anything by anybody? You got a bunch of kids who think they can play the *avant-garde* music of 1920. They got all kind of courage of amoebas. They don't believe in anything. Why don't they play the contemporaries? I played Charlie Ives when it was even a filthy word to even mention his name. Now they play the fashionable, voguish modern composers. That's all they care about. Richard Strauss *Symphonia Domestica*. What a weird city: it's got to make up the deficit of the symphony orchestra by going to the East Coast. Why can't they play commissioned works every year the way the Boston Symphony did or the New York Philharmonic before Lennie Bernstein got there? I mean, you mustn't make something holy about a concert hall; it isn't.

ZADOR: I see what you mean. [*To Rose:*] To give you an example of what Mr. Herrmann is talking about, he wrote an opera called *Wuthering Heights* and part of the music of Act I, scene i he used in a score called *The Ghost and Mrs. Muir*.

HERRMANN: No, I didn't. That's f'Chr . . . completely false.

ZADOR: But it sounds just like it.

HERRMANN: That's because it happens to be me. I was the composer of both. I sound like myself. It didn't come from that picture, and I resent that. It doesn't. I mean, I have certain earmarks as a composer, and if it shows up in my film music or in my opera or my symphony or string quartet, that's my music. I mean, hell, Copland sounds like Copland no matter what he's writing. Any composer sounds like himself no matter what he's doing. I mean Prokofiev, uh,

War and Peace has got a lot of his film music, it sounds like, but that's nothing to do with *War and Peace* being a great opera, and both things were written by Prokofiev.

ZADOR: Well, then that's just my point. It all sounds characteristically like Bernard Herrmann's music, and one *could* put portions of the music *The Ghost and Mrs. Muir* in your opera, I think . . .

HERRMANN: No, you couldn't. Because they're totally different. Only thing that might be, is stylistic music. It's the style of my own style.

ROSE: The structure's not the same.

HERRMANN: No, of course not. Might be a few notes that are coincidentally like it, but that's all.

ZADOR: The salami is awfully good.

HERRMANN: Yeah, I didn't make it. Where did you find out that it sounded like *The Ghost and Mrs. Muir*? That interests me. Where did you get this bit of startling information?

ZADOR: I saw *The Ghost and Mrs. Muir* on television a couple times, and then got the record of your opera.

HERRMANN: Well, there might be . . . there's a couple of phrases that I'm very fond of might sound alike, but so what? Who the hell cares? What's that got to do, one or the other?

ZADOR: They're both good.

HERRMANN: Yeah, but that's nothing to do with it. I didn't take somebody else's music. It's my own music. It's the way I write. So if it sounds like something else that I wrote, I can't help that. Bach wrote ten thousand pieces. They all sound in a certain way alike, 'cause he used a certain style in which to write music. Hell, Miklós Rózsa has written a hundred pieces. They all sound alike too, because that's his

A Conversation with Bernard Herrmann

style as a composer, or Shostakovitch, or anybody else. Each composer has his own fingerprints. But he doesn't take from one and put to the other. It's just that's how it is.

ZADOR: You conducted the CBS Orchestra for Orson Welles at the time of the "War of the Worlds" broadcast. I think that your connection with Orson Welles, the broadcast, and so forth would be of interest to our readers.

HERRMANN: I don't want to go into all that. I'm not interested in doing my life's story.

ZADOR: Do you think you could tell us just a little, though?

HERRMANN: Well, I had a long association with Orson Welles before he made *Kane*. And that was only one radio broadcast we did.

ROSE: Did you enjoy working with Mr. Welles?

HERRMANN: Yes, very much.

ZADOR: How did you meet him?

HERRMANN: Oh, I don't remember. That's forty years ago, forty-five.

ZADOR: Did you find him easy to get along with?

HERRMANN: I always find difficult people easy. I only find glad-harrys difficult and vacuous. Nice guys are difficult. It's because they're a bunch of empty-heads, that's why they're nice guys. They pretend to be nice guys. It's a disguise. They're not nice. They're vicious, vindictive people who make sure that anything good hasn't got a chance.

ZADOR: Then Orson Welles, who's a difficult person, gave you a chance . . .

HERRMANN: He didn't give me any chance! I gave him a chance. I had a job, and he was just an actor who we used. What the hell? He didn't give me any job!

ZADOR: Well, for *Citizen Kane* and *The Magnificent Ambersons* . . .

HERRMANN: He didn't give me a job. It was to his advantage to have me do the music for him. He didn't give me a job, or break, or anything. I did so much music for him, I was the man he wanted to do the films. It wasn't a question of you give somebody a job, or a break. For Christ's sakes, what is it working there, an accounting department?

ZADOR: A lot of times a film composer can write a score, and then the director will come to him and tell him he doesn't like it; he likes what the composer did in his last score.

HERRMANN: They never told me that, because I don't work for those kind of people. I tell them to get somebody else, and leave the job.

ZADOR: So you would say that you've had control over . . .

HERRMANN: Every score I've ever done, I've written exactly what I wanted to write.

ZADOR: Have you selected the passages in the picture?

HERRMANN: Yes, I do that. That's my profession, not theirs.

ZADOR: Well, you're sure good at it.

HERRMANN: Well, that's my talent. What do I need some half-wit to tell me what he thinks?

ROSE: You say that a composer is a composer, and I agree with you. But don't you also think that a composer must have a sense for cinema to be a film composer?

A Conversation with Bernard Herrmann

HERRMANN: Yes, certainly. Puccini was a great opera composer, but he couldn't write a symphony. Or at least his mind didn't think that way. You have to have a dramatic sense to be a good cinema composer. But not anymore, because cinema music today is only hoping to find a pop song or a pop hit. They don't care about the picture.

ROSE: That seemed to be coming for a while over the years, gradually. And now it seems to be . . .

HERRMANN: Complete now. It's part of the pop culture we're now exposed to. All film and television music today sounds exactly the same. It's made by one machine. It's stupid. It has no originality. It has no identity with the characters.

ROSE: Are you still associated with Alfred Hitchcock?

HERRMANN: No, I haven't worked with Hitchcock for many years, not since *Torn Curtain*. We had a disagreement about *Torn Curtain*.

ROSE: How did that come about?

HERRMANN: Well, it was not him. The studio wanted a pop score, and I said I'm not a pop composer . . . get a pop composer. So I didn't do it. And he went along with them, but it was a mistake in judgment, because a good score would have helped the picture. A pop score helped ruin it. [*John Addison wrote a second score, which was used.*]

ZADOR: But still, what made me so angry . . .

HERRMANN: Well, what are you worried about angry? You've got to face the fact that the people who make pictures are, you know, vacuous stupid people, and they only know what they read on the charts. They think, "We'll have a great pop score for *Torn Curtain* and we'll sell ten million records," and of course what *Torn Curtain* needed was music that didn't make these people into ludicrous TV characters, but into reality. So instead they got a kind of pop-y, simple kind of TV music like the rest of their product. They've done a great job to strangle Hitchcock.

ZADOR: You made a remark earlier that the difficult people, you find, are the easiest to get along with.

HERRMANN: They know what they're doing. They're not "doing their thing." They're artists. Anybody can "do their thing." What they call "doing their thing" means you don't know what the hell you're doing, and you're hopin' how it's gonna be all right. [*Rose and Zador laugh.*]

ZADOR: I suppose a guy like Orson Welles, if he said, "I want Bernard Herrmann to score *Citizen Kane* for me," and somebody gave him a hard time, he'd fight 'em.

HERRMANN: Yeah, but it wasn't that way.

ZADOR: I've heard from Miklós Rózsa that Alfred Hitchcock doesn't know very much about music.

HERRMANN: No, but he knows, uh . . . I had a very nice association with him for many years.

ZADOR: How did that begin?

HERRMANN: He asked me to do *The Trouble with Harry*. I mean, you seem to have an idea that you need a patronage in order to get yourself a film. They asked me because they thought I was the right man to do it. Today it's not done by people who got the right man. Every job is an opportunity for your friends who have as little talent as you have. I mean, that's how you get a job. You get a job today if the first requisite is that you have absolutely no talent. You're a nice guy who won't rock their boat. Whatever it is. That's why the business is where it is today.

ZADOR: What I meant when I asked you about how you began with Hitchcock . . .

HERRMANN: Well, I had already done forty films, so he wanted me to do a film, so he wrote me a letter and said will I do it, so I said yes. What has to be more than that?

A Conversation with Bernard Herrmann

ROSE: Have you ever accepted a film that you have regretted afterwards?

HERRMANN: Yeah, a lot of 'em, but I don't want to talk about it. Everybody does.

ZADOR: Which scores do you care for the most of the ones you've done?

HERRMANN: I like them all, but I don't have any favorites particularly. I forget about them after I do them. I don't ever think about them after I finish. I don't remember them, I don't wanna. It's always a surprise to me when I hear them again. You can't go on to write new music and think about old music.

ZADOR: It's encouraging that years after these pictures came out, we can hear the music now for the first time on record.

HERRMANN: Well, a new one's coming out in November. It'll have *Kane* and different ones ... *Kane, Jane Eyre, Kilimanjaro*.

ZADOR: *Citizen Kane*? That won't be the same ...

HERRMANN: Well, it's a different company; it's the same music.

ZADOR: Will it have *The Devil and Daniel Webster*?

HERRMANN: Yeah.

ZADOR: But *The Devil and Daniel Webster* and *Citizen Kane* take up an album alone.

HERRMANN: Well, it's different music, not the suites. I don't mind. You can have as many performances of the same piece ... I like it. I don't think a performance on a record is the definitive thing anyhow. I think records are a self-defeating process, because once the piece is performed, no matter how brilliantly, after two or three times you've had it.

ROSE: Has your view of the music changed? With respect to tempos, anything else?

HERRMANN: I don't think that way. I think that music lives by each performance being different. That's what's essentially the matter with all pop music and everything. That's the reason I think you sell more records, is people get . . . they don't really know, but they get fed up with the same repetition. Even the greatest performance by Toscanini, after a while you say, "It's no good; I heard that now."

ZADOR: Do you have an ash tray for me?

HERRMANN: I don't smoke, but I'll get you one. I gave it up a year ago.

ROSE: In your film scores, *Psycho* and *Vertigo*, the performances on the record are different. The overall conducting on the record is different from the way it is in the film. I wonder if you could elaborate on that.

HERRMANN: Well, one was the tempo for the film, and the other is the tempo for a concert piece. The tempo that's used in the film is based upon visual relationships. In a straight piece of music, the relationships are musical.

ROSE: And if you had made the record immediately after the film . . .

HERRMANN: It still would have been different. The film has adjustments that are made for the film. Who says that a piece has got to be the same? That's why I hate soundtrack performances, there's something wrong with them, because they're catching cues. And it's fine with the film, but it's not fine for music. They'll speed it up to catch some broad falling down the stairs. And it works in the picture marvelously, but then when you listen to it on the soundtrack album, you wonder why it's getting so fast on me . . . what's it all about?

ROSE: Well one part, in the love music from *Vertigo*, it has this stillness about it, this building to a crescendo, because you have this steady tempo . . .

HERRMANN: Well, you couldn't have that in the picture, because the picture jumped too much and cut across with the montaging. I don't like my soundtrack albums. I never play them. I don't even have one in the house. They've been all given away for that reason. I love it in the picture. Because film music in a picture is different. It's like accompanying a singer. You go down to an opera house, and you don't worry the orchestra is playing the "Habanera" differently than it is on the record, because the singer at that performance is doing it differently. Music is a living art. It's not a gelatined art. And all conductors play my works . . . everybody plays it different. I love it. I think that's what music is about. I don't understand Stravinsky who thinks music has got to be exactly one way and no other way.

ROSE: I don't recall him saying that.

HERRMANN: Well, he does. He fusses all the time. It's too slow; it's too fast; you didn't follow the metronome; you didn't do this; you didn't do that. I know. I know him very well. He's a very, very great man, but I think he's wrong on that point. Because music is a fluid art; it's a living art. And "living art" means that each time it's played it's reborn. So it's no point in your wanting to go hear whatever the piece is and wanting it just like you heard it before. Hell, I mean, you can hear Toscanini do the Beethoven *Eroica* symphony fifty times in his career . . . well I heard him do it ten times . . . and each one was different than the other. And when I said something to him about it . . . it was different from last year . . . he said, "Oh yes, last year I was a fool." Because that's the convictions. You're talking now about film music, but today's music for film isn't film music, it's one steady beat and it goes on no matter what the hell they're doing. Nothing fits, nothing works. They just play . . . it goes along with . . . instead of music being *with* the picture, it's what I call, "goes along" it; it's another strip of sound.

ZADOR: It works against the film.

HERRMANN: Yeah, it just goes along—against it or with it—it doesn't matter how it falls. It's like Muzak.

ROSE: There seems to be a certain soulfulness and literary quality that films have been lacking recently. Films seem to lack a point of view, and an emotional potency. It would help to have a better score for a contemporary picture; but, as you seem to say, it's just part of the pop culture we're in.

HERRMANN: Yeah, and besides that it has to do with other things. Today's world is all full of only sensationalism. And a beat score in a picture that just deals with the physical response, whether it be to nudity or to drugs or to the music, but it has nothing to do with the higher level of intellectual and emotional feeling. I mean, a picture like *Jane Eyre* makes no sense today, really. Today, it would be either she goes to bed with him or she don't. All the nuance of a story or people's relationship to one another is not portrayed, therefore the music that they have that "goes along" is primitive music that suits the inarticulateness of the story itself. Look at the language. It comes all from the drunken dance bands of back rooms. It's become the current language of intellectual communication. "Get with it." "Get off it." You tell me what the hell it means. You know what it means, and I do. But look at it in daylight, and you tell me what the word means.

ROSE: Do you think it's a passing phase? Do you think the higher standards will return?

HERRMANN: No, I don't think it's a passing phase. At the present moment, it's not a passing phase. It'll only pass when a new generation of young people come in who have different attitudes to life, that's all.

ZADOR: You know, *Jane Eyre* was shown recently at one of the revival houses. So there is a "silent minority" that still likes quality films very much.

HERRMANN: Well, I was asked to do a film on *Wuthering Heights*. I didn't do it, because when I read the script, there wasn't one word of Brontë in it. Not one word of the language. "Oh," they said, "we don't have to use that crappy old-fashioned language. It's not relevant today." So I said, "Then why do *Wuthering Heights*?" "Oh," they said, "we want to make it into a boot-hill western kind of picture." I said, "Then why do this great novel? Why don't you do a great western?" Why take characters who are linked to the living English language and to an attitude ... And it starts off, the first thing they have to do is, they have to have a great sex life. Well, the story of *Wuthering Heights* is that Cathy and Heathcliff didn't have a sex life together. They had other things that existed for them that were much more important in their lives: the way they both responded to the living environment that they were in, in nature. That's why they both married different people. Well, this point is not done in the picture at all.

ROSE: It's totally distorted.

HERRMANN: Well, I don't know; I don't know why they bothered to make it. Anyhow, I didn't do it. Michel Legrand will do it; I'm sure he'll give them just what they're looking for. But I saw no reason to have any part to do with the debasing of something beautiful.

ZADOR: Michel Legrand is doing it?

HERRMANN: That's what they said.

ROSE: Michel Legrand ...

HERRMANN: Well, that's his business.

ROSE: He did an album which I like very much called "I Love Paris." It's a very nice album of popular French tunes, and he never seems to have done anything like that again. He became a very, very happy composer, like so many others I know of.

HERRMANN: Well, I don't know why you're really interested in what he does, except I was interested in what they wanted me to do to pictures, so I'm telling you why I didn't want to do it. And also they told me they were going to have Olivier, Richardson, Susan Hampshire, all kinds of important actors. But none of these actors ... I guess after they read the script, they reacted to it the way I did, so they had nothing to do with it. I mean, I think in your life, you have to have certain lines where you don't go past.

ZADOR: Who are playing the parts?

HERRMANN: They got totally unknowns, small people, doing it. I don't know, they might be fine for it. I'm not grumbling about the casting. I realize that everybody gets older and you have to use different people. But I don't think you have a right to use the name of *Wuthering Heights* and then write a lot of garbage and say, "Well, that's the new way to look at it." I don't need their new way of looking at *Wuthering Heights*. I like the old way. The great way.

ZADOR: So do I. Fantastic opera!

HERRMANN: So, what's the point of doing it, it's the way it is today? Today, for kicks, you take some of the great things of the past and you make fun of them. We've always had vacuous, stupid, empty-headed people like that in the arts ... paint you pictures of a Mona Lisa with a mustache and then you're supposed to take them seriously as artists. Why don't you paint your own pictures without Mona Lisa and create your own world the way da Vinci created his? I mean, the great masters didn't create their work poking fun of somebody else or improving the vision of somebody else. You know what I mean.

ROSE: Of course. Do you plan to do a film again soon?

HERRMANN: Well, if they ask me, I'll do one. They haven't asked me.

ROSE: There's nothing in the works right now?

HERRMANN: No. I don't miss it.

ROSE: Are you currently composing anything?

HERRMANN: Yeah, I'm working on some things of mine, but I'd rather not talk about them. I never talk about works till they're finished.

ROSE: Do you try to compose every day?

HERRMANN: No.

ZADOR: When will we hear your symphony on record?

HERRMANN: Well, they want to record it, but I feel I have to revise it a lot, and I'm not ready to do that yet.

ZADOR: And your Christmas operas.

HERRMANN: Yeah, I did a Christmas opera, *A Christmas Carol*, with Maxwell Anderson, which is still shown on television.

ZADOR: Do you have a recording of it?

HERRMANN: No, I don't have a recording of it, no. Fredric March was the lead in it. And now I read they're making a new *Christmas Carol* with Bacharach, and you'd think this was the first one, this is the only one that was ever . . . it's got to become the big perennial. Well, this *Christmas Carol* that I did fifteen years ago is played every Christmas all over the world . . . on television. It was the first television musical, really.

ZADOR: It will be on this year?

HERRMANN: It's on every year. CBS shows it some time or other. It's in color. Fredric March and Basil Rathbone, and Marilyn Horne sang for me the music. That was her first big break.

ROSE: She's a marvelous singer.

HERRMANN: Yeah. When I got her, she was just a chorus singer with Roger Wagner.

ROSE: She stopped singing large vocal roles. It seems she doesn't want to do that any more. It's unfortunate.

HERRMANN: I have a lot of works of mine that aren't recorded. But there's no point . . .

ZADOR: I know I've asked you this several times, but I have to ask you again: can any of this material be made available? Are there any tapes we could copy?

HERRMANN: I haven't got them.

ZADOR: So there's nothing of Bernard Herrmann's that isn't on commercial records?

HERRMANN: That's right. All the rest is not worth trying for. I haven't got them. A lot of that stuff was all put on acetates. In those days, they all had glass backing. They break by themselves. The grooves break down. Even if you put it in a vault. The other day I took one out, it was all just fine glass dust... the way the acetate just breaks up. Even RCA had that with a lot of Toscanini they've never been able to clean up.

ROSE: Yes. How much of the year do you spend in England?

HERRMANN: About six months a year.

ROSE: And I take it you compose there also?

HERRMANN: Well, I compose when I feel like it. I don't believe in composing unless you have to.

ROSE: Do you find it easier to compose in Europe?

HERRMANN: I find it easier to compose any place if I get an idea, that's all. I don't compose all that much because today one lives in an environment where the romantic attitude towards the art is looked down on. Today, everything's got to be fashionable with some group or other. "Doing your thing" must be doing your thing in relationship to the approval of another group that're doing their thing. It has to be with them. That's why today you got electronic school, you got your synthesizer school, you got the percussion school, you got all this rubbish where the orchestra makes up what it likes.

ZADOR: It almost seems as though films and concert music...

A Conversation with Bernard Herrmann

HERRMANN: It's all the same rubbish. It's not music. And the audience is smarter than all of them. It's bored.

ZADOR: Which composers do you admire?

HERRMANN: Oh, I admire many of them. I admire many, many composers. I admire any composer who, I feel, is genuine, whether I'm sympathetic to him or not. I only don't like what I consider opportunists and frauds.

ROSE: Are there any composers in your youth that you felt were influential on your own music?

HERRMANN: When I was young? Well, Ives was an influence on me, because I knew him when I was about sixteen.

ZADOR: And you premiered much of his music?

HERRMANN: Yes.

ZADOR: Was that in England?

HERRMANN: No, in America. We did six weeks of his works for CBS. Across the whole network. Five concerts a week for six weeks. Thirty concerts altogether.

ROSE: How was the CBS orchestra?

HERRMANN: One of the greatest orchestras of the history of orchestras. Just like NBC. A great orchestra.

ROSE: Why could it happen then and not now?

HERRMANN: Because it was a different time. The people who were in charge of the popular entertainment felt that they owed something to the people who had other needs ... that fourteen million people listening to a symphony concert was important enough to spend money to supply them with music. Not today. Fourteen million people is regarded, "Take it away ... get rid of it ... no good." The only place where you still have it [is] in England, where the BBC has Channel Three, where they do have a symphony orchestra and they continue with the commissioning and playing of new works. I think if I was a composer today, a young man today, rather than was going to be a composer, I wouldn't; I'd give it up. I see no opportunity today for a young composer. Because you can fake being a young conductor with publicity and all kind of rubbish, but you can't fake being a composer. I mean, when I was a youngster, and people got a Koussevitzky to do a symphony, they couldn't have a symphony where the orchestra made it up as they went along. You tell me . . . you're more in touch with it than I am . . . who are the young people today who are composing? I don't ever see their music or hear it.

ROSE: I don't listen to much of it myself. There's . . .

HERRMANN: Well, there's something wrong.

ROSE: There are many composers today who are under thirty and are composing.

HERRMANN: I think if you want to do yourself a good turn and make a lot of fuss, why don't you attack the L.A. Philharmonic as to why the devil they don't play contemporary works. I have it on the best word around here that we were told, from Miklós Rózsa too, that the management don't like playing local composers.

ZADOR: Why?

HERRMANN: I don't know. I didn't make the rule. They make it. We're local composers. *Wuthering Heights*, I know, I submitted to Dr. Popper at UCLA. He said, "I'm not interested in an opera by a local composer." He didn't even look at it. Local composer.

ROSE: I suppose that if Stravinsky had handed him a score . . .

HERRMANN: What did they do for Stravinsky while he was here, come to think about it, or Schoenberg? Nothing! No, they didn't do anything. When Schoenberg and Stravinsky lived here, they didn't get played here. No, I'm only pointing out to you, I think it's terrible times. I think that's why I didn't really want to give you the interview. I find it so depressing I'd rather not talk about it. I feel it's like the Dark Ages have settled on the arts, and just a few people are gonna preserve the text. Some people have got to preserve the beauty of the past. It's important to preserve the past, because you can't have a present and a future if you have no past. I mean, just because you have people that have no training and have no ability to transmit their ideas in a great art form, there's no reason that the art must be destroyed. I mean, it would be like if nobody could paint a decent picture, we must burn Titian. I mean this is the most brutal attitude. I don't know what's going to become . . . some people got to preserve the great culture of the past. I'm not saying to be a reactionary. I'm saying, write for anything you like, but let me hear what you've written!

ZADOR: I think they *are* playing the works of the past, because they don't have anyone to write today. You certainly hear Beethoven . . .

HERRMANN: Yeah, but that's only because of the fact that you have a lot of music today on local stations because they're first of all a bunch of pirates. They play records and pay nothing for playing them. They're getting free music.

ZADOR: But I'm talking about symphony orchestras.

HERRMANN: Yeah, but suppose they had to pay $5.00 every time they played a Beethoven symphony, do you think you'd get it? Symphony orchestra! I have friends of mine, they don't want to play a piece of Ravel because they have to pay $25.00 for the rental of the parts. I had a friend the other day call me up, shocked because there was $50.00 rental to do *The Carnival of Animals*. The Saint-Saëns estate is not to make any . . . not even a drink of beer from it! And all these stations the same. That's why you don't have the NBC and CBS orchestras. Because at that time they didn't tolerate the playing of records on the air. When radio was the thing, both networks said if you hear it on NBC or CBS, it's alive. You had the Philharmonic, or the Boston, or the Philadelphia, or whatever.

But today . . . these things . . . even copyright music, I receive nothing for it, because they refuse to pay to ASCAP or BMI anything. And the other day I had to call them up . . . I'm sitting listening to

Mozart, and they finished, and the guy says, "You know, today I died," and proceeded to get me sick to my stomach while he's doing a plug for Forest Lawn. And the station said, "Oh, well, we don't scrutinize what they . . . they only buy time." But I said, "The FCC says *you* are supposed to scrutinize what they say. It's *offensive* what he's talking about." And I said, "I don't understand. You are a station that plays classical music, and your commercials are full of the stinkingest lousy rock music, so commercial and stinking! What makes you think that a fellow who sits and listens to a Mozart quartet wants a commercial with a background of that?"

ROSE: Which station are you talking about?

HERRMANN: Your station.

ROSE: Oh yes, I know that very well.

HERRMANN: Christ, I for one am not going to listen to it. I said, "There are stations that play rock-and-roll all day. And when they have a Tang ad, good, so it's like the music they play. But you are playing a Haydn symphony, and you break in at the end of the second movement with this outlandish shriek and caterwauling."

ROSE: I know. It bothers me more than you can imagine. But, it's just the . . .

HERRMANN: Look, you're asking me why I think . . . I'm explaining to you why, in answer to him, that Beethoven and Bach and Mozart are not popular composers. It's just that their material is available without any charge. If they had to pay, it wouldn't be that available. Because in England you have to pay. The English don't allow anybody . . . you have to pay for everything you do. And if you play a gramophone record, you can only play it . . . I think twice in the first year after it's issued for publicity purposes and then the Union fines you. You have to pay every musician who's played in it.

ROSE: On any recordings?

A Conversation with Bernard Herrmann

HERRMANN: Any recordings. They stop it. They say, "You don't have enough? Hire more musicians." That's the idea! Look at the BBC. They have there altogether about four hundred musicians. They have four symphony orchestras. I admit many of the records might be better musically than there, than the Scottish Orchestra, but it's still the Scottish Orchestra that's sitting in Glasgow playing the concert that you're listening to. And I feel . . . one of the sad things about it is that none of these stations like your or . . . there's so many . . . YMCA in New York . . . I mean, they don't do anything for music. They don't have one program a month where they commission composers to write a string quartet or a quintet and subsidize it and get a quartet to rehearse and play it.

ZADOR: Did they used to?

HERRMANN: All stations used to. At CBS we had ten commissions a year. Ten American composers a year were commissioned to write anything they liked. Symphonies, anything else; opera even. They made as much as $10,000 a commission.

ZADOR: People liked classical music more a long time ago than they do today.

HERRMANN: They don't like classical music. They get it because it's available.

ZADOR: Only 8% of all records sold are classical music, and it's going down.

HERRMANN: It's less than that. But I'm only saying to you that I . . . you asked me how I feel about it. I don't think that people love the music of the past. I think the orchestras here, our symphony orchestras, play Brahms and Beethoven and all of that because the audiences are comfortable with it. I mean, at least they're not bothered too much. And you can't tell me that the audience go, and they got to hear Brahms conducted by a fellow who has never conducted Brahms in his life. You know, the two things make no sense. So it's a show— somebody coming on, putting on a big show. It's what Reynaldo Hahn, the great French composer says: "I never saw why we go to a concert to admire a conductor's dance routines instead of what kind of sounds he makes in an orchestra." But it will pass. Everything passes and changes.

ZADOR: Look. The average soundtrack lasts about a year. After a year you can't get it. Now, years and years after these pictures came out, your records are doing well. So somewhere, they *do* recognize . . .

HERRMANN: But it's not recognized by the people who make pictures today. Pictures today don't want that audience, to buy their records. They're looking for another audience. They're looking for a different standard. What they hope is that you'll have a piece like *Doctor Zhivago*, which will sell millions. That's what they want. They made more money out of the record of *Zhivago* than they made out of the film.

ZADOR: Did they?

HERRMANN: Yeah.

ROSE: That's incredible.

ZADOR: That's funny.

HERRMANN: But you know what the chances are of that happening again. Very slight.

ZADOR: How many copies did that record sell?

HERRMANN: I don't know, it sold millions. But as far as I'm concerned . . . I mean, you should write music because it's not "doing your thing" or any of that. You're doing it because part of the thing of being alive and being an artist is in the pursuit of beauty, and music is a beautiful art—if not the greatest of all the arts. For that reason. It's the kind of beauty that lives in time and space and in each performance over and over again. All different kinds, to keep revealing what's in a piece. There's no one performance of a piece that can ever reveal the whole piece. That's why Beethoven is Beethoven. You can play Beethoven . . . conductor Stokowski once said to me, he said, "I might have conducted it in my life," he said, "in fifty years maybe three hundred times." He says, "And I'm still unhappy the way I do it, but Beethoven wrote it and said 'finished.'"

ZADOR: But it's not finished.

HERRMANN: It's not finished. It goes on and on and on. Each performance reveals something new about it again. And the young people who cut away from themselves the unique experience of being involved with the great arts . . .

ZADOR: I must turn over the tape.

[*As the tape is turned over, Herrmann autographs his guests' records. He becomes interested in Zador's four-track reel-to-reel tape of the Hitchcock album on London Phase Four.*]

HERRMANN: I didn't even know they had this out. I know they're bringing *The Planets* out. If it's selling well I don't know.

ZADOR: Well, I found it in a couple stores.

HERRMANN: So it sounds well on tape?

ZADOR: Oh, yeah. Would you like to borrow it?

HERRMANN: I haven't got a machine to play it. Norma will tell you we have no interest in playing pieces of mine once they're finished. I share that with Stokowski. I'm not as bad as he, but he hasn't got one recording of his. I once tried to find a performance that he did with the Philadelphia Orchestra. He said, "I don't have it." I said, "Why?" He said, "I'm not interested in how I did something. I'm only interested in how I'm going to do it tomorrow." Once he finishes it, that's the end of it. He never hears it again. He doesn't want to.

ROSE: Do you think that's possibly a subconscious reaction to a fear of becoming decadent?

HERRMANN: No, I don't think so. I mean, I think any artist is only interested in his renewal, not in his past. I mean, what's the use of sitting and saying, "Oh, look how marvelously I did that ten years ago or twenty years ago or last year"? How am I going to do it today or tomorrow—tomorrow particularly. You have to. That's the only way you live and grow.

ROSE: Do you compose at the piano?

HERRMANN: No, not particularly. What's the advantage in composing at the piano or not? I don't understand. It's just a ... it's a musical crutch. Some composers need it more than others. It's not of much interest.

ZADOR: My father uses it.

HERRMANN: It's nothing wrong, Stravinsky does. He likes to be "in touch with the sound" as he says. Ravel did. Wagner didn't. Strauss didn't. I don't think there are any rules.

ROSE: Do you have a specific way of structuring a work that you're composing?

HERRMANN: Yeah, well everybody has their own way of writing. The most important is the form, the shape of it. That's the important thing.

ROSE: Do you compose sometimes parts of the middle of the composition ...

HERRMANN: No, I like to start from the beginning to the end. I like to know where you're going all the time. Oh, when you first sketch it, you might have all kinds of ideas. Lots of people don't feel that you should really recognize your piece. I mean, there have been many examples, particularly in Europe, where they play new pieces where the composer didn't even know they were playing it. Because all they care about is how it looks, not how it sounds. In London they gave a few years ago a big art exhibit to pieces of music just on the looks. Nothing to do with ...

A Conversation with Bernard Herrmann

ROSE: Something not right about that.

HERRMANN: Well, some music... most of the way I view it is... a fine piece of music always looks fine too.

ROSE: That's true. But it's not in itself a work of art.

HERRMANN: Well, I know. But the Arts Council had an exhibition. Some of them looked very nice. Most of them I can't read, so it doesn't matter. I can't read their diagrams. I mean today, you get somebody who is "doing their thing," you have to first of all brainwash your brains and learn how to read the way *he* writes music. Which has nothing to do with the way anyone else has ever written it. And then you go and get some words to the special philosophical system to learn how to listen to it and then how to conduct it. You don't have to do that when you want to listen to other music, but you do if you listen to his.

ROSE: Do you compose in the small score and then orchestrate?

HERRMANN: No, I like to orchestrate right away. I mean, I don't think I have one way of composing. There are many ways of composing. You compose because you want to do it. You do it because it's going to please you. You do it because somebody else might be pleased, if you wrote it for them. The only thing that I ever did do that was foolhardy was to write an opera.

ZADOR: How long did it take you to write it?

HERRMANN: Seven years. A big undertaking, an opera—three hours, three and half hours of music.

ZADOR: Were you working on other pieces at the same time?

HERRMANN: Yeah, that's right. Franz Liszt said that you have to have the soul of a hero to write an opera and the mentality of a lackey to have it produced. It's true. I mean, people aren't even interested. It's been mostly turned down with the remark, "It's not problematical. We would like a problematical opera, experimental opera." So, I'm not interested in that.

ROSE: They premiered an opera at UCLA, the West Coast premiere of Richard Rodney Bennett's...

HERRMANN: Yeah, I heard it.

ROSE: I must say I didn't like it very much. It seemed not to have very many ideas. It seemed to be very slick.

HERRMANN: Well, that's what they wanted to do, so they did it.

ROSE: They wanted to do *Wozzeck*.

HERRMANN: *Wozzeck* is a very great original work. But they weren't dying to do that here until thirty-five years later.

ROSE: Strange, the tastes of the people that are in control of the arts.

HERRMANN: They're very safe tastes! They are the new conservatives of our time! In the worst way! They love any modern music, as I told you, that's forty years, fifty years old. Like Ives. He finished writing by 1914. Why didn't they play him when he was alive? Nobody played him except a few of us, a handful. Now it's safe: you play Ives, and you play Berg, and you play Schoenberg, and you play the imitations of it. Or you play the fashionable, voguish music of the moment. Which I don't object to their doing that, I think that's all right. But what I object to... they're not interested... a great work like *War and Peace* has never been done by a major opera company outside of Russia, outside of one performance at the Florence Festival. It's never been done by any company. And that's by a *great* composer of the twentieth century! Because it's not "problematical."

ZADOR: What do you mean, "problematical"?

HERRMANN: Well, I don't know. You have to ask them.

ZADOR: I never understood what that word meant.

HERRMANN: Because originally opera went through a whole series of things. In the eighteenth century to the third quarter of the nineteenth century, people went to opera to hear the singers. Whoever was singing on the stage was the focus of attention. Then about 1880, it began to drift from them to who was conducting the opera. Then from that to the beginning of World War II, the most important thing in an opera was not who was singing, but who was conducting it. This was the most important aspect. Since World War II it's ... then the next phase became who is producing it. Now you hear "Webster's" *Carmen*, "Bing's" *Tristan*. You'd think Wagner never wrote it, that it's something the general manager of the Met ... "his" *Tristan*. And suddenly the conductors are all nonentities. They're nobodies. The singers are very poor. But it's the new producer's thing.

ZADOR: And this is the way it is today?

HERRMANN: No, it's going ahead further. And that's the present moment, but it's now coming from that to the next stage, which is the stage that I see. Which is how much critical space do you get about the value of the work? How much does the critics write about it? And how problematical is it, so it'll make a big stir? Not the production, whether it's terrible, it's dreadful, it's ...

ZADOR: Wait a minute. What do you mean, "problematical"?

HERRMANN: Well, that's the word they use. They mean that it creates furor, because it's a problem.

ROSE: Controversial?

HERRMANN: Controversial.

ZADOR: Do you mean the theme of the opera is controversial?

HERRMANN: Yes, and the way it's presented. I mean, if you did a new performance of Tristan ...

ZADOR: Oh, how *new* it is.

HERRMANN: How *new* it is, and "copy" ... how much publicity does it make.

ZADOR: Yeah. Like *Hair* or something ...

HERRMANN: That's the idea. You can have the equivalent in an opera. It's that kind of idea.

ZADOR: Touching on the subject of film music again, which film composers do you admire?

HERRMANN: Who, in film music? I like William Walton ... Prokofiev ...

ZADOR: *Alexander Nevsky*?

HERRMANN: Oh, well, one of the greatest scores ever written. I like some of the ... I thought Copland did a lot of interesting film music. I can't say I admire a lot ... I don't admire music that panders beneath itself. I like music that is proud of itself. I mean, I don't like a guy who says, "I know it's a good idea, but it's too good for these creeps who come to look at a movie, so I'll debase it."

ZADOR: Well, that's not always done by choice.

HERRMANN: No! It *is* done by choice! You don't have to do it! You can walk away from it! I'm sorry. A composer can walk away from it. You say, "I'm not your man; get somebody else." I mean, after all, don't tell me that he has to make a buck. Look what Schubert put up with. I never cheapened a piece because somebody said that's what they want. That to me is where you separate the composers from the frauds. Look at *The Battle of Britain*. They threw Walton's music out and put that piece of crap in it. [*Walton's score was largely replaced with music by Ron Goodwin.*] But you didn't see Walton debasing his music. He said, "Okay, don't use it."

ZADOR: They left about four or five minutes of it in.

HERRMANN: Yeah, but he didn't say you can take my music and cheapen it. Any composer who does that, who stands on his own guns, I respect. I don't have to agree with him on anything else.

ROSE: There have been film scores that have been recorded, and then when the film was released, all or part of the score was deleted.

HERRMANN: Well, I never had that hard luck. The only hard luck I ever had was my disagreement with Hitchcock about *Torn Curtain*, and we never recorded the music. So, I mean, somebody else just wrote a new score, which is fair enough. His score was played, not mine. That's fair enough. See, I wasn't willing to debase my music, because Universal Studios and Alfred Hitchcock said, "This is what we want to do." I knew they were wrong. And even if what they wanted to do was right, I was the wrong man to do it.

ZADOR: There seems so much justice in that *Torn Curtain* . . .

HERRMANN: What justice?! I mean, you talk like a kid! There's no justice in the world!

ZADOR: Listen to me a second.

HERRMANN: You talk like a kid.

ZADOR: *Torn Curtain* was recorded after the last four scores you did for Hitchcock were not. But now your music is available to the public and *Torn Curtain* has long since gone the way of the buffalo.

HERRMANN: Well, that's what I'm talking about, one's self-respect. If you create something that's real, it'll go on living, no matter what happens to it. Even if it's neglected, it lives. The libraries are full of music that nobody plays, but that doesn't mean it's dead music. I just recorded a symphony by Joachim Raff in London. There's nothing dead about that. The orchestra had a hell of a time trying to play it. They said they're all great at playing all the latest shit, you know, but they didn't do so good on Raff. It took a bit of doing to get them to play it. It's a great work. It was once very popular, one of the greatest played symphonies of its time. Suppose, let's say today, nobody had played

Tchaikovsky for a hundred years. And suddenly somebody came along and said, "We'll do the Sixth Symphony." You think an orchestra will just play it like that?

What I'm trying to say to you is that . . . [*he becomes emotional*] I don't care . . . producers who know what you should write . . . and don't know what you write . . . all they're trying to do is to sell cheap side goods on the dirty picture postcards that go with their movies! That's what they want. But I don't have to do it, do I? I don't do it! I could do ten pictures a year if I was willing to do that. I wouldn't do it. I wouldn't do it in television either. I did some of the greatest television shows ever done: *Twilight Zone*s and *The Alfred Hitchcock Hour*. I must have done 75 of the *Hour* series. But I don't want to write this kind of music . . . I don't want to write what these "colleagues" want. They say I'm their colleague, but I'm not *their* colleague! They're not *my* colleague! I refuse to put them in the same place. I think for a man to be my colleague, I have to know that he can write music. And that he has a respect for himself as an artist. And I don't want to hear all this stuff they gotta make a living. Every composer's gotta make a living. On that basis, nobody ever would have written any music. I feel if every composer would do the *best* he was capable of doing, we wouldn't have this terrible standard.

ZADOR: How do you mean?

HERRMANN: Well, they *don't*! They debase themselves!

ZADOR: Well, I think that a lot of them really aren't that talented.

HERRMANN: All right, I can't disagree. You said it, not me. I don't think it's a question of talent. I just think that they are what . . .

ZADOR: Lousy.

HERRMANN: Vaughan Williams once described them in the best term of all: "cheapjacks."

ZADOR: I think one who has gotten worse and worse each year is Maurice Jarre.

HERRMANN: Well, I don't care. Who the hell is Jarre? I'm not interested in him.

ROSE: He never did anything good.

ZADOR: *Lawrence of Arabia* wasn't too bad.

HERRMANN: Oh? Who do you know who wrote *Lawrence of Arabia*?

ZADOR: Maurice Jarre wrote that score.

HERRMANN: Well, I don't want to go into that.

ROSE: Please do.

HERRMANN: No, I can't. I'm not interested. Go to London and ask that question and find out. I mean, I'm not saying Jarre didn't write *Lawrence of Arabia*. Maybe he did; but that isn't what I hear. I don't know.

ZADOR: That's awfully funny.

HERRMANN: What the hell was important about *Lawrence of Arabia* anyhow? It was a lousy film to begin with. Complete distortion of T.E. Lawrence's life and what it was about. To me the music sounded like an up-to-date version of "In a Monastery Garden," "In a Persian Market Place." I thought the music was really cheap. And I don't know whether he wrote it or not. How can you say whether he wrote it or not? I don't know. I'm not saying he didn't. But I don't know. It doesn't sound to me like the work of one man. I don't know. Maybe he had three days to write the whole score. I don't want to make this thing an attack on Jarre. I don't think about Jarre one way or the other. See, I don't waste my time thinking about people like that. [*Two letters responding to Herrmann's comments appear at the end of the interview.*]

ZADOR: Well, there are quite a few good composers who are in the same situation as you are. They can't find good films. They are not in demand any more.

HERRMANN: So?

ZADOR: Miklós Rózsa, for example, is in very much the same situation.

HERRMANN: So... I never thought it was going to last forever.

ZADOR: Rózsa has written some fine music. Do you see him still?

HERRMANN: Yeah. He isn't worried about it. He's busy writing some other music of his own. A real composer doesn't worry about whether you want them... want them for pictures or not.

ROSE: A composer that I like very much who does film scores is Alex North.

HERRMANN: Well, he doesn't work.

ROSE: He isn't doing much lately.

HERRMANN: Nothing.

ZADOR: How long did it take you to write *Psycho*?

HERRMANN: Oh, five weeks.

ZADOR: *Vertigo*? That had much more music.

HERRMANN: Five or six weeks.

ZADOR: It only took you six weeks?

HERRMANN: Well, I don't remember. That's about what I remember. I'm not good at... you see... I don't... when I'm finished with it, it's out of my head. I don't think about it any more, how long it took, how did I feel, or what.

ROSE: Do you have a favorite Hitchcock film?

HERRMANN: No.

ROSE: Not from a musical standpoint, from a personal...

HERRMANN: No, I don't feel that... how can you feel that way?

ROSE: I feel that *Vertigo* touched on subjects and human feelings that no other Hitchcock film had.

HERRMANN: Well, I enjoyed that film.

ROSE: The obsession...

HERRMANN: Yeah, that's right.

ROSE: It's so marvelous.

ZADOR: In connection with the album you did for London Phase Four of the various Hitchcock scores, what made you decide to allot the time you did to each of the five scores represented? I notice, for example, that *Psycho* has about fifteen minutes, but *North by Northwest* only four minutes.

HERRMANN: Because *North by Northwest* doesn't have much music which can be played on its own without the film.

ROSE: Well, I have a tape off television of *North by Northwest*, which I have edited down, so that a lot of the music is there without the dialogue; and I find a lot of it interesting.

HERRMANN: Well, they couldn't get it all in. You can't do more than twenty minutes a side, so that's it.

ZADOR: I wish, of course, that it had been a double album.

HERRMANN: One of these days we'll bring out another record. They don't believe in double records. They say they don't sell: "It's the kiss of death." They say it's the kiss of death to have a double record.

ZADOR: It would have been nice, though, if we could have had a little bit more music from *North by Northwest*.

HERRMANN: Well, we'll maybe make another one; we can put some in.

ZADOR: But the Hitchcock album sells well?

HERRMANN: Yeah. Very well.

ZADOR: Is the opera selling well?

HERRMANN: The opera sold very well. It's a little over two years now out; it's sold a little over three thousand albums in England.

ZADOR: How many in America?

HERRMANN: I don't know. America is not much. They're very happy about it, because they say that they've had operas which ... the *Capriccio* of Strauss has sold in the same period twelve hundred. After all, they said, it's a four-record album; it's an expensive piece. They're going to reissue it anyhow; on the Unicorn label next April they're going to bring it out much cheaper.

ZADOR: Also on four records?

HERRMANN: Yeah, but it's going to be much cheaper. They're going to bring it down about a third in price.

ZADOR: Oh, fantastic.

HERRMANN: They want to remix it. I don't know, they want to put it through the Dolby system. To get rid of all the pre-echoes which the opera has, which is what's current at that time, but which you don't have any more with the Dolby. It's the same performance. They'll just ... get rid of it. They thought of putting it on three records, they could physically do it, but the acts would come out all lopwise. I mean, part of one act would only begin on one side, then you'd have to take away. The opera is laid out now so that each act is complete. And when it does break in the middle, it breaks at a dramatic point. You haven't lost the continuity.

ZADOR: The opera has been performed?

HERRMANN: No, it hasn't been performed. It's been performed on records, which I prefer more than a half-baked production in an opera house . . .

ROSE: Still, it would be nice to see it.

HERRMANN: Well, they're not interested. As I told you, they say it's not "problematical" . . . "experimental."

ROSE: One thing that I've been discussing with friends of mine is the possibility of starting up another symphony orchestra in the Los Angeles area.

HERRMANN: Oh, go on.

ROSE: Forget it?

HERRMANN: Forget it. You don't know what money it'd cost you. It'd cost you a million dollars a year. The right thing to do in this town is to . . . instead of wasting your energies is to let the newspapers go for the L.A. Orchestra, but really go for them. And who the hell is Zubin Mehta with his patronizing attitude I mean towards the community and the composers? And the rubbish they write about him! I like it . . . when he did the Ninth Symphony last time, it was terrible; this new one was great. I was going to write a letter and say, "How about your guest conductors? When they turn in a lousy performance, you don't let them come back a second time, do you?"

ROSE: I was hoping that there could be a symphony orchestra that would be slightly related to performing film music as well as other music.

HERRMANN: They'll never do it.

Bernard Herrmann in London, 1972, conducting Charles Ives' Second Symphony for English Decca (*photo courtesy of Steven Smith*).

ROSE: There's no orchestra in the world that plays film music at concerts.

HERRMANN: No, there's no orchestra that wants to play anything!

ZADOR: There was a concert given about six or seven years ago at the Hollywood Bowl . . . some very good film music. I wonder why they never did anything like that again?

HERRMANN: They had a record out on that, but they withdrew that; that's no longer in circulation.

ZADOR: But I wonder why they never had a repeat of that because they had such fantastic . . .

HERRMANN: Johnny Green took it all over. It became his own personal evening. We all had fifteen minutes to rehearse our piece, but he had two hours . . . and ran us a big deficit.

ZADOR: I'm sorry, I don't understand that.

HERRMANN: We had to rehearse . . . any piece we did . . . we had fifteen minutes to do it. He took two hours for his. That ran us a big deficit.

ZADOR: Oh, I see. And he probably didn't even write all of it.

HERRMANN: Well, I'm not going into that. You say what you like. I'm not saying . . . you might some day go see a lot of people, do an article on ghost-writing.

ROSE: You might also find yourself with a knife in your back one night.

HERRMANN: Well, I don't think they feel that way about it, many of 'em, they feel it's perfectly okay. They say, "It's the biz."

ROSE: Yes, but it's such a sad situation, that Hollywood became that way.

HERRMANN: I would suggest, why don't you do a program on KFAC where you play motion picture scores and talk about them?

ROSE: We do have a show on Sunday on which, I told you, I would be featuring your music.

HERRMANN: Well, I'm talking about a special program devoted to film music.

ROSE: So far it's been hard to have programs like that, because they don't want to have programs like that, because what they want is to have music, then commercials, and then more music.

HERRMANN: Yeah, but if they don't stop it, the FCC... I was going to write them, they're getting to do five commercials for every minute of music. They're in violation of the whole FCC license. This morning, I counted, they played the Brahms Haydn Variations, they had five commercials after it.

ZADOR: Mr. Herrmann, I have a plane to catch.

HERRMANN: Where are you going?

ZADOR: San Francisco.

HERRMANN: Oh, well, okay. I've given you enough crap anyhow. [*To Rose:*] I think you should have an hour devoted to film music; and you go and tell them that it's a very good commercial idea. You can have a guest on each one and get all the big... everybody in this crappy town will all come and talk to you. And you can ask them what you want to ask them about, and you'll have a big audience here.

ROSE: I'd like to do it.

HERRMANN: Why don't they? They do it... the BBC... I can't go to London, I'm not there for forty-eight hours before they're on my tail to be on television about film music. They give me forty-five minutes to talk. And when I did *The Bride Wore Black*, they sent the camera crew all the way to Paris to photograph me recording it. I mean, they're interested in getting audiences. I think you got a good idea there; I think you ought to follow it through.

ROSE: I'd like to.

ZADOR: So the sad state of the arts, you would say, is more common in America than in England.

HERRMANN: It's more common to America because America, when it gets an enthusiasm, has got to kill everything else all for the current enthusiasm. I mean, if rock's in, then everything else has got to drop dead. Just think, we live in a culture where a great composer, Engelbert Humperdinck, who's got children still alive, a fellow whose name . . . what was his name? . . .

NORMA: Dorsey.

HERRMANN: Dorsey was a singer who never made it with anybody . . . took the name of a great composer . . . it's not his name . . . a great composer like Engelbert Humperdinck suddenly has got to become the handle for a . . .

NORMA: He didn't take that name because it was a great name. He took it because it was funny.

HERRMANN: Yeah, he thought it was funny, or whatever . . .

NORMA: It is funny.

HERRMANN: What . . . it's a German name, Engelbert Humperdinck. Humperdinck is a straight German name. I bet in any German telephone book you'll find there hundreds of Humperdincks. I mean, I think it's dreadful. And you can't do anything about that. So anyhow, well, they have to go and get a plane.

ZADOR: As I said, I'll see you in about a week.

HERRMANN: Okay, if you want to. Maybe I'll pick up some better ideas for you. [*He chuckles.*]

At the Editor's request, Maurice Jarre and Gerard Schurmann replied to Herrmann's remarks about the score for Lawrence of Arabia. Their letters are here reproduced in full.

Los Angeles
July 12th, 1987

Dear Mr. McCarty:

Thank you for sending me the passage of the interview with Bernard Herrmann.

I must say I am amazed that a composer of the stature of Bernard Herrmann would be involved in this kind of gossipy interview with an undercurrent of slander.

First of all, *I* wrote the entire original score for the film *Lawrence of Arabia* and *I* was the only composer. (The British military march "The Voices of the Guns" by K.J. Alford was used as source music for a visual band during a short scene.)

What is interesting in this denunciation of the film by Mr. Herrmann is the fact that Bernard Herrmann wrote a letter to the producer of the film, Sam Spiegel, who showed me the letter at that time, begging him to do the music for this "wonderful and amazing picture" and asking fifty thousand dollars to be associated to this great project!

Also I realize that the date of this interview (1970) was just after Alfred Hitchcock had rejected Herrmann's score of *Torn Curtain* and asked me to do his next film, *Topaz*.

I only can excuse these insulting, malevolent words because of the bitterness and the jealousy of an old man for a younger and successful colleague.

About "lousy cheapjacks," it's probably the same people who judged the work of Bernard Herrmann and gave me three Oscars, many nominations, a British Academy award, a French "Cesar," two "Premio Italia," a German "Golden Europa," the Sydney film critics circle award and a "Grand prix de musique contemporaine" for a work in the memory of Arthur Honegger, my Master.

As you promised me, I would appreciate if you publish my entire reply as an adjunct to this interview.

Sincerely,
Maurice Jarre

Los Angeles
November 11th, 1987

Dear Mr. McCarty:

Although Sam Spiegel originally invited me to work on the score of *Lawrence of Arabia* as one of two composers with equal responsibility, the contract that I finally signed put me in charge of the arrangements and orchestrations, and I therefore do *not* claim to have co-composed the music.

I don't think that Maurice Jarre ever liked any of my orchestral 'arrangements', at least he never expressed an opinion either way except to complain over and over again (in a score containing two hours of music completed in six weeks) that there were some wrong notes in one of the military band marches!

If, as many people have remarked, the orchestral score of *Lawrence* sounds unlike any other by Jarre, I am content to accept the responsibility for that difference, and take it that it could be something to do with my personal stamp or style.

Yours sincerely,
Gerard Schurmann

The Film Composer in Concert and the Concert Composer in Film

Eddy Lawrence Manson

Oscar-winner Ernest Gold, when asked how he became a composer for films, tells of the time when as a young composer he had a piano concerto performed in New York, and the critics said it sounded like "movie music." Instead of screaming epithets at the critics, he took the cue and set out for Hollywood. He met with Morris Stoloff, music director of Columbia Pictures, and played his piano concerto for him, whereupon Stoloff said, "It sounds like movie music," and promptly put Gold to work. His career since has been among the most notable in film music.

Heitor Villa-Lobos, the eminent South American composer, was hired by MGM to write the score to a film called *Green Mansions*. A script was sent to him and translated into his native Portuguese. Without ever seeing the film and with no apparent knowledge of film technique, Villa-Lobos delivered a complete score to MGM! Had the music been less than attractive, and beautifully composed, the score would probably have been rejected. As it was, Bronislau Kaper, then under contract to MGM, skillfully adapted Villa-Lobos' music for the film and it was saved. Eventually the score became a concert suite which was recorded.

The relationship between music for the concert stage and the movies has not been clearly delineated. Regrettably, some concert composers have been all but traumatized by unfruitful attempts at film scoring. One such case was my own teacher, the eminent Vittorio Giannini. Back in the forties Giannini was invited to Hollywood by a major studio, to score a film and possibly join its staff of composers. When faced with the demands of film, particularly the stop watch, he fled, never to return.

Concert composers, when exposed to the constraints of film scoring—the stop watch, the mathematics, having to "time down" to so many frames of film per beat, constantly playing a supportive role to what is happening on the silver screen, and relating to an unmusical producer—are inclined to simply stay away from Hollywood.

The talented young composers who do come to Hollywood may find that the film producers who do the hiring are often wary of them, fearing they may write "strange" music, or music that stands nicely on its own two feet but bears little relation to the film. These same producers are even more wary of composers fresh out of the university or conservatory, who can defend every note they've written by citing chapter and verse from scores by greats such as Ives, Elliott Carter, Varèse, Penderecki, and Stravinsky. All the producer knows is the bottom line: "It may be great music, but it doesn't work for the film"... or: "This guy may be a hot shot on the concert stage, but he can't write a decent melody"... or: "Can't use him... he can't write 'pop'"... or: "He takes too long... fusses too much... costs run up..." *ad infinitum.* A producer is more likely to chance a "pop" composer with hit songs and a "hot" reputation, guided if necessary by an experienced film composer/orchestrator. The concert composer would quickly resent having another composer looking over his shoulder.

With the demise of active music departments and music directors who had enviable autonomy over the composers and music they furnished for the studio's output, the producer is now in control of who scores a film, and how it is scored. In their day, men like Alfred Newman at Fox, Leo Forbstein at Warners, John Green at MGM, and Stoloff at Columbia knew how to work with and encourage fledgling film scorers. They also had the taste, knowledge, and judgment to gracefully veto a producer's choice of composer or at least to furnish an experienced back-up composer to help the helpless, often conducting the product of the inexperienced composer themselves. Today, if a Villa-Lobos were to deliver a score as he did out of sheer innocence and total ignorance of scoring technique, it would be blithely discarded, and a new composer brought in to do the job over. At least John Green and the

MGM music department appreciated the fundamental quality and brilliance of Villa-Lobos's score and salvaged what they could.

Film producers are often talented and knowledgeable in the visual arts, but they seldom evidence any degree of musical sophistication. The first time a producer or filmmaker lets go of his creation is when he turns the film over to the strange creature called "composer," a person over whom he has little or no control during the act of writing music, as he does over the actors, director, writers, editors, cameramen, etc. Until the filmmaker hears the music on the scoring stage, he does not know what the composer has done to his vision. Understandably, he is wary of the whole process of musicalization. Consequently, he feels safer with a composer whose music he can at least identify with.

While movies such as *Fame, Flashdance, Saturday Night Fever,* and *Purple Rain* benefit from a pop records/music video kind of score, other films are burdened by it rather than helped. If they could, some producers would score a period piece, say about Restoration England, with a "top forty" sound, delighting the record company and the music publisher no end, and thoroughly damaging the film. Into this morass of ignorance and "top forty" thinking goeth the young, innocent concert composer, often never to be heard from again. Pity.

On the other hand, experienced film composers, while they are prone to the slings and arrows of outrageous opinions, can deal with this by (a) knowing the producer personally, (b) exhibiting an understanding for the film's needs, (c) being able to argue the merits and demerits of the filmmaker's musical ideas on the filmmaker's terms ... and the terms of the film, and (d) being ready to adapt to any style the movie might require, seldom saying, "But I can't write *that* kind of music."

Being able to compose in almost any idiom or period is a mainstay in the cine-composer's armament. At UCLA and other schools, I have often told film-scoring students: "Learn to write the very music you hate; you never know when you'll need it." Yet, this kind of pliability and versatility is often anathema to the concert composer.

The concert composer has been trained and over-trained. Not only has he learned his composition, orchestration, and electronics, he has also been a loyal subject of his teachers, most of whom have had minimal experience outside the school or concert hall. He adores their thinking, smokes their cigars, goes to their parties, and drinks not only their wine but their doctrines. He often becomes a clone of his master.

This might be regarded as a perfectly normal stage in a composer's development, provided he eventually finds his own way. Eclecticism is historic. Mozart's influence over Beethoven is evident in the first and second symphonies, until Beethoven becomes his own man in the third symphony. Regrettably, many talents today never become "their own man."

"Disciple-ism" is the sincerest form of flattery to a composer-teacher and bolsters the sagging egos of men impacted in academic esoterica, for which they receive low pay with very little recognition—recognition of a talent that often deserves much more. But the really good teacher should wean his students and encourage participation out there in the "real world," which of course includes film.

Composer Quincy Jones speaks of the musicians who come from the "street" as opposed to those who come from the schools. A common denominator in all successful film composers is the combination of "street" and school. Nearly all of them have had not only a background of serious training, but also their share of writing and playing "people-music." They have all had practical, hard-fought encounters with rock, jazz, bar mitzvahs, theater, night clubs, and so forth. (In my own case, I started by playing harmonica on the Coney Island boardwalk for whatever people threw at me—sometimes it wasn't money.) These men are totally unencumbered by "disciple-ism," and are as practical and versatile as the industry demands. Some of them served as rehearsal pianists: David Shire, Billy Goldenberg, Marvin Hamlisch, and Elmer Bernstein, who was trained as a concert pianist until he caught the Broadway bug. Bert Shefter, with one hundred films to his credit and nine hundred TV shows, trained at Curtis under Josef Hofmann and then worked as a pianist throughout the music business, notably with George Gershwin. John Williams, Dave Grusin, and Artie Kane were successful studio pianists before becoming cine-composers. Jerry Goldsmith, following his studies at USC and with Jacob Gimpel, went to work at CBS—as a clerk-typist. In time, CBS discovered his talents and assigned radio and TV scoring chores to him. Hugo Friedhofer started as a cellist who subsequently orchestrated for Max Steiner and Erich Korngold before earning his wings as a full-fledged film composer. Steiner, who trained at the Imperial Conservatory in Vienna, conducted opera and Broadway shows for several years before Hollywood discovered him. Quincy Jones studied at Seattle University, at Berkeley, and with Nadia Boulanger, all the time immersing himself in the field of jazz and pop as a very successful arranger prior to having a film career.

Throughout my own career, I always worked while studying. I had performed with various bands as both an arranger and harmonica specialist throughout the country before enrolling at the Juilliard School. I then supported myself by playing in night clubs and burlesque shows while still in school. To this day, I am still a "working student," still learning, I hope.

Movie-scorers are not just practical, experienced musicians; they have a fund of human experience to draw on, an audience instinct, and are what composer Earle Hagen calls "applied psychologists." For me, it is a sixth sense that determines every note I write—an audience sense, a manipulative sense—what do I want my audience to feel? This instinct for communication and manipulation is not taught in the schools. Some have it, and others don't; it must be developed. The street is the great developer, if the talent is there. Dr. Tom Backer, a psychologist and film music scholar, suggests that a basic course in psychology should also be a part of the film composer's training.[1]

Paul Chihara, who has had a notable career as a concert composer with a long list of commissions and awards, eventually turned to film and has had a fine career. Paul taught at UCLA and experienced academia. He was never really anyone's disciple and always tried to do his own thing. He considers himself pliable and versatile enough to do the job, and is careful never to let his considerable craft run away with the film. "If music calls attention to itself instead of supporting, moving or coloring a given scene, it will in all likelihood be removed or dubbed down to an almost inaudible level."[2] Paul confesses a long-time love affair with movies, and it is evident in his dramatic ability and intelligence as a composer. He points out the need to become part of the working team that is creating the film. "You have to love movies—love them so much that you want to contribute the right score to that picture without being cheap or being a showoff. The movie was not created as a showcase for the composer."

Probing the position of the film composer venturing into the concert field, Chihara notes that they sometimes have difficulty with abstract forms: ". . . they tend to use the old-fashioned forms when writing a string quartet or symphonic work, the forms that are no longer relevant in today's classical field, as on the other hand—someone who comes from the classical field and tries to justify bad film scoring by quoting other composers—'Stravinsky did it in such and such a piece (therefore it's good).' He must realize that he cannot use the film as a vehicle for himself; whereas in concert, we are always using the concert stage as a vehicle for our own expression. Sometimes the composer falls into the trap of saying, 'Ah, here's a chance for me to write a fugue or to spring my new twelve-tone discovery,' when it is totally inappropriate to the movie."

Ernest Gold gainsays by suggesting that musical forms often prevent monotony in long, drawn-out "cues" (the normally short music sequences that comprise the film score). In *The Secret of Santa Vittoria* there is an unusually long sequence of eight minutes in which only a single action occurs, the passing of wine bottles through an everlasting line of people in an effort to save the rare wine from the approaching German army. Instead of getting drunk or kicking his dog, Gold solved the problem by composing a complete piece in *theme and variations* form (the theme had been introduced earlier, a catchy Italian street song associated with the people of the town).

"There are scores written by people who are specifically equipped to deal with sound track and nothing else," says Gold. "The best scores, however, are written by composers used to writing music intended to be listened to. One can adopt or adapt methods from concert music which support the picture and still leave the audience with that marvelous feeling that comes from having heard a well written piece of music." Gold points out that the effect is *cumulative*. It is possible to do naught but push a favorite theme around the film, resulting in little more than selling a song (with or without words). Conversely, thirty minutes of music in a two-hour film, if well composed with a sense of story concept, may result in something the producer did not ask for, or the audience may not understand, but it nonetheless benefits the film with that sense of progression and feeling of fulfillment one gets from a story well told or a tone-poem dynamically constructed. Harry Lojewski, MGM's music director, calls the tone-poem (*e.g.*, Strauss' *Till Eulenspiegel* and *Thus Spake Zarathustra*) "a score to an invisible film." Consequently, a well-composed movie score in the cumulative sense adds up to a tone-poem with a "visible" film.

Musical forms can unify a scene. In *Lovers and Lollipops*, Morris Engel's film about a New York couple with a testy child, I was faced with a scene in which the little girl, Peggy, decides to sail her toy boat in the pond of the Museum of Modern Art while her mother and friend are engaged in art appreciation. The little boat, floating out to the middle of the pond, is becalmed. Peggy tries to stimulate the current with her hands, to little avail. One by one, persons fill the scene trying to help, offering directions and wetting themselves down, splashing the calm water. Finally the boat is retrieved, and Petty is scolded. The entire scene was a single long shot, completely silent, to be carried by music. To me it suggested a visual fugue and I built a charming and complete fugue based on Peggy's theme. The effect was magical and funny. More than that, it gave flow to a scene that easily could have bogged down, requiring cutting.

Form can point up transitions and development in the story line. I've seldom composed a music cue that did not have a beginning, a middle, and an end, as does a sentence, a paragraph, and, in an abstract way, a photograph or painting. Music affects the visual, and the visual affects the music.

Still, even with a strong sense of form, the film composer falls into certain traps in the concert hall, which irritates the critics and the concert sophisticates. As Chihara points out, the movie writer tends to use the classic forms to offset his inability to handle abstract form. Thus he forces himself into tonal music, not unlike that which he uses in film. His tonal music often sounds derivative of other well-known composers. While this eclecticism is useful in movies, it is downright corny in a purely musical environment and would be best confined to pops concerts. Even if he belongs to the *avant-garde*, leaving tonality behind, or is involved in electronics with all manner of strange, new, and even cosmic sounds, he can fail. He fails simply because he can think only in short, evocative episodes, with no sense of development or feeling of beginning, middle, and end—*a total experience*, which the concert-trained composer might be better equipped to provide. Often, instead of a gradual metamorphosis, the film composer blows his big theme in the very beginning, with no place to go but down after that, or rambles through new but irrelevant material begging for an ending. John Green puts it succinctly: "The salient difference between the film composer and the concert composer is the difference between the short episode and the long line."

Recently I heard a recording of a concert piece by Max Steiner taken from a film called *Four Wives*. It bore the ostentatious title of "Symphonie Moderne," replete with a Straussian-sized orchestra, a piano solo played by Earl Wild, part-Rachmaninoff and part-Gershwin, and a grand theme that never stopped. I kept waiting for the development, but instead of intelligent variation, all I heard was turgid pomposity, which did nought but "sell the theme." As for its modernism, it would have been "Moderne" perhaps in the early 1900s. I don't know whose idea it was to call it "Symphonie Moderne" or to do it as a concert piece, but it would have worked much better had it been introduced simply as "Theme from the Film *Four Wives*" and arranged with contrast instead of bombast. Steiner's legacy deserves better treatment.[3]

Not long ago I heard a piece by a well-known film composer, written for a jazz group and symphony orchestra. It was intended as a piece of Americana and had some fine compositional moments in it. Still, the total effect was a rambling one, with little sense of progression.

Leonard Rosenman, whose training and primary thrust is the concert field, notwithstanding his Oscars and years in films, has composed notable pieces in the serial and *avant-garde* idioms for the concert stage. He says that in classical music, whatever the style, "*the process is revealed.*" He would rather write a fresh piece for the concert stage than re-do one of his film scores for concert presentation. Rosenman says that sometimes he wonders if movie music is really music at all, because of its *a priori* condition—the constraints, the pre-ordained set of its boundaries, and the lack of opportunity to develop a musical cue any further than a woefully short period. Shoving a square peg into the proverbial round hole can be frustrating.

Lalo Schifrin, no stranger to the concert field, once said that "listening to a piece of film music without the picture is like listening to a Bach two-part invention with one part missing." There are those who quarrel with that contention, pointing out such stalwarts as Prokofiev's *Alexander Nevsky* and *Lieutenant Kije*, Copland's suites from *The Red Pony* and *Our Town*, Miklós Rózsa's *Spellbound Concerto* and *Quo Vadis Suite*, among others. These pieces, however, were all re-composed for pure listening, and the film composer must start from "square one," developing material from the soundtrack to meet the requirements of extended form.

Sometimes the concert composer who succeeds in film is accused of "selling out," which points out the sea of ignorance that separates the two worlds. A composer who scores films is writing *Gebrauchsmusik*, music that is functional and made to order—

customized music as it were. Within that "made to order" parameter some very great music has been written for the theater, for the ballet, for special occasions, for dedications. Can one put down Stravinsky's work for Diaghilev's *Rite of Spring*, for example, as *kitsch*? Can one put down Copland's ballet, *Appalachian Spring*, as *kitsch*? Can one put down Gershwin's *Porgy and Bess* as *kitsch*? Can one put down Purcell's charming and elegant "Trumpet Voluntary" as *kitsch*? Certainly the aforementioned film scores by Prokofiev, Copland, and Rózsa stand beautifully as arranged for the concert hall and are awesome as film music.

One certainly cannot call Bernard Herrmann's score to *Citizen Kane* "junk," let alone Steiner's score to *Gone with the Wind*, Korngold's *Captain Blood*, Elmer Bernstein's thoughtful work in *To Kill a Mockingbird*, and Jerry Goldsmith's touching score to *A Patch of Blue*. True, some of this music might not stand up in the naked light of the concert hall while still in soundtrack form, but it works magnificently as a "visual" tone-poem when viewing the film.

Most contemporary music played today in concert is highly sophisticated in its "process," moving from episode to episode without repetition, yet carrying the listener through a very subjective experience, and an original one at that. The music is often very dramatic and evocative, as is film music. One would think that many good film composers could come from the classical field, but they don't.

Another difficulty that young composers in the film field have is learning to write sparsely. John Green points out that *"thickness* is a cardinal sin in film orchestrating." One cannot have too much going on in the music, particularly when it has to combine with dialogue and sound. The tendency to overwrite can be tolerated on the concert stage but is disastrous in movies. The best writing is both transparent and economical, making use of a simple device to score emotional points rather than the use of complex texture. The technique of writing a different part for everyone in the orchestra, with much of it aleatoric, produces an interesting chaos and excitement on the concert stage but does little more than confuse in movies. An exception is Lalo Schifrin's work in *The Hellstrom Chronicle*, where he had to create a chaotic and fearsome effect for the sequence showing an army of ants devouring a live animal. His music worked because it was high-pitched for the most part and performed "in the clear," without the encumbrance of dialogue and sound. However, that kind of music *under* sound and dialogue simply washes out, becoming little more than distracting noise.

Morton Stevens, the composer of TV's *Hawaii 5-O* and *Police Woman* and past music director for CBS-TV, says that no matter how much study and work a composer has had prior to film involvement, he must learn composition all over again. He must learn the street techniques—people music—and how to "hook" an audience with a memorable turn of melody or phrase, so it can be used as a basis for dramatic variations as the script requires. There is no time for gradual evolvement of a theme; it must be clearly and emphatically stated. He must learn flexibility, switching say from twelve-tone to a Greek mode, or from Baroque to rock, or from far-out jazz to society music. He must learn simplicity of construction and ease of performance (there is no time for practicing a difficult or unplayable part in the studios). He must learn to think electrically, since the microphone changes all he ever knew about orchestration. The use of synthesizers, organs, and various electronic processors must be dealt with. Foremost, he must develop film synchronization techniques, involving timing to a thousandth of a second, a knowledge of click tracks, visual pacing devices, how to measure drama in terms of time, and overlaying it all, he *must be a dramatist.*

There is no place in film music for the "absolute" composer, but certainly there is a place for the rhapsodic, romantic, descriptive composer who loves drama. The composer who writes for the ballet, the theater, and can also write a good song on occasion is welcome. Perhaps it is wisest for the aspiring cine-composer to carefully analyze his abilities before flying out to Hollywood. The first question he must ask himself is: "Am I a dramatic or absolute writer?"

Harry Lojewski points out that "Richard Strauss and Puccini were among the original film-scorers, only they didn't know it." In other words, film scoring is largely an extension of what the composers of opera, ballet, tone-poems, rhapsodies, and generally evocative music did for years, long before Edison. One difference between now and then is that the composer no longer possesses final authority over a work. In an opera or music drama the concept and working out of the piece are the composer's; even the libretto plays second fiddle to the music, let alone the staging. Large religious works—masses, cantatas, or Friday night services—are dominated by music, but not so in film. The composer must know that his is a supportive role, as a member of a creative team. He is "part of close synch with a number of people with a number of visions," says Paul Chihara, "and he cannot use the film as a vehicle for himself."

Nonetheless, *a middle ground does exist* for the movie and concert composer, and the concert stage itself can provide it.

I have witnessed several attempts at projecting film during the live performance of music, and the result is often entertaining and enlivening. Not only should more of this be encouraged, but the use of slides, split-screen and freeze-frame effects could nicely suggest a direction for the "theater of the mind," with the mind providing its own images to the music after a slide or two or three has shown the way.

At a concert of Aaron Copland's music at the Juilliard School some years ago, we were treated, following intermission, to the novelty of a large screen unfolding, the musicians leaving the stage, and a short film called *The City* being run with an enticing score by Copland. It was now Copland in a supportive position, which added to the interest of the evening.

On other occasions film music has been dramatized by running actual footage while a live orchestra played "in synch" to the film, just as in the studios. Audiences love this. It is perhaps the best way to enjoy film music in its original state. Carmine Coppola's score to the reconstruction of Abel Gance's *Napoléon* gives strong evidence of the value of *live* film music. Unencumbered by sound and dialogue, Coppola's symphonic score (sixty musicians in the pit) unashamedly soars on the wings of Gance's full-blown drama, with mighty climaxes and satisfying lengths in place of the usual truncations that recorded scores are prone to. While not terribly original, the music has a sense of form and completion and thus stands adequately on its own.

If film music is performed as a suite, rhapsody, or concerto, then perhaps a slide, reminiscent of the film from which it came, might serve as a provocative backdrop. Much new music, written expressly for the concert stage, could be helped by visual devices, planned carefully by the composer himself. A film audience, which is essentially a "pop" audience, will accept some far-out, *avant-garde* sounds if those sounds support what is up there on the screen.

An audience will accept strange-sounding music in film that it would not accept in the concert hall, because, I believe, the listener has no frame of ready reference in concert and does not like to be left at sea. Much contemporary music I have heard could stand a *visual* reference.

Program notes are not enough. Electronic pieces by the likes of Subotnick, Xenakis, Reynolds, and Badings could use a little visual help. It could also be an exciting opportunity for experimental filmmakers, music-video producers, and for abstract or impressionistic visualists. It can also be tremendously entertaining, as witness a demonstration some years ago of a technique developed in Czechoslovakia in which separate images were projected on several screens in synchronization with live action on the stage. Performers timed their bits to the film and vice versa. The effect often was one of the performer seemingly coming right out of the screen, and then melting back into it. Music was the unifying element, and a large orchestra played the original and provocative score.

Concert promoters and conductors would do well to consider a visual approach. But it should be done with taste, not with the gross effects of fireworks, laser beams, and sound effects while the orchestra plays John Williams' music.

Another middle ground, of course, is the phonograph record. Collecting records of film music scores is a national hobby of late. The scores of Elmer Bernstein, Hugo Friedhofer, David Raksin, Korngold, Rózsa, Steiner, Alex North, Bernard Herrmann, Mancini, Green, Williams, Schifrin, Walter Scharf, and many others from around the world are now available, freshly recorded and in some cases re-arranged.

David Raksin attributes the growth of "movie" records to the "big hole in the middle"—that is, between classical and pop. Apparently film music, with its "hookiness," its rich and entertaining textures, not to mention its evocation of images, fills a need for listenable music that does not demand the intellectual attention required of classical music but is more attractive, melodically and structurally, than rock or most pop songs.

There has been a vast void in people-music these last twenty years. Rock and pop supply little more than interesting rhythms and sounds; the record industry largely depends on production rather than memorability, let alone melodiousness, for its successes. Advertising jingles on the airwaves often provide the best tunes around, since memorability is a must (one recalls the tune and, it is hoped, the product by association). Consequently, in our need for good melody, we are reduced to humming the commercials.

But people out there want something more than rock, pop, and jingles. Movie scores often fill the bill. The film music heard on records, however, is little more than the original soundtrack with its miniature gems, or "cues," strung together.

A soundtrack score may justify a recording, but it does not make for concert listening. Nonetheless, if the public's taste is whetted enough by provocative, interesting, and colorful music, perhaps concert composers might break similar ground with contemporary tone-poems and evocative rhapsodia. There is already an incipient movement away from the *avant-garde* into "accessibility," or what is now conveniently labelled "neo-romanticism." Composers for the concert stage are rediscovering linear beauty, and some have already displayed a talent for melody, a talent that has been hidden behind the convenient cocoon of *avant-garde* experimentation and musical nihilism. In short, they have found that melodiousness, or at least a sense of line, attracts an audience, whereas bombast, self-indulgence, and intellectualism can drive said audience out of the hall. Consequently, there is now a mutual environment for both the concert and film composer.

As it stands, the film composer is already established in a comfortable and well-paying life style and is a recognized creator. He is often free to pursue interests in other fields and has the time to do it. If he chooses to race horses or sail boats, fine. If, on the other hand, he has to exercise his considerable talent on the concert stage, he can, on the basis of his name, wangle a commission, which might pay enough to cover his copying costs and perhaps his travel. Still, it is a working joy for him to compose music that stands on its own without the imposed architecture of a film. He must, however, deal with prejudice: film composers upon entering the concert hall are sometimes hurt by imperceptive critics. And he must achieve a mastery of extended forms.

The concert composer does not enjoy the material advantages of his peers in film. He often can't afford bus fare to the town where his work is to be performed, let alone copying costs, unless he is well commissioned. He struggles for minimal recognition and wants to get into the movies, more out of a need to survive than out of a love for film. He may even fantasize about how nice the house on the beach would be, the foreign car, the beautiful women, and the recognition to boot. Yet, unless he is thoroughly trained in film technique, has a dramatic talent, and is willing to constantly assume a supportive role on a creative (and ofttimes not-so-creative) team, it would be wise to hold onto his job at the college and continue to write good, unencumbered music.

The writing of this article poses an afterthought. There is a strong tendency among us to label a composer according to the medium in which he is most active, or has achieved the most success. We are known either as "film composer," "Broadway composer," "arranger" (recordings, variety shows), "jingle writer" (TV commercials), "university composer," or "songwriter." In some cases the composer labels himself, since he actually does specialize in one area and nothing else. Many songwriters should not be described as "composers" since they cannot write down their own music, and yet have had success as such. Other "songwriters" have had a solid background from the conservatory and are trained in composition and orchestration. Still they remain known as "songwriters." Witness Richard Rodgers, who studied at ten or so different schools, including Juilliard, Columbia University, and the New England Conservatory. Burt Bacharach is an erstwhile student of Darius Milhaud and Henry Cowell and an alumnus of the Mannes School of Music in New York. He can also do his own orchestrating. Marvin Hamlisch received his early training at the Juilliard School and Queens College in New York.

Among the composers in film, most are conservatory-trained and some have branched into the concert and theatrical fields, as has Walter Scharf. He has written an opera, *The Plot to Overthrow Xmas*, and two musicals, with a third on the way at this writing. Leonard Rosenman has had extensive experience in the concert field and enjoys a sizeable background of training (Roger Sessions, Schoenberg, Dallapiccola). John Green has extended himself into many media besides film. His list of hit songs is formidable. He has written Broadway shows; "Body and Soul," for instance, came from *Three's a Crowd*. Green is a busy conductor of symphonic pop concerts and recently premiered a major work with the Denver Symphony called *Mine Eyes Have Seen*. Henry Mancini has a conservatory background (Juilliard, Carnegie Tech, and private studies). He has conducted his own music in concert halls and on campuses for many years and has made substantial contributions to the educational field as well.

Still, these men are known as "film composers," instead of composers who happen to score films. Why should anyone be labelled a "university" composer, or a "jingle" composer, "Broadway" composer, *ad infinitum*? The labelling often prevents them from crossing into other fields, the assumption being that they are capable in only one area. The assumption is a silly one, but nonetheless real. In the field of acting it is called "type-casting"; in a more general sense, it's called "pigeonholing." Why does it exist?

Since film is seen by millions around the globe and is publicized to the tune of multi-million-dollar promotion budgets, the composer in a successful film is almost immediately labelled "movie" composer, or worse, "Hollywood" composer, a term that can be the proverbial kiss of death in the concert field. "Hollywood composers" are conceived of as "writers of cheap music," "university composers" are "ivory tower," "jingle composers" can only write "catchy phrases," songwriters are "musical illiterates," arrangers "cannot compose their own music," *ad nauseam.*

Perhaps we have become too specialized. Each of these fields in which a composer earns his living is highly insular, and there is little overlapping. What has Madison Avenue got to do with the universities? What has Tin Pan Alley got to do with the concert field? Certainly not enough to pave the way for the crossover of a composer from one area into the next, regardless of his qualifications and training. We are to some extent ghettoized, and from that stems prejudice. This pigeonholing of a music writer makes it doubly tough for the "film composer" to succeed in concert and for the "concert composer" to break into film.

Labelling has posed a problem for this writer, on a different level. I have a thirty-five-year history as a composer and arranger, with some recognition and a bunch of awards. Yet I am primarily known, internationally, as an artist on the humble harmonica. However, when my agent calls a producer for my next composing assignment, she might be told: "I hear that Manson composes tunes on his harmonica and then has someone write them down for him."

You just can't win.

NOTES

[1] See "In the Key of Feeling" by Thomas E. Backer and Eddy Lawrence Manson, *Human Behavior*, February 1978, pp. 63–67.

[2] This quotation, and all subsequent quotations from musicians, come either from tape-recorded interviews or from their taped lectures to my classes at UCLA.

[3] The version of *Symphonie Moderne* referred to was released in 1973 on the album *Now, Voyager: The Classic Film Scores of Max Steiner* (RCA ARL1-0136). This version was not Steiner's original, but was newly arranged and expanded by Charles Gerhardt, who also conducted the National Philharmonic Orchestra, which at 92 musicians was almost twice the size of the Warner Bros. studio orchestra heard on the film's sound track.—Ed.

Contributors

Rudy Behlmer is a lecturer in film studies at UCLA, California State University, Northridge, and Art Center College in Pasadena. For 32 years he produced and directed for television. He has written on films for several periodicals, and wrote the booklet accompanying Warner Bros.' record set, *Fifty Years of Film Music* (1973), and pamphlet notes for five of RCA's Classic Film Scores series (1973–75). His books include *Memo from David O. Selznick* (1972), *America's Favorite Movies: Behind the Scenes* (1982), and *Inside Warner Bros. (1935–1951)* (1985). For the 1988 Criterion laserdisc, *Scaramouche*, Behlmer did the audio essay.

Richard H. Bush is operations manager of NASDAQ, Inc., in New York, a division of the National Association of Security Dealers. He has made a special study of the music for Universal Pictures during the 1930s. "The Music for Flash Gordon and Buck Rogers" is his first full-length article on film music.

Dennis James has been the resident organist for the Ohio Theatre in Columbus since 1975. In 1981 he was the organist for the world tour of Abel Gance's *Napoléon*, and has subsequently toured with *The Passion of Joan of Arc*, *Nosferatu*, and other silent films. He has performed at many film festivals and film series under the auspices of the American Film Institute, the Museum of Modern Art, and other sponsors. He is dedicated to furthering public interest in the theater pipe organ and to the continuation of the theatrical traditions of organ performance.

Kathryn Kalinak is an associate professor of English at Rhode Island College in Providence, where she teaches literature and film studies.

She has published in *Film Reader*, *Jump Cut*, and *Film Quarterly*. Her previous work includes analyses of the representation of women in Hollywood film, the impact of race on the representation of gender, and the function of gender in the construction of the film score. She is currently at work on a book on the Hollywood film score.

Clifford McCarty is Vice President of the Society for the Preservation of Film Music, and from 1984–1987 edited its quarterly newsletter, *The Cue Sheet*. His writings on film music have appeared in *Film and TV Music*, *Films in Review*, *Notes*, and other periodicals. He compiled the first filmography of composers, *Film Composers in America: A Checklist of Their Work* (1953; reprinted 1972), and a new edition is in progress. He wrote or contributed to over twenty other books and wrote the entries on six film composers for *The New Grove Dictionary of American Music* (1986).

Eddy Lawrence Manson wrote the scores for *Little Fugitive*, *Lovers and Lollipops*, *Weddings and Babies*, *Three Bites of the Apple*, and the Oscar-winning short subject, *The Day of the Painter*. He composed music for hundreds of industrial films, documentaries, animated films, and commercials, and his television credits include *Ben Casey*, *Slattery's People*, *The Virginian*, and several TV features. At UCLA he taught courses in film scoring, arranging, and orchestrating. He is a celebrated harmonica soloist, who in 1942 premiered the first work for that instrument by a major composer, Darius Milhaud's *Suite for Harmonica and Orchestra*.

David Raksin first came to Hollywood to assist Charlie Chaplin with the score of *Modern Times*. He has since composed music for many films, including *Laura*, *Forever Amber*, *Force of Evil*, and *The Bad and the Beautiful*, as well as some 300 television shows. He wrote and narrated "The Subject Is Film Music," a series of 64 hour-long radio programs, and has taught film music at UCLA and USC. *Wonderful Inventions* (1985) includes 65 pages devoted to his work and two 12-inch records of his film music. His latest work (1987) is *Oedipus Memneitai (Oedipus Remembers)*, an Elizabeth Sprague Coolidge commission from the Library of Congress.

William H. Rosar is the founder and President of the Society for the Preservation of Film Music. His academic training is in research psychology and music history. Articles by him on film music have appeared in *Film Music Notebook*, *The Quarterly Journal of the Library of Congress*, *The Cue Sheet*, and *CinemaScore*. He is editor of the National Union Catalogue of Film Music.

Gregory Rose has held positions at several Los Angeles radio stations, where he produced and hosted classical music programs and conducted interviews with many film composers. He assisted Tony Thomas in producing the series of seminars on film music for Filmex L.A., in 1976, and wrote the liner notes for the Citadel recording of Jerry Goldsmith's *Freud*.

Fred Steiner is a noted composer for films (*Run for the Sun*, *Time Limit*, *First to Fight*) and television (*Gunsmoke*, *Perry Mason*, *Mannix*, *Star Trek*, *Twilight Zone*, *Amazing Stories*). He has conducted several film music recordings, lectured widely on film music, and taught composition and orchestration at the University of Southern California. He received his Ph.D. in musicology in 1981 with a dissertation, "The Making of an American Film Composer: A Study of Alfred Newman's Music in the First Decade of the Sound Era." He has written on film music for *Film Music Notebook*, *The Quarterly Journal of the Library of Congress*, and *The New Grove Dictionary of American Music*.

Steven D. Wescott is a composer and historian specializing in the history of twentieth century music and musical culture in America. A Ph.D. candidate in musicology at the University of Minnesota in Minneapolis, he is completing a dissertation, "Miklós Rózsa: A Portrait of the Composer as Seen Through an Analysis of His Early Works for Feature Films and the Concert Stage." He compiled *A Comprehensive Bibliography of Music for Film and Television* (1985), an indispensable tool for film music research.

H. Stephen Wright is Music Librarian and Assistant Professor at Northern Illinois University (DeKalb). He attended Indiana University, receiving a master of music degree in instrumental conducting in 1981 and a master of library science degree in 1983. He studied conducting at the Aspen Music Festival and is a former associate conductor of the Houston Civic Symphony. He currently is coordinator of the Music Library Association Film Music Roundtable.

Leslie T. Zador is the Secretary of the Society for the Preservation of Film Music and has edited and written for *The Cue Sheet*, the quarterly newsletter of the Society. In 1970 and 1971 he wrote a column of interviews with film composers, "Music and the Movies," for the *Los Angeles Free Press*. He heads a property management company and practices law in Los Angeles.

Index

Adams, George, 172
Adamson, Harold, 111
Addison, John, 219
Adorno, Theodor, 205
Affron, Charles, 142
Alexander, Jeff, 12
Alexander Nevsky, 7, 240, 262
Alford, K.J., 252
All Quiet on the Western Front (1930), 155
All That Money Can Buy, see *The Devil and Daniel Webster*
Altered States, 8
Anderson, Gillian B., 16
Anderson, Maxwell, 227
Antheil, George, x, 82, 90, 92, 100–101, 105
Appalachian Spring, 263
Armitage, Merle, 112, 117
Arnaud, Leo, 119, 121
Axt, William, 12, 26, 32, 74

Bach, Johann Sebastian, 216
Bacharach, Burt, 227, 268
Backer, Dr. Thomas E., 259, 269
Balanchine, George, 178, 180, 181
Baravalle, Victor, 111
Baron, Maurice, 32, 74

Bassett, R.H. (Rex), 111, 174
Bassman, George, 122
The Battle of Britain, 240
The Battle of Neretva, 215
Beau Geste (1926), 27
Beebe, Ford, 148, 151
Beecher, Milton, 111
Beethoven, Ludwig van, 234
Behind the Screen: How Films Are Made, 107, 122
Behlmer, Rudy, xv, 162, 271
Belasco, David, 139
Bemberg, H., 29
Ben-Hur (1925), 24–25, 30, 33–34, 35, 38, 39
Ben-Hur (1959), 7, 183–207
Benjamin, Arthur, 82, 100, 101, 103, 105
Bennett, Richard Rodney, 238
Berlioz, Hector, 54
Bernstein, Elmer, xi, 9, 15, 16, 258, 263
Bernstein, Leonard, 7, 13, 52, 215
Big Business (1928), 62
The Black Cat (1934), 147, 155, 161, 163
Bliss, Arthur, 90
Blitzstein, Marc, 82, 97, 99, 105

The Blue Max, 8
Bogdonavich, Peter, 141
La Bohème (1926), 31
Bombay Mail (1934), 146, 150, 154, 155, 161
Booth, Margaret, 191, 206
Borch, Gaston, 68
Bordwell, David, 141
Boulanger, Nadia, 258
Bourne (publisher), 3
Bowes, Major Edward, 74
Bowles, Paul, 82, 96–97, 105
Bradford, James C., 29, 30, 32, 52
Brahms, Johannes, 155
Bride of Frankenstein (1935), 148, 150, 151, 156, 161, 162
The Bride Wore Black, 250
Broken Blossoms (1919), 54, 67–70, 77
Brown, Nacio Herb, 111
Brown, Royal S., 4, 15
Browne, Nick, 141
Buck Rogers (1939), 151–152, 165
Buck Rogers vs. the Planet Outlaws (1939), 153, 165
Bukofzer, Manfred F., 14, 17
Burton, Val, 111
Bush, Richard H., 271
Buttolph, David, 168, 170, 172, 173

California State University at Long Beach, 11, 12, 16
Calvocoressi, M.D., 83, 90, 93, 105
Capriccio Espagnol, 76

Captain Blood (1935), 90, 263
Carmichael, Hoagy, 63
Carnival of the Animals, 50, 231
Carter, Gaylord, 19–59, 63
Case, Anna, 77
Chang, 38
Chaplin, Charlie, 53
Charles, Milton, 42, 45
Chavez, Carlos, 81, 83, 90, 96, 105
Chell, Samuel, 142
Chertok, Jack, 151
Chihara, Paul, 259, 261, 265
Chopin, Frédéric François, 155
Christlieb, Don, 122
A Christmas Carol (1954), 227
Le Cid (Massenet), 75
Cimarron (1931), 123, 130
Cinema Journal, 15
CinemaScore, xii
The Circus, 53
Citizen Kane, 7, 12, 214, 218, 220, 221, 263
The City, 7, 265
Closson, Hermann, 85, 87, 105
Cokayne, A.H., 72
Columbia Broadcasting System, 9
Composing for the Films, xiv
A Comprehensive Bibliography of Music for Film and Television, xiv
Connor, Edward, 77
Cook, Page, xi
Cook, Pam, 141
Copland, Aaron, xi, 5, 7, 13, 15, 215, 240, 262, 263, 265
Copley, Richard, 118

Coppola, Carmine, 74, 265
Copyright Office, 13, 161
Corigliano, John, 8
The Covered Wagon (1923), 20
Cowell, Henry, 268
Crabbe, Larry "Buster", 144, 151
Craft, Robert, 109, 117, 118, 119, 120, 122
Crawford, Jesse, 42

Daehler, Carl, 77
Dahl, Ingolf, 120
D'Amato, Tony, 209
Davey, Charles, 106
Davis, Carolyn, 207
Day, Jim, 53
Dearth, Earl, 172
De Koven, Reginald, 72
Del Castillo, Lloyd, 44
Destination Unknown (1933), 146, 149, 156
The Devil and Daniel Webster, 214, 221
The Devil Dancer, 26, 30
Directory of Music Research Libraries: Volume I, Canada and the United States, 14
The Docks of New York, 20
Doctor Zhivago, 234
Don Juan (1926), 72, 74–77
Don Quixote, 120
Donaldson, Walter, 111
Dorsey, Arnold (Engelbert Humperdinck), 251
Dracula's Daughter (1936), 148, 152, 157
Dragon, Carmen, 12
Drigo, Riccardo, 30

Duke, Vernon, 180
Duning, George, 12
Dushkin, Samuel, 109, 112
Dvořák, Antonin 140

East of Java (1935), 148
Eastman School of Music, 45
Einstein, Alfred, 83
Eisenberg, Emanuel, 141
Eisler, Hanns, 82, 86, 93, 97, 106, 205
Elinor, Carli, 27, 28, 51
The End of St. Petersburg, 121
Entr'acte Recording Society, 3
Erwin, Lee, 63
Etude, x
Evans, Mark, 119

Fame, 257
La Fanciulla del West, 139–140
Faust, 63
Fiedel, Robert, 13, 16
Film and TV Music, xi
Film Composers in America: A Checklist of Their Work, xiv
Film Music, 94, 106
Film Music Notebook, xi, xv, 15, 16
Film Music Notes, xi
Film Score: The View from the Podium, 15, 142
Films, x
Films in Review, xi, 16
The Firebird, 112, 115, 119, 121
Flashdance, 257
Flash Gordon (1936), 143–147, 154, 157, 165

Flash Gordon Conquers the Universe (1940), 150–151, 153, 154
Flash Gordon's Trip to Mars (1938), 147–150, 152, 161, 165
Footnotes to the Film, 106
Forbstein, Leo, 24, 26, 27, 28, 30, 31, 36–37, 38, 174, 256
Ford, John, 93, 124–125
Foster, Stephen, 62, 170
Fotoplayer, 48–49
Four Wives, 261–262
Frankenstein, Alfred, 120
Freed, Arthur, 111
Freed, Ralph, 164
The Freshman, 55
Friedhofer, Hugo, 167, 172, 176, 178, 180–181, 258
Fry, Stephen M., 12, 16

Gall, Thom, 74
Geduld, Harry, 61
The General, 59
George Arents Research Library, 162, 207
Gerhardt, Charles, 10, 16, 270
Gershwin, George, 178, 180, 258, 263
Gershwin, Ira, 178
The Ghost and Mrs. Muir (1947), 215–216
Giannini, Vittorio, 255
Gimpel, Jacob, 258
The Girl of the Golden West, 139
Gluck, Joseph, 154, 162, 164, 165
Gold, Ernest, 12, 255, 260

The Gold Rush, 53
Goldenberg, Billy, 258
Goldsmith, Jerry, xii, 8, 214, 258, 263
Goldwyn, Samuel, 26, 30, 172, 177
The Goldwyn Follies, 178, 180, 181
Gone with the Wind, 130, 151, 263
Goodkind, Saul, 151, 164
Goodwin, Ron, 240
Gottschalk, Louis F., 67, 68, 77
Gounod, Charles François, 63
Grauman, Sid, 52, 74
Great Expectations (1934), 149, 157
The Great Impersonation (1935), 152, 157
The Great Train Robbery (1903), 61, 63
Greed, 62
Green, John, 213, 249, 256, 261, 263, 268
Green Mansions, 255
Griffith, D. W., 167
Gruenberg, Louis, xi
Grusin, Dave, 258
Gutman, John A., 83, 103, 106

Hadley, Henry, 75
Hagen, Earle, 259
Hahn, Reynaldo, 233
Hajos, Karl, 147, 158, 160, 161
Hall, Ben M., 67
Hall, John, 141
Hamlisch, Marvin, 258, 268
Hammond, Richard, 88, 106

Harling, W. Franke, 146, 149, 156
Heindorf, Ray, 37
The Heiress, 13
The Hellstrom Chronicle, 263
Henie, Sonja, 170
Hennessee, Don A., 16
Herrmann, Bernard, xii, 4, 7, 10, 12, 209–252, 263
Herrmann, Norma, 209
High Fidelity, 15
Highsmith, Harry, 111
Hill, Robert, 148
Hitchcock, Alfred, 4, 219, 220, 241, 244–245, 252
Hofmann, Josef, 258
Hollywood Bowl, 249
Hollywood Quarterly, xi, xv, 15
Honegger, Arthur, 99, 252
Hope-Jones, Robert, 47
Horn, Maurice, 164
Horne, Marilyn, 227
Huber, Fred, 40
Humperdinck, Engelbert, 251
Huntley, John, 104

Ilyinsky, Alexander, 149, 159
The Indians Are Coming, 152
The Informer, 90, 93, 123–142
International Pictures, 153
The Invisible Man (1933), 146, 150, 154, 157
Ivan the Terrible, 5
Ives, Charles, 215, 229, 238, 248

James, Dennis, 44, 271
Jane Eyre (1944), 221, 224
Janssen, Werner, x
Jarre, Maurice, 11, 12, 242–243, 252, 253
Jason, Will, 111
Jaubert, Maurice, 82, 93–94, 95–96, 99, 101, 106
The Jazz Singer (1927), 81, 167
Jones, Isabel Morse, 117, 118
Jones, Quincy, 258
Joplin, Scott, 62
Journal of the University Film and Video Association, xiv
Julius Caesar (1953), 184, 205
Jurmann, Walter, 111

Kahn, Gus, 111
Kalinak, Kathryn, 271
Kall, Dr. Alexis, 111, 112
Kane, Artie, 258
Kaper, Bronislau, 12, 111, 122, 255
Kaun, Bernhard, 119, 129, 147, 149, 157
Kaun, Hugo, 119, 147
Kaylin, Samuel, 168
Keaton, Buster, 53
Kennedy, Joseph P., 124
Kern, Herb, 43
Ketelbey, Albert, 30
Keystone Kops, 40
The Kid Brother, 58
King Kong (1933), 3–4, 6, 15, 123
The King of Kings (1927), 25, 52
Klapholz, Ernest, 111
Klatzkin, David, 159
Klemperer, Otto, 109
Knight, Arthur, 106
Knudson, Carroll, 172, 175–176

Koldys, Mark, 205
Korngold, Erich Wolfgang, xi, 11, 13, 90, 258, 263
Krummel, D.W., 14, 16
Kubik, Gail, 12

Laemmle, Carl, 146, 164
Lambert, Constant, 83, 89, 99, 106
Lane, Burton, 111
LanFranchi, C.P., 25, 26, 28, 30 31, 33, 36, 37, 38, 41
Lange, Arthur, 168
Lanterman, Frank, 27
Lasher, John Steven, 3, 15
Lasky, Jesse, 172
The Last Command (1928), 20, 28, 62
Laura, 8, 12
Laurel and Hardy, 56, 62
Lava, William, 12
Lawrence, T.E., 243
Lawrence of Arabia, 243, 252–253
Leaf, Ann, 44
Lebrecht, Norman, 118
Lees, Gene, 15, 16
Legrand, Michel, 225
Lehmann, Liza, 29
Leigh, Walter, 82, 89, 98, 100, 106
Levant, Oscar, x, 122
Library of Congress Music Division, 12–13
Lieutenant Kije, 262
Lightning Express, 152
Lilac Time, 66, 67
Liszt, Franz, 146–150, 154, 155, 159, 237

Lloyd, Harold, 23, 53, 54–55, 57, 58
Lojewski, Harry, 260, 264
London, Kurt, 94–95, 97, 98, 103, 104, 106
The Lost Patrol, 123
Lovers and Lollipops, 260
Luders, Gustav, 27

MacLeish, Archibald, xii
MacRae, Henry, 144
Madame Butterfly, 68
The Magnificent Ambersons, 7, 218
Main Title, 15
Malotte, Albert Hay, 43
Mancini, Henry, 12, 268
Manson, Eddy Lawrence, 269, 272
Manvell, Roger, 104
Maria Chapdelaine, 97
The Mark of Zorro (1920), 53, 63
Marks, Martin, ix, xiv, 5, 15
Mars Attacks the World, 152, 165
Massenet, Jules, 75
Max Steiner Music Society, xii
Maxwell, Charles, 111, 168
Mayer, Louis B., 113, 114, 119
McCarty, Clifford, xiv, 16, 174, 272
Mehr, Linda Harris, 14, 16
Mehta, Zubin, 247
Melos, 83
Mendelssohn, Felix, 50
Mendoza, David, 26, 32, 74
Merovich, Alexander, 111, 112, 118

Index

Metro-Goldwyn-Mayer, 11, 108–122
Mickey-Mousing, 55–56, 99, 125–126
The Midnight Sun (1926), 146, 147, 157
Midsummer Night's Dream, 50
Miklós Rózsa Society, xii
Milhaud, Darius, 82, 85, 107, 268
Mockridge, Cyril, 168, 170, 172, 173
Modern Music, x, 83, 90, 96
Morton, Arthur, 122
Morton, Lawrence, ix, xi, xiv, 122
Motion Pictures, Television, and Radio: A Union Catalogue of Manuscript and Special Collections in the Western United States, 14
Moving Picture World, ix
Muri, John, 44
Murtagh, Henry B., 43
Museum of Modern Art, 62
Music and Letters, 83
Music for Movies, 7
Music for the Films, xiv, 90
Music Library Association, 14
Musical Quarterly, x, 83
Musical Times, 83
Mussolini, Benito, 114, 118
Myers, Rollo, 83
Mystery of Edwin Drood (1935), 157

Napoléon (1927), 74, 265
Naumburg, Nancy, 107
Neale, Stephen, 141

A Neglected Art: A Critical Study of Music in Films, xiv
New World Symphony, 140
Newman, Alfred, 12, 175, 177, 178, 256
Newsom, Iris, xv
Nichols, Dudley, 124
North, Alex, 12, 244
North by Northwest, 214, 245, 246
Notes, xiv, 15, 16, 17

Of Mice and Men (1940), 7
O'Flaherty, Liam, 124
Old Ironsides, 20, 78
On the Waterfront, 7, 12
One Night of Love, 167
Orphans of the Storm, 77–78
Our Town, 7, 262

Pacific Coast Musician, x
Palmer, Christopher, 3–4, 16
Paramount Pictures, 10
A Patch of Blue, 263
Patton, 214
Perkoff, Leslie, 96, 107
Perry, Sam, 150, 152, 155, 158, 159, 161
Peters, William Frederick, 77, 167
Pétrouchka, 112, 116, 121
The Phantom of the Opera (1925), 22, 54, 63, 66
Pickford, Mary, 79
The Pines of Rome, 25
Popper, Dr. Jan, 230
Porgy and Bess, 263
Powell, Edward B., 176, 178, 180–181

Les Preludes, 150, 154
Prendergast, Roy M., ix, xiv
Previn, André, 12
Previn, Charles, 150, 159, 165
The Prince of Pilsen, 27
Pro Musica Sana, xi, 205
Prokofiev, Sergei, 5, 7, 215, 240, 262
Psycho, 10, 222, 244, 245
Puccini, Giacomo, 139, 219, 264
Purple Rain, 257

The Quarterly Journal of the Library of Congress, xii, 162
Quo Vadis (1951), 184, 205
Quo Vadis Suite, 262

Raab, Leonid, 111
Radin, Oscar, 111
Raff, Joachim, 241
Raintree County, 213
Raksin, David, 8, 12, 120, 122, 167–181, 266, 272
Raksin, Ruby, 175–176
Ransom, Cliff, 172
Rasch, Albertina, 119
Ravel, Maurice, 236
The Raven (1935), 158
Raybould, Clarence, 87, 101, 107
Raymond, Alex, 143
The Real Tinsel, 141
The Red Pony, xi, 7, 262
Reported Missing (1937), 160, 161
Requiem Mass, 141
Resources of American Music History: A Directory of Source Materials from Colonial Times to the Present, 14
Rienzi, 75
Riesenfeld, Hugo, 27, 30, 52
Rimsky-Korsakov, Nikolai, 76
Rite of Spring, 263
RKO, 3–4, 124
RKO General Pictures Archive, 3, 141
Robbins, Jack, 111
Roberts, Charles J., 149
Robin Hood (1922), 70–74
Rocketship, 165
Rodgers, Richard, 268
Roemheld, Heinz, 146, 148, 150–151, 152, 155, 156, 157, 158, 159, 162, 163, 164
Romberg, Sigmund, 27
Romeo and Juliet (Tchaikovsky), 147, 148, 163
Rosar, William H., xv, 3, 15, 162, 164, 273
Rose, Gene, 168, 172
Rose, Gregory, 210, 273
Rosenberg, Bernard, 141
Rosenman, Leonard, 8, 15, 262, 268
Rózsa, Miklós, 7, 12, 114, 117, 183–207, 216, 220, 230, 244, 262
Running Wild, 20

Sabaneev, Leonid, xiv, 83, 90–92, 93, 98–99, 100, 104, 107, 205
Safety Last, 66

Saint-Saëns, Charles Camille, 50, 163, 231
Salter, Hans J., 164, 165
Sarecky, Barney, 148
Saturday Night Fever, 257
Savino, Domenico, 30
Sawyer, Geneva, 171
The Scarlet Letter (1926), 25–26, 31
Scharf, Walter, 10, 12, 16, 168, 268
Scheherazade, 29
Schertzinger, Victor L., 70–74, 167
Schifrin, Lalo, 262, 263
Schneider, George G., 111
Schoenberg, Arnold, 230
Schoenberg, Chris, 111
Schoenfeld, Herm, 15
Schrager, Rudy, 172
Schreiner, Alexander, 43
Schurmann, Gerard, 253
Scott of the Antarctic, 7
The Secret of Santa Vittoria, 260
Selwyn, Arch, 172
Shattuck, Charles, 142
Shefter, Bert, 258
Shire, David, 258
Shostakovitch, Dmitri, 217
Sight and Sound, 83
Silvers, Louis, 81, 167–168, 169, 170, 171, 172, 173, 175, 177–178
Silverstein, Harry, 141
Simon, Geoff, 68
Sinclair, Andrew, 141
Sinfonia Antartica, 7

Skinner, Frank, 150, 158, 159, 164, 165
The Snows of Kilimanjaro, 221
Society for the Preservation of Film Music, xiii, xv
Son of Frankenstein (1939), 150, 158
Song of Ceylon, 89
Soundtrack: The Music of the Movies, 119
Spell of the Circus, 158
Spellbound Concerto, 262
Spencer, Herbert, 167, 168, 171, 172, 175, 176, 177, 178
Spiegel, Sam, 252, 253
Staiger, Janet, 141
Stanley and Livingstone (1939), 174
Star Wars, 8
State Historical Society of Wisconsin, 12
Steiner, Fred, xv, 3, 10, 16, 142, 273
Steiner, Lee (Mrs. Max), 3, 142
Steiner, Max, x, 3–4, 11, 82, 86, 90, 93, 107, 123–142, 151, 258, 261–262, 263, 270
Stephani, Frederick, 144
Stevens, Morton, 264
Stokowski, Leopold, 174, 234, 235
Stoloff, Morris, 255
Stothart, Herbert, x, 82, 102, 107, 111, 112, 115, 116, 118, 121–122
Strauss, Richard, 215, 236, 246, 260, 264

Stravinsky, Igor, 108–122, 223, 230, 236, 263
Stravinsky, Vera, 117, 118, 119, 120
Stringer, Robert Wilson, 121–122
The Student Prince (1927), 27
Suez, 171, 174
Sugerman, Harry, 46
The Sun Never Sets (1939), 150, 158
Sutak, Ken, 15
Sutter's Gold (1936), 153, 158, 162
Swan Lake, 37, 147
Symphonie Moderne, 261–262, 270
Syracuse University, 12, 162

Tailspin Tommy serials (1934, 1935), 143
Tarzan the Tiger (1929), 150, 158, 161
Tchaikovsky, Peter Ilich, 28, 147, 148, 163
Tell It to the Marines, 38
The Temptress, 23, 38
The Ten Commandments (1923), 20, 55
That's My Wife, 56
Theremin, 206
The Thief of Bagdad (1924), 29, 39, 53
Thielmann, Urban, 180
Things to Come, 90
Thomas, Kevin, 211
Thomas, Tony, xv, 15, 142
Thompson, Kristen, 141

Thomson, Virgil, x, 82, 83, 88, 92, 98, 107
Tim Tyler's Luck (1937), 149
Tiomkin, Dimitri, 12, 120
To Kill a Mockingbird, 263
Toch, Ernst, x, 12, 82, 102, 107, 168
Topaz, 252
Torn Curtain, 219, 241, 252
Toscanini, Arturo, 223, 228
Tower of London (1939), 150, 158, 164
Tracking, 144–45, 149
Tristan und Isolde, 140, 239
The Trouble with Harry, 220
Turner, George, 162
Twentieth Century-Fox, 167–178
Twisted Nerve, 214
2001: A Space Odyssey, 12

United Artists, 180, 181
Universal Pictures, 143, 144, 146, 148, 149, 150, 153, 154, 161, 162, 163, 165, 174, 241
University of California at Los Angeles, 12
University of California at Santa Barbara, 12
University of Cincinnati, 32
University of Oregon, 12
University of Santa Clara, 12
University of Southern California, 11, 12
University of Wyoming, 12, 207

van Loan, Paul, 168

Index

Vaughan, Clifford, 145, 153, 157, 158, 162, 163
Vaughan Williams, Ralph, 7, 242
Verdi, Giuseppe, 141
Vertigo, 214, 222, 244, 245
Villa-Lobos, Heitor, 255
Virgil, Jack, 168

Wagner, Richard, 75, 140, 146, 236, 239
Wagner, Roger, 227
Walton, William, 240
War and Peace (Prokofiev), 216, 238
Ward, Edward, 145, 149, 157
Warner Bros., 10–11, 174
Washington, Ned, 111
Watts, Stephen, 107, 122
Waxman, Franz, 12, 145, 148, 152, 153, 156, 161, 162, 163
Waxman, John, 161
Way Down East, 167
We Make the Movies, 107
Webber, W. Lloyd, 69
The Wedding March, 20
Welles, Orson, 7, 165, 217–218, 220
Welles Raises Kane, 7
Werewolf of London (1935), 147, 158, 160, 161
Wescott, Steven D., ix, xiv, 273
Whallon, Evan, 69
What to Listen For in Music, 15
The White Hell of Pitz Palu (1930), 150–151, 152, 158
The White Sister, 49, 50
Whiteman, Paul, 24

Wiener, Jean, 97
Wild, Earl, 261
William Tell (Rossini), 51
Williams, John, 8, 9, 15, 258
Wilson, Mortimer, 29
Wings, 20, 50
The Winning of Barbara Worth, 39, 40
The Wizard of Oz (1939), 121
Wonderful Inventions: Motion Pictures, Broadcasting, and Recorded Sound at the Library of Congress, xv
World Film News, 83
The World, the Flesh and the Devil, 206
Wozzeck (Alban Berg), 238
Wright, H. Stephen, 273
Wurtzel, Sol, 168
Wuthering Heights (Herrmann), 215, 226, 230
Wuthering Heights (1970), 224–226
Wyler, William, 184, 185, 205, 206

Zador, Eugene, 210
Zador, Leslie T., xv, 210, 274
Zamecnik, J.S., 30
Zanuck, Darryl, 178
Zanzibar, 154
Zéro de conduite, 93
Zimbalist, Sam, 184
Zissu, Leonard, 15
Zorina, Vera, 180, 181